PRIVATE AND FICTIONAL WORDS

For Phoebe and Miranda

PRIVATE AND FICTIONAL WORDS

Canadian women novelists
of the 1970s and 1980s

CORAL ANN HOWELLS

METHUEN · London and New York

First published in 1987 by Methuen & Co. Ltd
11 New Fetter Lane, London EC4P 4EE
Published in the USA by Methuen Inc.
29 West 35th Street, New York, NY 10001
© 1987 Coral Ann Howells

Photoset by Rowland Phototypesetting Ltd
Bury St Edmunds, Suffolk

Printed and Bound in Great Britain by
Biddles Ltd, Guildford and King's Lynn

British Library Cataloguing in Publication Data
Howells, Coral Ann
    Private and fictional words: Canadian
    women novelists of the 1970s and 1980s.
    1. Canadian fiction – Women authors –
    History and criticism   2. Canadian fiction
    – 20th century – History and criticism
    I. Title
    813'.54'099287   PR9192.W6/

    ISBN 0-416-37640-1
    ISBN 0-416-37650-9 Pbk

Library of Congress Cataloging in Publication Data
Howells, Coral Ann.
    Private and fictional words.

    Bibliography: p.
    Includes index.
    1. Canadian fiction – Women authors – History and
criticism   2. Canadian fiction – 20th century – History
and criticism.   3. Women and literature – Canada.
I. Title.
PR9188.H68   1987   813'.54'099287   87-1580

    ISBN 0-416-37640-1
    ISBN 0-416-37650-9 (pbk.)

Contents

Acknowledgements

I could not have written this book in England without the help of my friends in Canada. So many people have been generous with information, encouragement and hospitality that for every one I name there are many others whom I would like to mention as well. My first thanks are due to colleagues at the University of Guelph, Ontario, where I spent a year teaching and learning about Canadian literature, especially to Linda Marshall for her untiring intellectual and emotional support, also to Elizabeth Waterston, Doug Killam and Margaret Hundleby. To Clara Thomas of York University, who has been truly generous to me throughout this project, I owe a thousand thanks. There are two friends in Toronto without whom this book would certainly not have been written, and for very practical reasons: Judith Skelton Grant who sent me the copies of many of the novels I needed and Paula Bourne who has been an unfailingly generous hostess on my frequent visits. Others whom it is a pleasure to thank are James Carscallen, Bill Keith and Jay Macpherson at the University of Toronto, for reading parts of this book in its early stages and for their discriminating criticism when I most needed it.

I have many people to thank for bibliographical assistance:

Moshie Dahms and Robert Logan of Guelph University Library for expert help in carrying out the database search of the Canadian National Library; Cicely Blackstock and Rachel Grover of the Thomas Fisher Rare Book Library and Frieda Forman, Research Associate of the Women's Education Resource Centre at OISE, who generously made their Canadian collections available to me in Toronto. I am grateful for the friendly co-operation of those novelists to whom I wrote for supplementary information: Joan Barfoot, Marie-Claire Blais, Nicole Brossard, the late Marian Engel, Janette Turner Hospital, Alice Munro, Audrey Thomas; to Judith Skelton Grant for essential help with the bibliography of Mavis Gallant and to Louise Myette and Kathy Garay who helped in similar ways with Blais and Engel; also to Robin my husband for checking the French-Canadian holdings at the Bibliothèque Nationale in Paris.

I would like to thank Michael Hellyer and Elizabeth Ritchie of the Canadian High Commission in London, Peter Easingwood and Lynette Hunter of the BACS Literature Group, Bernard Koch of the Québec Délégation générale in London and Cedric May of Birmingham University, for their encouragement of my teaching and writing about Canadian literature. My thanks also to Simone Vauthier of the University of Strasbourg whose conferences on the Canadian short story have provided a congenial forum for discussions with European colleagues. I am indebted to the British Association for Canadian Studies, to the Foundation for Canadian Studies in the United Kingdom, and to the University of Reading Research Board for generous financial assistance with travel. And many thanks to Patrick Parrinder and to the students in my Canadian Literature classes at Reading University since 1982 for their bright ideas and discreet criticisms.

For editorial encouragement and help my thanks to Janice Price and Merrilyn Julian, and to Lilian Argrave and Ruth Kennedy for secretarial help which far exceeded the bounds of duty.

If this book begins to look like a collective effort then that is exactly right, for it seems to me that women's criticism has much in common with women's gossip. The best gossip is creative too, sharing information, finding new connections and so making better sense of things. My final thanks (or should they have come first?) to my husband and my two daughters Phoebe and Miranda. We have survived the writing of this book together.

Parts of Chapters 3 and 4 are based on my essay in *Gaining Ground: European Critics on Canadian Literature*, eds R. Kroetsch and R. Nischik (Edmonton: NeWest Press, 1985); an earlier version of my analysis of *Latakia* appeared in *Canadian Woman Studies*, 6(1), 1985; the section on *Bear* appeared as an essay in *Ariel*, 17(4), 1986.

Coral Ann Howells
London, August 1986

Introduction

The last two decades have seen a new flowering of fiction writing by women everywhere, but in the case of Canadian women the fiction being produced has specific implications which go beyond the feminist awareness which has nurtured it. Through readings of the fiction of eleven Canadian women writers this book attempts to map an exciting new territory of Commonwealth literature and to examine the ways in which these women's Canadianness informs their fiction. Many of the experiences these writers are chronicling cross national boundaries and are shared by writers elsewhere, but as a non-Canadian critic writing in England I am not trying to assimilate Canadian literature by re-reading it outside Canada; this book is not another version of imperialism. Instead it argues for the importance of nationality and gender in Canadian women's fiction, suggesting that the connections between the two have produced a literature that is distinctive, focusing on what the Canadian writer Alice Munro has noticed in a different context as 'those shifts of emphasis that throw the storyline open to question, the disarrangements which demand new judgments and solutions, and throw the windows open on inappropriate unforgettable scenery.'[1]

I began this book in an attempt to answer the question repeatedly asked outside Canada about Canadian fiction: 'Why are there so many good Canadian women writers?' The answers to such a question reveal interesting similarities between the search for visibility and identity so characteristic of women's fiction and the Canadian search for a distinctive cultural self-image. *Who Do You Think You Are?* is the Canadian title of a book by Alice Munro which was changed in Britain and the United States to *The Beggar Maid*. Evidently the Canadian self-questioning would not be likely to strike a responsive chord in readers abroad, and there lurks a shadow of the old imperialist attitude of superiority in that title change. In a sense this anecdote of a transformation encapsulates the problematic definition of feminine and Canadian identity in its subjective sense and its objective recognition by others. What does being a subject mean? If it means self-awareness, then it involves taking into account inconsistencies and contradictory impulses inside the self, so that the search for boundaries which self-definition implies would highlight multiple differences within and blur those very boundaries through which the self is constituted. If on the other hand being a subject refers to a political category, then self-definition is something imposed from outside by a superior power in a colonial situation and therefore reductive of inner diversity.

There are close parallels between the historical situation of women and of Canada as a nation, for women's experience of the power politics of gender and their problematic relation to patriarchal traditions of authority have affinities with Canada's attitude to the cultural imperialism of the United States as well as its ambivalence towards its European inheritance. Canada's colonial inheritance of English and French language and culture is complicated by the multiple origins of the Canadian population as a result of multi-ethnic patterns of immigration and settlement. While Canadians have strong loyalties to racial and cultural origins outside Canada, they also have a strong sense of marginality in relation to those cultures which have disinherited them as emigrants. So a question of inheritance frequently becomes a questioning of inheritance in contemporary Canadian literature, where attempts at revision are problematized by the knowledge that self-definition can take place only within the very traditions that are being questioned. The colonial inheritance of a postcolonial culture like Canada's includes an 'inescapable doubleness of vision', Margaret Atwood's phrase to describe the contradictory state of mind of a nineteenth-century English immigrant to Canada, Susanna Moodie.[2] Given the parallels, it seems entirely appropriate that Atwood should choose a woman as subject for her poetic meditation on the Canadian psyche.

The colonial mentality and Canada's recent emergence from it have close affinities with women's gendered perceptions of themselves, for the revivification of the feminist movement since the 1960s has created the conditions for a change in women's consciousness as they struggle to find their own voices through which to challenge traditions which have marginalized and excluded them from power. Looked at from the outside, it would seem that in Canada there is a connection between the preoccupations of nationalism and of women's fiction as strong though not as obvious as is to be found in many postcolonial Third World cultures. The ideological coincidence between nationalism and feminism would suggest one of the reasons why so much attention is being paid to women writers in Canada now. It might also be argued that women's stories could provide models for the story of Canada's national identity. The feminine insistence on a need for revision and a resistance to open confrontation or revolution might be said to characterize Canada's national image at home and abroad, while women's stories about procedures for self-discovery which are as yet (as always?) incomplete may be seen to parallel the contemporary Canadian situation.

Canadian arguments for coexistence and national policies that take into account its own multicultural diversity may be translated into the arguments of feminism, for the power politics of imperialism and of gender have much in common. The nature of power relationships between the sexes and the social and literary consequences of this have been brought to the forefront of public attention by the feminist movement, though of course the long history of such relationships has already been written into women's literature preceding the last twenty-five years. Contemporary Canadian women writers are aware of themselves as inheritors of a female literary tradition which includes both European and Canadian predecessors. Women's writing has always been characterized by the urge to 'throw the storyline [of traditional power structures] open to question' and to implement 'disarrangements which demand new judgments and solutions',[3] however obliquely such challenges may have been written into women's texts. Any politics of domination and submission is based on the principle of an absolute difference existing between two protagonists which vindicates the claim to superiority of one over the other. By now we have had the chance to learn that difference need not be a static irreducible separation between categories (like biological difference) but something rather less stable where, by a process of displacement, boundaries between categories like identity and gender may be blurred. Such awareness of instability undermines traditional structures of political authority, making it possible to envisage 'new solutions' where opposition is discredited in favour of a more pluralistic approach to questions of social and cultural order. The concept of difference which feminist theorists have appropriated and developed from Jacques Derrida's poststructuralist writing about texts is already there in women's fiction, and now as readers and critics we have been given a language through which to 'see' it.

The Canadian women's fictions discussed in this book are in no sense theoretical statements about feminism, though they are all written out of a conviction of the worth of women and the necessity for women to be critically conscious of their own roles in conventional social structures. Novels and short stories do what theory cannot do, for they deal with particularities of individual experience, problematizing theoretical issues by writing in the instabilities which are the very conditions of knowing. Many of these women's stories about the lives of girls and women between the 1950s and the 1980s are concerned with exploration and survival, crossing boundaries, challenging limits and glimpsing new prospects. Such a description makes them sound like stories of male heroism, yet they do not read like this and might even be seen as stories about uneventful private lives. The main reason for this difference is that heroism is redefined in these fictions, for these are stories about inner adventures which are often invisible to other people.[4] The limits they challenge are cultural and psychological and their discoveries may be of no importance to anybody but the characters themselves. Many of these novels have women writers as protagonists engaged in a struggle with language and inherited literary conventions to find more adequate ways of telling about women's experiences, fighting their way out of silence to project more authentic images of how women feel and what they do.

Shifts of emphasis are evident in their subject matter and their story-telling methods, as my discussions of particular texts will show. However, it is worth noting here how many of these novels and short stories suggest the limitations of traditional literary conventions in an attempt at more open forms of fiction. This revisionism can be done in many different ways, from Atwood's rewriting of popular genres like women's romance or science fiction in order to expose the dangerous fallibility of such fantasies, to Joy Kogawa's historical novel about the fate of the Japanese-Canadians where the official histories are discredited by the supplementary evidence of this feminized version. Perhaps the commonest feature of women's resistance to tradition is their mixing of genre codes – like those of gothic romance, history, gossip and Christian fable in a short story by Munro for example; or the mixing of history and legend, filmic images, extracts from private letters and novels in Margaret Laurence's *The Diviners*. Such interweaving of genres suggests a different aesthetic principle from the traditional one of 'whole-ness, harmony and radiance', for here the emphasis is on multiple perspectives, drawing attention to the process of fiction making itself. These strategies are not peculiar to women's writing for they are general characteristics of mod-ernist and postmodernist writing; the difference here is that these stories are all told from the woman's angle, registering a feminized awareness of dislocation within the very literary traditions in which they are writing.

The awareness of such multiplicity within these fictions and among the interests of the writers themselves has influenced my own critical approach. It is evident that different texts respond to different kinds of reading, so that novels and short stories written within a mode that is primarily realistic demand to be read differently from fragmented postmodernist fictions or from fantasy. It is equally true that with such mixed fictions as these any reading must be an active engagement with language and the structures of narrative, for none of them are simply texts to be uncritically consumed. Instead they challenge the reader's expectations as constantly as they challenge literary traditions. Modern reader response theory could provide a useful approach here, and I have used it in discussing those novels that rely for their effects on the reader's stock reactions to the formulae of popular fiction, especially women's romantic fantasy of the Mills & Boon variety. Although most of these novels expose the dangers of such fantasizing they also recog-nize its power, and it is one of Munro's adolescent narrators who catches this doubleness of response exactly:

> I thought at once that he was coming to stand beside me. Then I thought what nonsense; like a recognition in an opera, or some bad, sentimental, deeply stirring song.[5]

I have not rejected thematic criticism for, although it is out of fashion, it helps to establish a referential context for readers coming to Canadian fiction from outside. 'Where is here?' is

Northrop Frye's famous formulation of the question Canadians used to ask themselves, and a similar unfamiliarity with Canada's cultural and physical geography still afflicts many non-Canadian readers. My interpretative procedures may vary from one chapter to the next and often within a chapter several critical perspectives will be suggested. This flexibility of response to individual texts will not, I hope, obscure my general framework of reading which is designed to highlight the connections between Canadianness and feminine-gendered awareness in these fictions.

My study, with its selection of writers from different regional and cultural backgrounds, attempts to reflect the multivoiced Canadian tradition. It includes native-born and immigrant writers in English and French, expatriates from the United States and Australia now living and writing in Canada, also two Canadians (one writing in English and one in French) who have lived in France since the 1950s. The 'unforgettable scenery' of these fictions stretches across Canada from east to west, while several of them reflect Canadians' experiences abroad in Britain, Europe, the United States, India and the Caribbean. Inevitably there are gaps, and I would like to have been able to include the novels of Aritha van Herk and Sandra Birdsell's short stories as representative of the rich variety of prairie women's writing, also the lesbian writer Jane Rule from the West Coast, and the Québécois feminist writers of the *nouvelle écriture*, Nicole Brossard and Louky Bersianik. However, my book does not have the inclusive spaciousness of Canada. Even 'novelists', though it is a convenient title, is not a comprehensive description, for all these writers have worked within a variety of genres. Several of them are best known as short-story writers, four of them are poets, and two are also radio dramatists. Any formal categories are seen to be open to question and in need of perpetual revision.

I begin with Margaret Laurence, whose Manawaka cycle written in the 1960s and 1970s pioneered many of the themes and narrative techniques of contemporary English-Canadian

women's writing; and I end with the Québécoise Anne Hébert
who has been publishing poems, novels and short stories since
the 1940s, speaking for many years from the distance of metropolitan France. Within these parameters I have chosen writers
several of whom are well known internationally and all of whom
deserve to be more widely read, whose fictions demonstrate the
extensive range of women's imaginative responses to their social
and historical situation and pluralize the concept of Canadian
identity. Margaret Atwood is Canada's most versatile and
famous writer, 'quite simply the most distinguished novelist
under fifty currently writing in English', as a London critic of
The Handmaid's Tale remarked.[6] Her novels present Canadian
women's ambivalent relation to the literary and cultural traditions they have inherited through a variety of genres, all of
which combine her sense of the connections between a power
politics of nationality and gender with her sense of the imaginative possibilities of fictional language. Alice Munro's short-
story cycles and collections, while having no overtly political
engagement, subtly resist any authoritarian structures by subverting both realism and fantasy as modes of fictional discourse,
questioning masculine and feminine stereotypes and reminding
readers of the incompleteness of all forms of classification. With
their curious mixture of Canadian provincial ordinariness and
extraordinary insights her stories reveal the contradictions of
banality and secrecy within the daily lives of us all. Mavis
Gallant's internationalism (for she is a Canadian expatriate
living in Paris and writing stories about exiles and refugees in
Europe more often than in Canada) challenges any narrowly
nationalist definition of Canadianness, as lifestyle or literary
style. Her stories, with their interweaving of different cultural
codes, dissolve truth and certainty into a matter of perspective,
where displacement denies any fixed classification that a pass-
port would affirm. The concept of Canadianness is problematized further in my chapter on Marian Engel, Joy Kogawa and
Janette Turner Hospital, for the three novels I treat offer
different perspectives on modern women's wilderness experi-

ences in Canada and abroad and the writers themselves – one Ontario-born of Scottish descent, one Vancouver-born Japanese, and one Australian expatriate – embody that mixture of cultures which is characteristic of Canadian social geography. The novels of Audrey Thomas and Joan Barfoot both focus on women living alone and writing, one in Crete and one in a mental asylum in Ontario. Both casualties of colonialism in its gender sense, their disrupted postmodernist narratives register dislocation as a feature of their lives and of their story-telling at the same time as they highlight the diverse conditions of possibility out of which women's writing is produced.

Québécois novelists write out of a different literary tradition as well as a different culture, and in French, so that many English-speaking readers know their work only in translation. Clearly it is difficult for non-French-speaking critics who are also non-Canadians to discuss Quebec writers, yet equally clearly the French Fact is of striking interest to readers outside Canada, who see two very different Canadas imaged in Anglophone and Francophone literature. Anne Hébert and Marie-Claire Blais both have international reputations in the French-speaking world and have been read and written about by English Canadians like Atwood and Thomas. There is also very important experimental feminist writing in Quebec – undoubtedly the most radical women's writing in Canada – but little of it is available in English translation and to write about it would be to write a different book from this, perhaps more appropriately in French. Yet Quebec women's writing is an important component in the multivoiced tradition of fiction by Canadian women. It is evident that the recurrent themes of marginality and invisibility in Canadian women's writing are projected by Québécoises on to the wider screen of a whole French-speaking community, where difference is often literally driven underground. One of Marie-Claire Blais's novels is called *Les Nuits de l'Underground* (*Nights in the Underground*) where the Underground is the name of a lesbian bar in

Montreal; and Anne Hébert's *Héloïse*, a sinister gothic tale about a female vampire, uses the scenario of the Paris Metro, suggesting through its fantasy the deeply ambivalent attitude of the Québécois towards metropolitan France. Although the Québécois novels look very different from English-Canadian novels, there are some very interesting continuities which have to do with women taking risks to write their way out of silence and cultural dispossession in order to tell their own stories.

To read Canadian women's fiction of the past twenty years is to become aware of how a cultural map of Canadianness exceeds geographical limits, for national boundaries have to be extended at least imaginatively to accommodate the recognition of Canadians' multicultural inheritance. In an analogous way, traditional structures of patriarchal authority are shown to be in need of revision if women's alternative views are to be taken into account. The patterns of resistance that emerge to externally imposed systems of classification and definition are both characteristically Canadian and characteristically feminine. Paradoxically there is one single striking feature about Canadian women's fiction, and that is its multiplicity. As Margaret Laurence says in *The Diviners*, 'But there's no one version. There just isn't.'[7]

1

Canadianness and women's fiction

'Right, Jane,' said Professor Lotta Gutsa. 'Now, first of all we
need a title . . . I've got it. We'll call it *Wilderness Womb: The
Emergence of Canadian Women Writers* – that's a no-loser.
Women's Studies, Canadian Literature, the whole Bit.'

(Clara Thomas, 'How Jane Got Tenure'[1])

Canadian writing has always been pervaded by an awareness of
the wilderness, those vast areas of dark forests, endless prairies
or trackless wastes of snow which are geographical facts and
written into the history of Canada's exploration and settlement.
Throughout the Canadian literary tradition wilderness has
been and continues to be the dominant cultural myth, encoding
Canadians' imaginative responses to their landscape and history
as an image of national distinctiveness. Professor Lotta Gutsa's
comic suggestion of the fertility of the wilderness myth for
Canadian women writers points up the consistent feminization
of a national myth from its nineteenth-century occurrence in
pioneer women's tales to contemporary women's fiction, undergoing some modifications in writing which is responsive to
specific historical and social circumstances but retaining its
original power as an image of female imaginative space in texts

which both mirror the outside world and transform it into the interior landscape of the psyche. If we are looking for distinctive signs of Canadianness in women's novels of the 1970s and 1980s, I suggest that the most important of these may be found in the wilderness which provides the conditions of possibility for the emergence of Canadian women writers.

An important aspect of this study is the relationship of these contemporary women to their literary and cultural inheritance, where the historical resonance of wilderness cannot be neglected. All these stories scrutinize 'traditional cultural dependencies', a phrase Canadian critic Robert Kroetsch used to describe the efforts of the 'best Canadian artists'[2] and which may be used equally well of the 'best Canadian women writers' for it points up the feminine analogy with the colonial mentality through which Margaret Laurence described women's condition when in 1978 she said:

> These developing feelings [re Third World cultures] related very importantly to my growing awareness of the dilemma and powerlessness of women, the tendency of women to accept male definitions of ourselves, to be self-deprecating and uncertain, and to rage inwardly. The quest for physical and spiritual freedom . . . run[s] through my fiction.[3]

This colonial inheritance is there to be both recognized and resisted in postcolonial Canadian literature, which registers change and slippage from historical origins in its language and literary forms. Arguably this national sense is exacerbated in women's fiction by their sharpened gender sense of marginality and cultural dispossession. As we might expect in a society like Canada's where there are no single origins but multiple European and native inheritances, modern writers' relationship to tradition is extremely ambivalent, registering both awareness of displacement and the urge towards the definition of an independent identity. All these stories are crisscrossed by allusions to European and Canadian history, so signalling the traditions within which they are written just as they all attempt to revise these traditions to accommodate more adequately women's experience and knowledge. What we find are fictions that delight in the interplay of multiple codes of cultural and literary reference. The stories are structured through the interrelatedness of these different codes, not one of which may be taken as authoritative but all of which have to be taken into account for a more open reading of the complexity of reality.

Such multiplicity together with the refusal to privilege one kind of discourse or set of cultural values over others is characteristic of women's narratives in their urge to shift the emphasis and so throw the storyline of traditional structures of authority open to question. Shifts and questionings involve disruption, which is a common characteristic of all these fictions with their mixed genre codes as well as their chronological and narrative dislocations. Most of them look like realistic fictions registering the surface details of daily life, yet the conventions of realism are frequently disrupted by shifts into fantasy or moments of vision so that they become split-level discourses when alternative ways of seeing are contained within the same fictional structure. They are fictions characterized by their indeterminacy, a feature confirmed by their frequent open endings. The emphasis is on process and revision so that truth is only provisional and writing is not transparent but something to be decoded and reconstructed through the reader's collaborative efforts. As Margaret Atwood warns her readers:

> The true story is vicious
> and multiple and untrue
>
> after all. Why do you
> need it? Don't ever
>
> ask for the true story.[4]

Within this context of multiplicity and the rejection of fixed categories it is worth considering further the historical and imaginative significance of wilderness in the work of Canadian women writers. When the first Europeans came to Canada in the sixteenth century they confronted an alien landscape of silent forests in what is now Quebec and Ontario. Inevitably those first European responses were male ones recorded through the accounts of explorers and trappers, soldiers and missionaries. Canada was a hostile terrain with an implacable climate and filled with hidden dangers from indigenous Indians and wild beasts, where the European settlers felt their existence to be a heroic struggle for survival against multiple natural threats. The male response was either one of fear and recoil (which found its expression in Northrop Frye's famous 'garrison mentality') or an adventurous challenge to the unknown in journeys of exploration and later colonial exploitation and settlement. Gaile McGregor's recent book *The Wacousta Syndrome* offers an analysis of the Canadian myth of wilderness as alien and 'other'.[5] This is arguably the male myth of wilderness, but if we look at women's writing we find some important differences in female versions of the wilderness reflecting their very different experiences of colonization. Small numbers of European women came to Canada in the seventeenth and eighteenth centuries (Frenchwomen as early as 1604 to Acadia and 1617 to Quebec) and then they came as military wives, settlers, temporary visitors or, in the case of some Frenchwomen, as missionary nuns. It is however only with the best known nineteenth-century records of English women's pioneer experiences that I am concerned here and their stories of settlement as they rewrite male pioneer myths from the woman's point of view. The differences in many respects conform to stereotype gender differences, focusing on women's domestic and private experiences as they tried to establish homes for their families under harsh pioneer conditions. Their letters, journals, fictions and emigrants' guides written for those 'back home' record the facts of settlement with its privations and dangers and their responses to the challenge of the wilderness. Certainly terror of the unknown trackless forests is an

important component in their accounts, like the nineteenth-
century pioneer Susanna Moodie 'surrounded on all sides by
the dark forest' which she sees as 'the fitting abode of wolves and
bears' in *Roughing It In The Bush*.[6] Yet there is also a surrep-
titious kind of exhilaration, and we find in Mrs Moodie's
anxieties, as in other texts by nineteenth-century women, an
interesting doubleness of response to the wilderness. For the
vast Canadian solitudes provided precarious conditions of existence where women were forced to redefine themselves and
where the self was discovered to be something far more problematical than feminine stereotypes from 'home' had allowed
women to believe. The wilderness of environment seems to
have evoked a corresponding awareness of unknown psychic
territory within, so that the facts of settlement provided the
conditions of unsettlement as the wilderness became a screen on
to which women projected their silent fears and desires. The
wilderness was internalized as metaphor remarkably early as
Marian Fowler shows in her book *The Embroidered Tent: Five
Gentlewomen in Early Canada*:

> These five women had to tramp through dense bush, travel
> by canoe, sleep in tents and hovels, cope with sudden
> emergencies, improvise and adapt in a hundred ways. On an
> imaginative level the wilderness offered a mirror for the
> psyche, for all five discovered images there reflecting repres-
> sed areas of consciousness . . . Their psyches began to run
> wild along with the forest undergrowth and its furtive inhabi-
> tants. Now these women began to identify with white water,
> forest fires, giant trees, bald eagles. These images crowd the
> pages of their journals.[7]

The wilderness as the pathless image beyond the enclosure of
civilized life was appropriated by women as the symbol of
unmapped territory to be transformed through writing into
female imaginative space. It provides the perfect image for the
'wild zone', the 'mother country of liberated desire and female

authenticity' which Elaine Showalter projects as the repressed area of women's culture in her essay entitled 'Feminist criticism in the wilderness'.[8] Showalter suggests Atwood's *Surfacing* as one of the novels which create a feminist mythology on matriarchal principles 'at once biological and ecological', so directing attention towards this paradigmatic wilderness text and pointing the way towards the transformations that wilderness has undergone in twentieth-century Canadian women's writing.

The wilderness is still there in contemporary urban and small-town fiction as a feature of environment and available as metaphor or symbolic space for the exploration of female difference. *Surfacing* with its transitions between Toronto and the backwoods of Quebec exploits both the environmental and mythic aspects of wilderness in its story of a female psychic quest, and Marian Engel's *Bear* as another quest narrative journeys from a library in Toronto back to an island in northern Ontario where the protagonist finds in her close contact with a wilderness creature the necessary source for her own psychic renewal. In both these novels the wilderness remains deeply symbolic, never becoming a literal alternative to civilized living as it does in Joan Barfoot's *Gaining Ground*, but a place of refuge and rehabilitation which the protagonists leave when they are ready to return refreshed to the city. Both are feminized versions of the authentically Canadian ambivalence towards city living and survival in the wilderness. Pockets of wilderness survive in many of Atwood's urban fictions, where Toronto's ravines provide a wilder dimension to that city's neat lawns and ordered spaces in *The Edible Woman*, *Lady Oracle* and the short story 'Bluebeard's Egg'. What is true of Toronto is even truer in fictions about small towns like Margaret Laurence's prairie town of Manawaka or Alice Munro's southwest Ontario towns of Jubilee and Hanratty, where the enclosed community defines itself against the surrounding wilderness and where the edges of town signalled by the spots where the sidewalks and streetlights cease provide that wasteland occupied by the more marginal members of the community and by

the public rubbish dump. Munro's and Laurence's heroines are
brought up in such borderland territory and they retain their
doubleness of vision in their adult lives. Their perceptions that
the wilderness as place/state of mind is not something that can
be entirely shut out are written into their stories, resulting in
those moments of instability where cracks open in the realistic
surface to reveal dark secret places within social enclosures. Del
Jordan in *Lives of Girls and Women* knows that the memory of
the wilderness lies beneath the solid brick houses and neat
streets of her town just as surely as it is still there underneath the
bridge or down beside the Wawanash river, so that her stories
begin to look like mosaics of secret alternative worlds that
coexist with ordinariness as everything presents a double image
of itself. The same kind of doubleness exists for Morag Gunn in
The Diviners, where coming to terms with the past as an adult
involves a journey through the wilderness of memory to a
homecoming in a log farmhouse in Ontario far from the prairie
town where she grew up. As she knows, wilderness living
should be updated to fit the needs of women in the late
twentieth century. The updating of wilderness as myth or
metaphor includes the imaginative transformation of Toronto
itself into 'unexplored and threatening wilderness' in Atwood's
Journals of Susanna Moodie and Munro's *Lives of Girls and
Women*, of Montreal in Marie-Claire Blais's *Nights in the
Underground*, and perhaps most deviously in Anne Hébert's
Héloïse where the underground of Paris becomes the world
of the past which disrupts and destroys the world of the
living.

   Continuities may be seen in the way that Janette Turner
Hospital uses wilderness in her Indian novel *The Ivory Swing* as
symbolic space for the exploration of unknown regions of the
female self. Joy Kogawa's *Obasan* as the history of the dispossession of Japanese-Canadians uses a hostile prairie wilderness
as its setting so that this novel looks in many ways like a revision
of nineteenth-century Canadian immigrants' experiences of
solitude and unbelonging in the New World. However, in both

these novels, as in *Surfacing* and *Bear*, wilderness is not presented as an alternative to twentieth-century existence but rather as a place to be emerged from with strength renewed. Such a variety of treatments not only illustrates the transformations of the wilderness myth in women's fiction but also signals women's appropriation of wilderness as feminized space, the excess term which unsettles the boundaries of male power. These are not fictions which aspire towards androgyny but rather towards the rehabilitation of the feminine as an alternative source of power; wilderness provides the textual space for such imaginative revision.

The rehabilitation of the feminine is an important feature of Canadian women writers' sense of their relation to literary tradition, and a quotation from Marian Engel's novel *No Clouds of Glory* aptly focuses these concerns:

> Those of us who operate from bastard territory, disinherited countries and traditions, long always for our non-existent mothers. For this reason I devilled five years – six? When did I start? how many? – in the literature of Australians and Canadians, hoping to be the one to track her down.[9]

Engel has feminized the whole question of inheritance in colonial and postcolonial cultures by conflating mother country and literary tradition, so focusing on the sense of unbelonging and the search for origins which is a general characteristic of Commonwealth writing as well as a specific characteristic of much women's writing. Though my main interest is in the feminine literary traditions within which contemporary Canadian women are working, the question of literary inheritance relates to wider concerns of Commonwealth and women writers' perceptions of their relation to history. It was Virginia Woolf writing within the English tradition who said, 'As a woman, I have no country', a statement about unbelonging which is strikingly elaborated in the 1970s Canadian context by Atwood:

We are all immigrants to this place even if we were born here:
the country is too big for anyone to inhabit completely, and in
the parts unknown to us we move in fear, exiles and invaders.
This country is something that must be chosen – it is so easy
to leave – and if we choose it we are still choosing a violent
duality.[10]

This statement pushes beyond Woolf and Engel as it demonstrates clearly how being a Commonwealth writer and a woman
problematizes one's sense of cultural identity and demonstrates
dilemmas of allegiance. There is a complex of attitudes here
relating to lack of historical depth and continuity of tradition in
a New World society, and much postcolonial fiction is preoccupied with finding substitutes for this lack. The substitution
comes partly through a quest for the past or indeed the creation
of a past in legends of the new country and of the mother
country (or 'mother countries' in Canada, where inheritance is
multiple); partly it is achieved by taking up the languages and
literary traditions of the 'lost' mother cultures and modifying
them into discourse more appropriate to a place outside the
original discourses.[11] The aim of both these endeavours is to
establish possibilities for the coexistence of multiple cultures
within oneself which are perceived as different from one
another. As is clear in a number of these fictions, it is a process
which involves rejection as well as acceptance and the exercise
of imaginative reason till the protagonists see themselves as
inheritors and finally come to feel at home in Canada.

Turning to the question of how contemporary Canadian
women writers recuperate their literary inheritance, the first
thing we notice is that none of them has an exclusive preoccupation with the traditions of a single country or of a single
gender or literary genre. As inheritors whose historical and
cultural situation is different from their predecessors they are
eclectic in their choices. Margaret Laurence in *The Diviners*
acknowledges Virginia Woolf and works within the inheritance
of modernism at the same time as her protagonist is holding

imaginary conversations with the nineteenth-century pioneer Catherine Parr Traill, producing within the fiction one novel which is a feminist revision of Shakespeare's *Tempest* and another based on the legends of the prairie Métis. Canada's multicultural inheritance is written into many of these fictions with their mixture of genres as well – female gothic, sentimental romance, spy stories, animal stories, pastorals, science fiction – in the recognition that literary traditions have to be transformed in a process of perpetual revision. Only through story-telling can connections with the past be realized, for inheritance comes to possess reality only when it is re-imagined and when history and legend are so closely interwoven that no objective truth is possible.

The problems faced by Canadians are similar to those faced by any colonial culture like Australia or New Zealand or, earlier, the United States which has been up against the difficulty of inheriting a mother tongue together with its traditions and without a powerful infusion of indigenous culture as in Africa, India or the Caribbean – except that for Canadians the problems are further complicated by having two mother cultures and two national languages, English and French. How to find a distinctive voice for such a mixed society or to have that voice listened to abroad has always been a crucial difficulty. With Canada it seems to be resolving itself in division, as English-Canadian fiction becomes more widely known in the English-speaking Commonwealth and French-Canadian within the Francophone tradition. D. H. Lawrence focused the dilemma for American fiction when he wrote in 1923:

> It is hard to hear a new voice, as hard as it is to listen to an unknown language. We just don't listen. There is a new voice in the old American classics. The world has declined to hear it, or has babbled about children's stories.[12]

Though the invisibility of American literature has now become past history, Canadian literature is currently confronting the same problems of being heard as a 'new voice' while maintaining its 'difference', with all the instability that this word implies. Robert Kroetsch quoting Lawrence in 1978 suggested that paradigms of other literatures 'patently and blatantly' did not enable Canadians to respond to their own literature.[13] While that is true, it is also true that readers outside Canada come to its fiction with exactly those other literary paradigms in their heads. The range of intertextual references I have indicated signals the relatedness of Canadian literature to British and European traditions, which is to be expected for these are the traditions within which most Canadian writers have been educated. Canadian distinctiveness may be seen to lie in efforts towards autonomy through displacing the authority of other traditions in order to give a place to what has been traditionally regarded as marginal. As a process of decentralization it is characteristically Canadian. Such shifts of emphasis involve a good deal of ambivalence, which finds its most desperate and negative expression in the work of some Québécois writers where the weight of European history is seen to lie like a dead hand on the present, dispossessing the living and draining the life out of them, as in Hébert's vampire fable *Héloïse* where Paris itself becomes the site of the curse of the past.

While the search for 'lost mothers' abroad is an important aspect of Canadian literary tradition, this is not to deny that Canadian women writers have literary mothers of their own. Contemporary women's writing in Canada is the culmination of a strong feminine literary tradition and one of which modern writers are very conscious as reassuring evidence of their creative origins in their own country. Even that tradition is double, for while pioneer women wrote about their responses to the wilderness and their experiences as immigrants to Canada, there has also been since the late nineteenth century a movement in the opposite direction with Canadian women writing about cosmopolitan experiences, like Sara Jeanette Duncan in the 1890s who worked in the United States and in England and accompanied her husband to India; or more recently Elizabeth Smart (*By Grand Central Station I Sat Down and Wept*), Mavis Gallant and Anne Hébert, all of whom have lived as expatriates for long periods. Their internationalism forms an important strand in the multivoiced tradition of Canadian women's writing, though it is the national tradition where women have seen themselves in distinctively Canadian conditions to which I wish to pay more attention here.

The narratives of nineteenth-century pioneer women like the sisters Susanna Moodie and Catherine Parr Traill who came from England with their husbands in 1832 to take up farming in the wilds of Upper Canada express a very different imaginative response to the New World from what we find in early American or Australian fiction. In both those traditions masculine voices predominate in stories of the challenge of a wilderness of bushland or open plains, and the cultural myths projected are of the 'frontier' in the case of the United States and of pioneering and male mateship in the Australian tradition. Clearly the circumstances of colonization and the crises of colonial history were major factors in each country's created image of itself. Australia had its beginnings as a penal colony where the lives of men and women convicts were officially separated, while the great American movement west with its convoys of covered wagons and Indian Wars represented a massive exercise in aggressive male confrontation with wilderness. Neither of these phenomena has a parallel in Canadian history where patterns of colonization were more sporadic, beginning in the late sixteenth century with isolated French and English trading posts and military garrisons plus a few scattered settlements mainly in the east. So the pattern continued through the seventeenth century and the first half of the eighteenth, when two crucial events occurred: in 1759 the English defeated the French in Quebec and Quebec was ceded to Britain, and in 1776 the American Revolution sent an influx into Canada of those colonists who did not wish for independence from Britain. As W. J. Keith says,

It was this nucleus of Loyalist immigrants and settlers . . . –
that laid the foundations at once social, political and psychological – for what eventually cohered as the Canadian
nation.[14]

Only in the nineteenth century did British and European
settlers come to Canada in large numbers and to this period
belong Susanna Moodie and Catherine Parr Traill, both of
whom experienced the challenge of living in the backwoods of
Canada and wrote about it for readers back home in England,
especially prospective female settlers. Moodie's *Roughing It In
The Bush* (1852) is as much aimed at educating her readers
about conditions in the new colony as Traill's *Female Emigrant's Guide* (1854) which was reprinted as *The Canadian
Settlers' Guide*.

Neither *Roughing It In The Bush* nor *The Female Emigrant's
Guide* is fiction,[15] though both shape immigrant experiences in
relation to existing fictional models. Moodie with her responses
to sublime scenery and her sense of exile in dark forests writes in
the female gothic mode, while Traill takes a male model of
survival in the wilderness likening herself to Defoe's Robinson
Crusoe, for she possessed, as Marian Fowler argues, the same
combination of piety, practicality and determined optimism.
Clara Thomas points out that she was the 'ideal coloniser'
determined to name and order and control 'the maze of inter-
minable forest' according to her own imported cultural
values.[16] She is the personification of the Victorian Protestant
work ethic in its feminine form: 'In case of emergency it is folly
to fold one's hands . . . it is better to be up and doing', a
sentence of hers which Margaret Laurence quotes with rueful
admiration in *The Diviners*. Both Moodie and Traill write in
the genre of the female *Bildungsroman* which Maggie Butcher
perceives as a distinctive form in Commonwealth literature,
where women chronicle their emergence from the stereotype of
the proper lady into the Canadian pioneer of energetic
initiative.[17] Their emphasis is on women's strength in the

absence of men or even in the presence of husbands who are
unfitted for life in the backwoods. While Carol Shields points to
a pattern of reversal of sexual roles in these pioneer narratives,[18]
she neglects the doubleness of Victorian women's awareness
where wifely duty counterbalances their sense of their own
power, resulting in strategies of obliqueness in their narratives
of the split self which Atwood perceives a hundred years later as
so characteristic of Moodie's feminine consciousness.

The other remarkable nineteenth-century female narrative of
wilderness is Anna Jameson's *Winter Sketches and Summer
Rambles* (1838). She was not a settler but a visitor to Canada;
her husband was Attorney-General in Upper Canada and her
visit confirmed their plans for a separation, after which she
returned alone to England. As a widely travelled literary woman
who had already written books on the influence of women on
'men of genius' and one on Shakespeare's heroines, she came to
Canada in 1836 with the image of herself as a female hero in the
Byronic mode and undertook a two-month journey alone to
northern Ontario. As she wrote to her mother in triumph:

> I am just returned from the wildest and most extraordinary
> tour you can imagine, and am moreover the first English-
> woman – the first European female – who ever accomplished
> this journey. I have had *such* adventures and seen *such*
> strange things as never yet were rehearsed in prose or verse.[19]

These things never yet rehearsed gave Anna Jameson the
metaphorical language to describe her inner quest so that, as
Fowler claims, her narrative stands as archetype for many later
quests in Canadian women's fiction. *Surfacing* and *Bear* are the
most recent though not the only examples, and two earlier
narratives should be included to mark the continuity of this
tradition. First come Emily Carr's autobiographical accounts
of her journeys as a painter through the forests of British
Columbia between 1898 and the 1930s. Here she traces the
pattern of a visionary quest through the wilderness recording as

she passes signs of primitive female power in the abandoned Indian totem figures on the West Coast.[20] There is also Ethel Wilson's novel *The Swamp Angel* (1954) which begins as a woman's flight from the constraints of an unhappy marriage and becomes a journey of self-discovery for the heroine in the mountain wilderness of British Columbia. This Canadian female literary tradition gains its strength from women's recognition of their crucial importance in the history of settlement, for while women's work has been 'largely taken for granted as part of the natural backdrop against which important "man-made" history like railway construction or dominion-provincial relations occurs',[21] women have never taken it for granted and have redefined their relation to the 'natural backdrop'.[22] Contemporary writers use the same rhetoric of wilderness as their nineteenth-century predecessors, revising their inheritance to accommodate modern versions of similar experiences, but still multiplicity is the key in the multiple facets of the self and the multiple stories contained within the maze of narrative reconstruction.

The awareness of such multiplicity problematizes the sense of one's own identity for instead of the self being solid and unified it becomes a more shifting concept without fixed boundaries, something for which 'wilderness' would be an appropriate analogy. This feminine awareness finds interesting parallels in the problematic concept of Canadian national identity which has notoriously escaped definition, being variously described as 'negative', 'plural', or 'decentralized'.[23] All of these adjectives relate to historical problems of Canada's double colonial inheritance and its relationship to the United States, as well as reflecting the internal tensions of a linguistically divided culture of great ethnic diversity and conflicting regional interests. Canada evades any easy definition geographically or culturally. It does not have a unified image of itself as a nation, unlike the United States which has created and exported a myth of Americanness which is as easily identifiable in its literary and filmic images as in its political rhetoric. Of course there are

historical reasons for this positive self-definition of the US
which go back to the Declaration of Independence; Canadian
national ideology has no such base. As has been pointed out by
David Staines,[24] Canada's history has been shaped in a discon-
tinuous pattern by imperial power politics: Quebec was ceded
by France to England in 1763, the Dominion of Canada was
declared by England in 1867; only in 1965 did Canada choose
the maple-leaf flag as the symbol of its nationhood, and its
Constitution was repatriated from Britain in 1982. It has always
been easier to define 'Canadian' negatively, as Mavis Gallant's
young protagonist Linnet Muir does in one of the stories in
Home Truths: 'I did not feel a scrap British or English, but I
was not an American either.'[25] Two features of this statement
are interesting: Linnet's youth and her refusal to be defined
from outside. Like Linnet, Canada has refused the monolithic
stories of British or US imperialism and has been evolving from
its marginal position a self-definition based on an ideology of
decentralization which recognizes both its difference from
outside powers as well as its differences within. The Canadian
problem of identity may not be the problem of having no
identity but rather of having multiple identities, so that any
single national self-image is reductive and always open to
revision.

This coincidence of similar problems of self-definition in
nationalist and feminist ideology would go some way to explain
why so much attention is being paid to women writers in
Canada at the present time, for their stories seem the natural
expression of the insecurity and ambitions of their society and
in many ways they provide models for stories of Canadian
national identity. These are not the only models but I am
suggesting that the affinities help to explain the visibility of
women's writing in Canada, whereas women's voices are not so
congruent with the nation's story in Britain or the United
States. Women's fiction in Canada as elsewhere insistently
challenges authority, paying attention to what has been traditionally seen/unseen as marginal, questioning the stereotype

images and narratives of their culture together with the language of its value judgements. The deconstructionist urge to displace traditional authority structures is a basic feature of women's writing and has been seen as a basic feature of Canadian writing by Robert Kroetsch.[26] These women's fictions generate a double sense not only of women's difference but also of their complicity in traditional power arrangements and an awareness of their strategies of appeasement. In some, explicit connections are made between 'colonized' female perceptions and Canadianness, as with Atwood's women and Canadians and Americans in *Surfacing* or Kogawa's delicate but insistent analogy between women's silence and that of the Japanese-Canadians in World War II. If the narrative forms these stories take are often fragmented or fantastic this should come as no surprise, for these are stories about processes of discovery and recovery which are still incomplete, as the tentative endings of so many of them suggest.

Canadianness remains a problematic category in women's fiction, where multiple voices and points of view indicate the differences between writers. In *Surfacing*, *The Diviners*, *Lives of Girls and Women*, *Bear*, *Obasan* and *Nights in the Underground* the geographical signals locate narratives in specific Canadian places, yet the perspectives on Canadian social and cultural values are unmistakably plural. In *Latakia*, *The Ivory Swing* and some of the Gallant stories set abroad memories of Canada form a sub-text only, while for intensely subjective or fantastic narratives like *Dancing in the Dark* and *Héloïse* referentiality to any world outside the fiction is unimportant. *Héloïse* and *The Handmaid's Tale* only allude to Canada as the impossible haven of escape, and for the narrator of *Dancing in the Dark* to be anywhere else but 'home' was 'to be nowhere at all'. Though in some of these novels signs of national identity may be difficult to decipher for readers outside the culture, the signs of gender identity are plain and there is no way any reader would not know that they were all written by women. The question arises as to whether there are identifiable features in women's narratives which are gender specific (i.e. found only in women's writing).[27] I am not at all sure that there are, but there are habitual ways of looking at the self and the world reflected in configurations of imagery and narrative strategies which because of their frequent occurrence may be seen as gender distinctive. As is to be expected on such an issue as gender, the question of difference is one of dominant characteristics rather than mutually exclusive categories, and arguably it is the overlap between feminine and masculine gender characteristics which is most interesting in literature. All of which is not to compromise the difference of women's fiction but merely to acknowledge that it is a matter of degree and not of kind – as again is to be expected given that interrelatedness rather than separateness is the common human condition. Women are deeply implicated in the existing structures of the social world as mothers, daughters, lovers and wives, so that it is a paradox of most women's position that any search for new ways of restructuring their lives and their stories has to acknowledge their genuine need for affective relations and responsibilities at the same time as they register resistance to such constraints.

Women's fiction is insistently double in the recognition of contradictions within the self and the perceptions of incongruity between social surfaces and what is hidden beneath them. It is interesting to find gothic fantasy, that old devious literature of female dread and desire, surviving in the fiction of Atwood, Munro and Hébert, updated certainly but still retaining its original charge of menace, mystery and malignancy. In all these stories there is an intricate balance between the urge for self-discovery and women's self-doubts, between the celebration of new freedoms and a sense of precariousness. Where such tensions form not only the material but also the method of story-telling, women's narratives are seen to share many of the characteristic features of modernist and postmodernist writing as it has developed since the 1920s. In these mixed fictions realism is often disrupted by fantasy, and fragmentation and multiplicity coexist with moments of vision and order. They all have their moments of unity where the protagonist feels in serene possession of herself, though such unity quickly disintegrates into ambiguity and contradiction. However, such holistic moments are always written in, so generating the energy for the protagonist to go on and celebrating the triumph of the female imagination through art.

It is worth looking briefly at women's attitudes to writing as presented in these fictions, many of which have women writers as protagonists. As the novelist Morag Gunn says in *The Diviners*,

> A daft profession Weaving fabrications . . . Yet, with typical ambiguity, convinced that fiction was more true than fact. Or that fact was in fact fiction.[28]

Morag suggests the multiple functions of fiction writing for women as a way of creating the illusion of order out of the random contingencies of experience, as a way of restructuring the past, as a way of self-assertion out of social or economic constraints. Audrey Thomas's letter-writing heroine in *Latakia* is most strongly aware of writing as order in the midst of disorder: 'Art is merely the organisation of that look at chaos.'[29] Most of these novels may be read as revisions of history told from a marginalized feminine perspective, like the history of the Japanese-Canadians in World War II in Joy Kogawa's *Obasan* or the story of one woman who has been dead (or undead) for eight hundred years in Anne Hébert's *Héloïse* where writing becomes a fantastic resurrection. Alice Munro's *Lives of Girls and Women* is a female *Bildungsroman* with distinct revisionist tendencies, for as the chronicler of her own life Del Jordan also writes in the secret lives of earlier generations of women in her family which support her from the past, so creating through her fiction a mosaic of alternative female worlds that have been hidden within the 'living body' of social history. The implications for women's writing as dissent from existing structures of authority are explored in Margaret

Atwood's *Bodily Harm* and *The Handmaid's Tale* both of which are forms of prison narrative where a woman's only way of defiance against abuses of political power is her ability to make things visible through words. Paradoxically these fictions of confinement create the textual space for the protagonists' self-revisions as powerfully as those fictions of wilderness like *Surfacing* and *Bear* where self-transformation occurs within myths and legends of landscape.

Women's writing often celebrates the power of the female imagination yet such celebration is frequently accompanied by a deep unease about the activity and the purposes of writing. There are obvious dissatisfactions with the duplicitous nature of language and fiction-making for professional writers like Morag Gunn, Del Jordan or Thomas's Rachel who are aware of the status of fiction and never mistake it for reality. Writing is a deliberate displacement, a 'fabrication' as Morag calls it, 'an illusion' to use Rachel's words. Del Jordan registers the separation between the two in the epilogue to *Lives* :

> Such questions persist, in spite of novels. It is a shock, when you have dealt so cunningly, powerfully, with reality, to come back and find it still there.[30]

Perhaps the most serious doubts about the efficacy of writing are expressed by the amateur narrator Edna Cormick who writes obsessionally in the lunatic asylum of Joan Barfoot's *Dancing in the Dark* :

> What good are pages and pages of neat precise letters spiralling into tidy words and paragraphs, if they only look good? Underneath it is a mess.[31]

Fiction is always and only metaphor, a recognition signalled in the titles of most of these novels and of which the protagonists, some of whom would prefer to paint or to dance or to act on the stage rather than write, are aware. This ambivalence towards writing comes from the double recognition of its power as much as its limitations. For Alice Munro there lurks a possible treachery in writing in her fears of the distortion of truth through language:

> And even as I most feverishly practise it, I am a little afraid that the work with words may turn out to be a questionable trick, an evasion . . . an unavoidable lie.[32]

There is another kind of treachery of which Munro's and Atwood's protagonists are sometimes conscious, that of writing as illegitimate exposure when secret unseen things are made accessible to view. This moral anxiety about fiction as scientific experiment finds its language in the traditional image of the exposed heart which goes back to the glass hive of eighteenth-century sentimental fiction, though there it expressed the novelist's desire for transparent access to the mysteries of the human heart.[33] Atwood and Munro write stories where the behaviour of the living heart is displayed electronically, and in both primitive fear is the dominant feeling conveyed:

> He seemed so distant, absorbed in his machine, taking the measure of her heart, which was beating over there all by itself, detached from her, exposed and under his control.[34]

And:

> It seemed to me that paying such close attention – in fact, dramatizing what ought to be a most secret activity – was asking for trouble.[35]

The novelist's urge to make everything visible seems to be in conflict with traditional feminine codes of decorum so that the activity of writing itself is problematized in these fictions. Modern women's ambitions are still haunted by an older in-hibiting tradition of femininity, and their efforts to write new

versions of old stories involve the double process of disestab-
lishment and redefinition of their feminine inheritance.

I shall end this chapter where Margaret Laurence ended *The
Diviners* with a homecoming and a new departure:

> Morag returned to the house, to write the remaining private
> and fictional words, and to set down her title.[36]

Margaret Laurence's words have given me the title for this book
as 'private and fictional' characterizes all these novels and short
stories. They are 'private' because they are wrought out of
personal and often unconscious emotion and 'fictional' because
the experiences have been transformed into the controlled
multivoiced discourse of art. As invented worlds which reinvent and reshape reality, they offer readers new possibilities
and new perspectives.

2

Margaret Laurence
A BIRD IN THE HOUSE, THE DIVINERS

> Morag returned to the house, to write the remaining private
> and fictional words, and to set down her title.
>
> (*The Diviners*[1])

These last words of *The Diviners* serve a double function in this
book, providing its title and also an emblem for women's
fiction. Here is the celebratory image of a woman writing,
acknowledging the doubleness of her activity yet achieving
through it a confident homecoming as she writes her way into
possession of herself and her inheritance. Yet such a moment of
triumph in Margaret Laurence's fiction is inevitably double-
faced, like the snapshots Morag keeps 'not for what they show
but for what is hidden in them' (6). What is hidden is a woman's
journey through the wilderness of memory in an attempt to
trace her own identity and her own place, gaining in the process
an awareness of her relation to the literary and cultural traditions which have made her what she is, for 'here and now is not
an island' (357). The narrative to which she finally sets down
her title is her creation of a fictional order out of the multiplicity
of a life's experiences.

Margaret Laurence as a writer within the tradition of prairie fiction is a regional and historical novelist who is peculiarly conscious of a personal need for the imaginative revision of history:

> My writing then has been my own attempt to come to terms with the past. I see this process as the gradual one of freeing oneself . . . while at the same time beginning to see its true value.[2]

Like her protagonists and unlike other modern prairie novelists such as Rudy Wiebe and Robert Kroetsch, she moved away from the prairies before she started writing about them. Her fiction is her attempt to recreate a local community and a way of life which has already passed and which shapes itself differently in every one of her novels. A great deal has been written about Manawaka, that small prairie town in Manitoba which she creates through five books so that in the end the reader has the sense of a place as well known as anywhere in a nineteenth-century panoramic novel. Indeed the documentation is so consistent that, as Clara Thomas shows in her excellent chapter in *The Manawaka World of Margaret Laurence*, the town with its streets and its buildings can be mapped.[3] Similarly precise are the local history details since its settlement in the 1880s through the Depression and droughts of the 1930s up to the early 1970s when it has become, as one of the characters remarks, 'Prosperous town, I'd say' (233). Manawaka is based on Laurence's home town of Neepawa yet it is not Neepawa for the real town has been remembered and reinvented in fiction:

> Manawaka is not my hometown of Neepawa – it has elements of Neepawa especially in some of the descriptions of places, such as the cemetery on the hill or the Wachakwa valley through which ran the small brown river which was the river of my childhood. In almost every way, however, Manawaka is not so much any one prairie town as an amalgam of many prairie towns. Most of all, I like to think it is simply itself, a town of the mind, my own private world.[4]

The growth of this invented world was very like the organic growth of a real town expanding by its own logic of accretion. As Laurence says:

> When I wrote *The Stone Angel* [the first of these novels] I did not have any idea that I would write *The Diviners* [the fifth] nor even that I would write another book out of the fictional town of Manawaka . . . You write what there is to write, whatever is given you to write, you know.[5]

Manawaka is a fictional world structured through the stories the characters tell. Yet it is more than a realistic chronicle, and though it is possible to construct a map of Manawaka from these stories, what strikes the reader is its multiplicity. Manawaka is reinvented by every narrator in her own idiom, from ninety-year-old Hagar Shipley in *The Stone Angel* to the middle-aged narrators of the other fictions, all of whom are engaged in coming to terms with the past, recalling a childhood place from which they have moved away. For them, as for Laurence, Manawaka has become a place of the mind. Her protagonists are always aware of the discontinuities in their relation to the past yet also of their strong need for connections with that lost community and its history. Their story-telling represents the imaginative effort to write oneself into one's inheritance by recreating it from personal memory combined with the local history and legends of that community.

Everybody is an inheritor, and Laurence's fiction investigates how far every individual exists separately yet at the same time as part of a wider historical continuum that goes beyond an individual life span back into the past and forward into the future. The Canadian multi-ethnic inheritance is focused through the history and population of Manawaka, where its tales of Scots and Irish settlers and the survivors of the pioneer generation coexist with the tragic history of the indigenous Métis population who were dispossessed of their prairie lands. The Métis family of the Tonnerres still lived on the edge of town in the 1930s with their fragmented language that was 'neither Cree nor French' and their broken English 'full of obscenities', displaced persons on their own territory:

> They did not belong among the Cree of the Galloping Mountain reservation, further north, and they did not belong among the Scots-Irish and Ukrainians of Manawaka, either.[6]

Theirs too is a colonial inheritance, the other side of the history of European prairie settlement, and the coexistence of these two separate traditions is registered in all the Manawaka fictions. Only in *The Diviners* is there any reconciliation across the gap of history and social custom when Morag Gunn's child by Jules Tonnerre becomes the inheritor of both traditions. Yet any colonial inheritance, for white immigrants as for indigenous peoples, is inevitably as much about displacement as it is about entering into possession, and what Laurence registers is the pluralism of Canadian history with its sense of slippage from historical origins together with the urge to reinvent the past in order to feel at home. These fictions with their imaginative reordering of history and legend are based on multiplicity, for they are as much about multiple inheritances as they are about multiplicities within the subjective selves of the narrators.

It is this engagement with multiplicity that I wish to investigate in *A Bird in the House* and *The Diviners*, for Laurence addresses the question central to feminist writing of how women find a language and narrative form to write about ourselves, and in these texts she offers two different kinds of model for women's stories. Both of them are stories about girls growing up in Manawaka from very different social backgrounds but at the same time, during the Depression up to the mid 1940s when they leave Manawaka to go to college in Winnipeg. *A Bird in the House* is a short-story cycle or 'story sequence',[7] while *The Diviners* is a modernist novel. Between these apparently different fictional forms there are strong connections. Both narratives are fragmented yet both insist on hidden continuities through their narrators' efforts to reorder the past and so create acceptable fictions within which they can assume their own separate identities. Both are structured as double narratives of Now and Then, though the method is more completely developed in the novel where each of these narratives is multiplied through first- and third-person narration and the use of different voices.

While *A Bird in the House* appears to be a much neater book than *The Diviners*, to call it a story sequence is to suggest an orderliness which is belied by the narrative method, for the chronological sequence of Vanessa MacLeod's growing up is frequently interrupted by flashbacks to earlier childhood or flashes forward both within stories and between them, confounding the reader's sense of linear arrangement between past, present and future. Vanessa's ordered world is constantly disrupted, and there is a crucial break at the centre of the book when her father dies and 'the whole order of life was torn' (*A Bird in the House*, 144). After his death she loses any sense of a harmoniously ordered world and her narratives record fragmentation, loss and separations. In many ways *A Bird in the House* prefigures *The Diviners* in narrative method, for the latter offers a more extreme version of experience as contradictory and multiple, 'flowing both ways' like the river that Morag Gunn watches from her window as she writes (*The Diviners*, 453). *The Diviners* has all the characteristics of a modernist novel like *To the Lighthouse* with its registration of instability together with the strong imaginative urge to reconcile contradictions in a final moment of created order and self-possession. Because of their similarities, it is tempting to try to read *A Bird in the House* as a modernist fiction too, given that the short-story sequence is a characteristic modernist genre. However, these stories do not follow the modernist shape for they do not work towards moments of insight or epiphany on the model of Joyce's *Dubliners*. Nor are they fixed within the limits of an older realistic tradition. Instead, the narrative method may be described as that of supplementarity, for after the central anecdote there is always something more to be added, an unexpected event or a realization by the narrator years later which produces disarrangements and necessitates a further reordering. As a story-telling technique it has striking similarities with Alice Munro's 'shifts of emphasis' in *Lives of Girls and Women* and *The Beggar Maid* where the human desire for order is endlessly in conflict with the disorder of reality. Like those sequences, *A Bird in the House* may be seen as an attempt to disestablish realism in its resistance to any fictional ordering or any final interpretation.

Laurence has said that *A Bird in the House* is based on her own childhood, 'the only semi-autobiographical fiction I have ever written'.[8] Knowing this gives the stories a personal interest but it would be a mistake to read them as artless self-revelations, to reduce them to private words and to forget that they are fictional words as well. This sequence is remarkable for Laurence's rich abundance of memory material which is reshaped in order to create the identity of the narrator persona, Vanessa MacLeod. Arguably the main impulse behind Laurence's fiction has been biographical if not autobiographical, for she is centrally concerned with women as the subjects of their own fictions and the forms these fictions might appropriately take:

> I am concerned mainly, I think, with finding a form which enables a novel to reveal itself, a form through which the characters can breathe.[9]

The idea of characters being able to breathe emphasizes the importance of the subject in Laurence's fiction and what being a subject means. The problems her narrators face are those faced by any biographer: how to present one's subject as a coherent invention while acknowledging that there always remain dimensions of unknowability about any human being. Any attempt at ordered presentation of the subject is precariously liable to break down, and these problems are multiplied when the subject being 'invented' is oneself. Defining the self, or rather creating images of the self through a continual process of revision, is one of the recurrent themes in contemporary women's writing. It may well be that women's experience tends to highlight the inherently unstable nature of all human subjectivity and that this perception of fragmentation affects the way women write about themselves in narratives that emphasize discontinuities within the self, till the words 'I' and 'self' look like an inadequate shorthand.

The fictional form of *A Bird in the House*, with its breaks between stories and its twin narrative voices of Vanessa the child and Vanessa the remembering adult within every story, which parallel Vanessa's awareness of disparities within herself and within her world, enables her to breathe. The stories focus on Vanessa between the ages of ten and thirteen with some anecdotes referring back to earlier childhood and some that go forward till she is twenty, so that her growing up provides the narrative framework. Yet there is a doubleness about this seemingly conventional structure, for Vanessa's life story is haunted by ghosts; it is an elegy to her father and grandfather whose deaths are the most important events in the book. The established order of her childhood passes away before her eyes, so that by the time she is twenty her Manawaka world has vanished; its icons have gone and the rest of her family have scattered west and east to Vancouver and to Nova Scotia.

The earlier stories, with their domestic icons of Grandfather Connor and Grandmother MacLeod, look like fairly programmatic statements about inherited ideas of order, yet every story is fissured by the revelations of family secrets and the child's awareness of the gaps between appearances and the lives beneath them. 'To Set Our House in Order', the story about Grandmother MacLeod, actually contradicts itself between the title and its final paragraph:

I could not really comprehend these things, but I sensed their strangeness, their disarray. I felt that whatever God might love in this world, it was certainly not order. (59)

These stories are Vanessa's look at the eminent Victorians in their Canadian context and her revision of that iconography of Pioneer and Patriarch, the Angel in the House and the Lady. As she gradually comes to understand 'many years too late', those stereotype images always possessed the double face of the legendary and the human, like the duality of the bear mask through whose empty eyeholes the adult Vanessa glimpses the humanness of 'the Great Bear' her Grandfather Connor:

> Many years later . . . I saw one day in a museum the Bear Mask of the Haida Indians. It was a weird mask. The features were ugly and yet powerful . . . The eyes were empty caverns revealing nothing. Yet as I looked, they seemed to draw my own eyes towards them, until I imagined I could see somewhere within that darkness a look which I knew, a lurking bewilderment. I remembered then that in the days before it became a museum piece, the mask had concealed a man. (87–8)

Such supplementary knowledge at the end of one early story does not prevent Grandfather Connor from lumbering through Vanessa's other stories nor does it discredit her adolescent image of him as domestic tyrant; but it does hint at the provisional status of her presentation and looks forward to the revisions that will be necessary before his elegy can be written.

The crucial break in the order of Vanessa's life comes with her father's sudden death when she is twelve, recorded in the title story:

> Everything seemed to have stopped, not only time but my own heart and blood as well. (107)

The title itself, with its image of the trapped sparrow's panic and the hired girl's folk wisdom ('A bird in the house means a death in the house' (102)), suggests the characteristic division between the domestic and the inexplicable in a story where oddities and Vanessa's intuitions of unaccountable connections between apparently separate events form a multistranded narrative. Her later discovery of the French girl's photograph in the secret drawer at the back of her father's desk gives Vanessa a fleeting glimpse into another corner of her father's experiences as a young soldier during World War I. Of course this untold story offers no confirmation of anything except her own sense of missed opportunities:

> Now that we might have talked together, it was many years too late. Perhaps it would not have been possible anyway. I did not know. (112–13)

While that story records Vanessa's shock of loss, her mourning for her father continues in the next two stories, 'The Loons' and 'Horses of the Night', both of which look back to the time before her father's death. These are the strongest stories of alienation in the collection, and though Vanessa deliberately distances herself from the life and death of the Métis girl Piquette Tonnerre, as she does from her shell-shocked cousin Chris, her choosing to write about them suggests that 'in some unconscious and totally unrecognised way' (127) she is silently displacing her own feelings into their stories. They are both wilderness stories in their evocation of the Canadian land as a place that exists alongside but in a different dimension from human society. The call of the loons belonged 'to a world separated by aeons from our neat world of summer cottages' (121), just like the lake on Chris's farm up north:

> No human word could be applied. The lake was not lonely or untamed. These words relate to people, and there was nothing of people here. There was no feeling about the place. It existed in some world in which man was not yet born. I looked at the grey reaches of it and felt threatened. It was like the view of God which I had held since my father's death. Distant, indestructible, totally indifferent. (147–8)

While both Piquette and Chris belong to that prehistoric world, Vanessa does not, and these stories of her recognitions and rejections highlight the unbridgeable gaps between the present and the past, between reality and dream, as between Vanessa and the subjects of her stories.

The spaciousness of those stories emphasizes limits of power as well as limits of understanding, which in turn provide a context for Vanessa's last story, 'Jericho's Brick Battlements', which is her taking stock and taking leave of her past, having created her personal mythology. The story which is framed by her father's death at the beginning and her grandfather's death at the end is Vanessa's chronicle of herself and her family. It is also the most disrupted story in the collection, with its fragmentation clearly signalled in the breaks between sections, all of which present Vanessa at different ages in a series of family crises from the move to Grandfather Connor's house at the beginning, through the events of her Aunt Edna's marriage and Vanessa's first boyfriend, to her departure for college and her grandfather's funeral. By this 'accumulation of happenings which can never entirely be thrown away' (202) Vanessa registers the multiplicity within her own and her family's past.

To this last story a supplement is added:

> Twenty years later, I went back to Manawaka again. I had not been back in all that time . . . Everything had changed in the family which had been my childhood one. (206)

It has all the characteristic doubleness of Vanessa's narrative method, as she comes to recognize her Manawaka inheritance only when everything that had belonged to her has passed away. There is nothing left except gravestones, memories and Grandfather Connor's Brick House 'not ours, not mine'. By then she has become a different self with a family of her own who lives somewhere else, and she takes her leave in the final sentence: 'I looked at it [the Brick House] only for a moment, and then I drove away' (207). It is an elegiac ending which focuses on loss

and dissolution rather than on stability or inheritance. Yet
Vanessa's departure is balanced by the knowledge that she is
herself the living monument to her parents and her grand-
parents, and that she will carry Manawaka inside her head for as
long as she lives. In this she is like Morag Gunn and both of
them are like Margaret Laurence:

> I may not always write fiction set in Canada. But somewhere
> . . . Manawaka will probably always be there simply because
> whatever I am was shaped and formed in that sort of place.[10]

Vanessa has written herself out of dispossession into her
inheritance, but the ending where so much is left unaccounted
for offers no solutions to the enigmas of history or of the self.
Her consciousness of identity does not reveal an authentic core
of selfhood but rather an awareness of multiple selves at
different ages. Her last story, with its selection of those different selves, writes in her sense of separation from that past yet
also her awareness of her mature self as continuous with them.
Interestingly, Vanessa leaves Manawaka twice, first as a girl of
eighteen leaving for college, when she is surprised to find that
'in some way which I could not define or understand, I did not
feel nearly as free as I'd expected to feel' (203), and then again
twenty-three years later when she drives away for the last time,
no longer expecting to be free, 'knowing that there's a certain
amount of mental baggage which you're stuck with'.[11] Her
resistance to the past is transformed into a revision of the past as
she comes to accept her role as inheritor as well as accepting
the multiplicities within herself. She is both 'successive and
continuous', a phrase Virginia Woolf used to describe her
recognition of herself in a diary entry in 1929.[12]

One of the traits which Vanessa inherits as a story-teller is her
family's sense of decorum. Unlike Morag Gunn whose fragmentation is signalled from the beginning of *The Diviners*,
Vanessa's sense of her own self-divisions is written far more
discreetly into her narrative through her need to memorialize

her father and her grandfather, as through the fragmented form
of her story sequence with its breaks and its supplements. What
emerges is Vanessa's consciousness of a self always incompletely
understood existing in a world where order is insistently disrupted and meaning is constantly deferred. *The Diviners* on the
other hand is a self-consciously modernist fiction which insists
on the multiplicity of its subject on every page. The 47-year-old
novelist Morag Gunn is like Vanessa MacLeod writing about
herself and through her stories trying to make sense of her life
and the person she has become. It is in many ways a more
obvious treatment of Vanessa's dilemma which might be
summarized as the investigation of 'subject and object and the
nature of reality', the way that one of Morag's literary mothers
described her novel *To the Lighthouse*.[13]

What is most striking about *The Diviners* from the beginning
is its registration of contradictions:

> The river flowed both ways. The current moved from north
> to south, but the wind usually came from the south, rippling
> the bronze-green water in the opposite direction. This
> apparently impossible contradiction, made apparent and
> possible, still fascinated Morag, even after the years of
> river-watching. (3)

As Morag sits watching from her window it becomes clear that
'apparently impossible contradiction' is the condition of her
own life. In this room of her own which is not her own because
she is endlessly interrupted, where her kitchen table doubles as
her writing desk, Morag thinks about her dual roles as writer of
novels and reader of her daughter Pique's letters. Her thoughts
about Pique's leaving to go out west on her own are mixed:

> Pique was eighteen. Only. Not dry behind the ears. Yes, she
> was, though. If only there hadn't been that other time when
> Pique took off, that really bad time. That wouldn't happen
> again, not like before. Morag was pretty sure it wouldn't. Not
> sure enough, probably. (3–4)

Perceptions are as unstable as language is unreliable, and both are likely to be inaccurate:

> The river, which was moving quietly, its surface wrinkled by the breeze, each crease of water outlined by the sun. Naturally the river wasn't wrinkled or creased at all – wrong words . . . I used to think words could do anything. Magic. Sorcery. Even miracle. But no, only occasionally. (4–5)

It is with this sense of the provisional nature of things that the novel opens.

Morag contemplates herself as subject and her relation to reality, wondering to what extent 'it must all be in the head' (5). This very title *The Diviners* is a reminder that there is no unmediated access to reality, either through perception or through memory. The world is not readily decipherable and 'divining' is a necessary activity for readers just as it is for Morag the writer who has herself borrowed the term from her old neighbour who is a water diviner. Reality like a text presents signs to be decoded and there are always gaps. Morag is aware that objectivity as a condition of mind is an illusion, which does not mean that there is no objective reality but only that she cannot read its signs reliably. Her perceptions about the surface of the river note what is apparent but not true, for in fact the river does flow only one way, just as this novel though it looks circular in its structure does move through time and changes do occur. If perception in the present is unreliable, it is also true that memories of the past cannot fix reality either. Morag has peculiar faith in her collection of old photographs from her early childhood for at least these are images of past facts fixed on paper. But seen by her remembering eye, they become notoriously shifting shadows as what is there dissolves into what is not there: 'I keep the snapshots not for what they show but for what is hidden in them' (6). The very activity of remembering is itself a process of reinvention or 're-filming, a scene deleted here, another added there' (28). It is the awareness of how things shape themselves differently in memory that Virginia Woolf recreated in her novels and which is Laurence's inheritance from this literary mother. In her turn, Morag refashions the Woolfian narrative method to contain the multiple stories she needs to tell:

> Whatever is happening to Pique is not what I think is happening, whatever that may be. What happened to me wasn't what anyone else thought was happening, and maybe not even what I thought was happening at the time. A popular misconception is that we can't change the past – everyone is constantly changing their own past, recalling it, revising it. What really happened? A meaningless question. But one I keep trying to answer, knowing there is no answer. (60)

This recognition of instability and contradiction is basic to Morag's imaginative effort of writing fiction:

> A daft profession . . . Weaving fabrications. Yet, with typical ambiguity, convinced that fiction was more true than fact. Or that fact was in fact fiction. (25)

For all its ambiguity writing is of crucial importance to Morag, as it is her way of creating an order through art which her life does not possess. Interestingly *The Diviners* is the only Manawaka novel where art is celebrated both as activity and as artefact. Morag's novel-writing engages with lived experience and with memory in ways that are only implicit in Vanessa's story-telling and in a way that is the opposite of the Stone Angel, that imported eyeless artefact in the prairie cemetery where art only memorializes the dead. Morag comes to recognize how European cultural symbols remain always at a distance from Canadian life and that they have to be transformed in the crucible of the individual imagination before they can enter one's private mythology. Certainly she writes into her story Christie Logan's legends of the Sutherland immigrants at the time of the Highland Clearances and Jules Tonnerre's Métis legends of the Riel Rebellion, just as she includes talismans like a Scottish plaid pin and an old hunting knife. But the way these things appear and disappear only to reappear (first in *The Stone Angel* and then in *The Diviners*) suggests the transformations that stories and objects have undergone in being passed down through generations living in another place. As Morag realizes, 'The myths are my reality. Something like that' (390), for history is only real 'by adoption'. Morag is literally an orphan brought up on the margins of Manawaka by Christie Logan the town scavenger and it is only through writing that she is able to recreate and so possess her inheritance. It is a long journey both geographically and psychologically for Morag to the point where she recognizes in Scotland that her birthright is in Canada, 'where I was born' (391). Only then does she come 'home' with her daughter – not to the prairies but to Ontario where she buys a log house built a hundred years ago by a pioneer family named Cooper which she modernizes to suit her late-twentieth-century lifestyle as a novelist, being neither 'an old nor a new pioneer' (406).

The only kind of power that Morag has ever possessed is the transforming power of language. Nourished by Christie's tales of Piper Gunn and his wife Morag, as a child she created an alternative heroic world of words which, unlike Vanessa MacLeod's, was not always threatening to break down:

> She does not know where it came from. It comes into your head, and when you write it down, it surprises you, because you never knew what was going to happen until you put it down. (87)

Morag never entirely loses this primitive sense of writing as inspiration, as her later image of herself as a diviner suggests. Writing is the means through which she achieves not only her imaginative freedom but also her freedom in the real world. Being paid as a reporter on the *Manawaka Banner* brings in some of the money necessary for her escape from Manawaka to college in Winnipeg; later, writing her first novel is the means by which she frees herself from an oppressive marriage. Only when it is accepted by a publisher does she gain the economic independence to leave. As she tells her husband,

> Brooke, I'm withdrawing the money I earned from the novel . . . I'm going to Vancouver. And I'm sorry. But I just have to take off by myself. (278)

And it is as a professional writer that she survives into this, her fourth novel. Every section opens with Morag in her house writing or preparing to write, except the last one which opens with her talking to her daughter and ends with her sitting down again to write.

Not surprisingly writing is a double-edged advantage for Morag. It is through her story in the university magazine that she attracts the attention of one of her English Literature lecturers, Dr Brooke Skelton, with whom she falls in love and then marries. It is ironic that just at the point when Morag is beginning to challenge the traditional notion that men have all the authority she should fall under the spell of Brooke Skelton, the image of British male cultural imperialism. 'He is an Englishman (I mean, from England)' (204) with an impressive accent and a British Raj childhood to boot! Falling in love with him means falling into the old romantic fantasy of feminine submission and self-abnegation. As Mrs Brooke Skelton she abandons her past, going to live in Toronto for four years, writing short stories and then tearing them up, till one day much to her own surprise, 'she throws a Benares ashtray through the kitchen window' (122). Only at this point of crisis does Morag begin writing her first novel, *Spear of Innocence*, 'almost unexpectedly, though Lilac has been in her mind for some time' (225). Such psychic insurrection has been a characteristic of women's fiction since the gothic novel and it is explored in many modern fictions such as Margaret Atwood's

The Edible Woman and Joan Barfoot's *Dancing in the Dark*.
Writing her novel is Morag's active resistance to an oppression
of which she only becomes conscious as she writes. Fiction is for
her a double process, for writing her story of Lilac Stonehouse
is also her means of writing her way out of her marriage.
However, separating herself from a romantic fantasy which is
also a living relationship inevitably involves suffering, as she
finds in the confrontation with her husband over her novel.
When Brooke offers to 'take a quick run through it' she refuses:

> It's not that. It's – I know you know a lot about novels. But I
> know something, as well. Different from reading or teaching.
> (260)

Brooke's resentment that Morag is engaging with him on his
own territory reveals in all its nakedness the power politics
behind the situation. Of course Morag publishes the novel
under her own name of Gunn, for this is her work not Mrs
Skelton's, but her struggle for self-definition is long and painful. Beset by guilt and doubt, she does not have the strength to
complete the process on her own. She needs help which comes
in the form of a male rescuer, for Morag cannot at one blow
completely rewrite the traditional plot of a woman's life story
just as the process of emancipation cannot be entirely effected
through words.

Feeling 'separated from herself' (263) Morag meets Jules
Tonnerre her old school friend and lover on a Toronto street:

> She wants only to touch him, someone from a long way back,
> someone related to her in ways she cannot define and feels no
> need of defining. (267)

It is through going to bed with Jules (her 'shaman' as he
ironically remarks) that she reforges the connections with her
past that free her from her 'inner chains' (271). Out of this
encounter she finds the strength to get away and to survive her

terrible struggle with Brooke. She goes to Vancouver, putting the distance of the Canadian continent between them.

Living and writing fiction are intertwined activities, as Morag's story shows in its insistent emphasis on the conditions out of which she writes. She has always written at home in relation to domestic circumstances, *Spear of Innocence* being written in her living-room and put away when her husband returned, and though she wrote her way out of that situation all her novel writing is done 'in between or as well as everything else' (366) amid the multiple demands which are the real conditions of a woman's life. As if to underline the importance of biology for women, Morag finds herself pregnant with Jules's child when she goes to Vancouver, so that having attained a room of her own she feels 'too tired and lousy most evenings to do any writing at all' (294). Yet she needs a child just as she needs to write, and her chronicle of novel-writing is also the record of her daughter Piquette's birth and growing up. Morag's story is one of conflicting needs, counterbalancing demands and mixed feelings, for 'nothing gets simpler' and 'I'm still fighting the same bloody battles as always, inside the skull' (289). Domestic interruption is the necessary condition of her life and her writing:

> Hi, Ma. You working? . . .
> This had been the pattern of life for how long?
> Morag at this table, working, and people arriving and saying, in effect, *Please don't let me interrupt you.* But they *did* interrupt her, damn it. The only thing that could be said for it was that if no one ever entered that door, the situation would be infinitely worse. (349)

This is Morag's statement of the relation between herself as subject and the nature of reality, where separateness and relatedness are the conditions of being. Relationships are necessary but fragmentary and understanding is closer to divining than it is to knowledge, for there are always gaps just as there are always doubts and guilt.

Like Vanessa, Morag suffers anxiety over her possible betrayals of other people in her desperate struggle to find her own
way, and it might be demonstrated that part of the awkwardness
of Pique's presentation in the novel stems from her mother's
sense of guilt. Pique also suffers from the weight of too much
thematic relevance, having to serve as role model for a Canadian
multi-ethnic future. 'I clobbered her with a hell of a situation to
live in' (99) Morag thinks, and her comment can bear more than
one interpretation. Characteristically, Morag does not have any
prescription for her daughter's future, nor does she seem to be
able to escape the idea that Pique is the sacrifice for her own
flouting of social conventions; some part of her still believes the
old story that there is a price to be paid for a woman's assertion
of freedom. 'I know it doesn't work that way. God, I know it but
I don't believe it. My head knows perfectly well that retribution
is unreal. But my blood somehow retains it from ancient times'
(328). I suspect that her attitude to Pique with its combination
of permissiveness and self-castigation is one of the darker
sub-plots in the story of a woman's gaining her freedom, and it
is part of Laurence's honesty to write in this unresolved
dilemma as well.

By the end Morag manages to achieve a kind of equilibrium,
not through any process of logic but through acceptance of all
the ambiguities and contradictions that make up her life and her
writing: 'Too many years. No brief summary possible. Accept
it and let it go' (438). Though there is not much sign of her
letting anything go, she learns to accept her life as part of a
continuous historical process. Everything may seem to be
'inside the head' but there is also an objective reality, and even if
things flow both ways in the mind, time, like the river, flows
only one way. Her situation is different by the end for Pique has
gone west to find her father's family, Jules is dead, she is left
alone and she finishes her novel. Though Morag's sense of coming to the end is very strong, her statements of achievement are
somewhat destabilized by the pervasive images of water which
she uses. The analogy she chooses for writing is water divining:

> At least Royland knew he had been a true diviner . . .
> Morag's magic tricks were of a different order. She would
> never know whether they actually worked or not, or to what
> extent. That wasn't given her to know. In a sense it did not
> matter. The necessary doing of the thing – that mattered.
> (452)

And:

> How far could anyone see into the river? Not far. Near shore,
> in the shallows, the water was clear . . . Only slightly further
> out, the water deepened and kept its life from sight. (453)

With this emblem of reality as both lucid and impenetrable,
Morag turns back to the house 'to write the remaining private
and fictional words, and to set down her title' (453). Unlike
Vanessa, Morag does not drive away, but stays to celebrate her
power as an artist who has created her own place to stand on
through her reordering of multiple stories of the past, some of
which are her own and some of which she has made her own 'by
adoption' (432). Of course she knows that this order is gener-
ated by her imagination out of the chaos which is lived experience and that it is a 'fabrication' which only a naïve reader and
not a professional novelist would mistake for reality. As Morag
had earlier reminded her daughter, 'But there's no one version.
There just isn't' (350).

Creativity and multiplicity, Morag realizes, are causes for
celebration, as Margaret Laurence so optimistically affirms
elsewhere:

> I think that human society wherever it is, anywhere in the
> whole world, needs fiction and poetry in the same way that
> human cultures forever have needed their storytellers and
> their poets and their singers of songs . . .
>   There really is room for an unlimited number of different
> points of view.[14]

3

Margaret Atwood *BODILY HARM,*
THE HANDMAID'S TALE

> When you read a book, it matters how old you are and when you read it and whether you're male or female, or from Canada or India. There is no such thing as a truly universal literature, partly because there are no truly universal readers. It is my contention that the process of reading is part of the process of writing, the necessary completion without which writing can hardly be said to exist.
>
> (Margaret Atwood, 'An end to audience?'[1])

It is characteristic of Margaret Atwood, who has done more single-handedly to put Canadian literature on the international map than anyone else, that she should make a statement about fiction that resists any essentialist approach based on nationality, gender or genre. Though her writing is grounded in her own strong sense of cultural identity as Canadian and female, she refuses to limit texts to the original conditions of their creation either as printed words or as culturally defined statements. Her recognition that texts are created by their readers as much as by their writers (reading being 'the necessary completion without which writing can hardly be said to exist') displaces the concepts of writerly authority and absolute meaning in favour of a more open and pluralistic approach to the availability of fiction. It is both paradox and consequence of Atwood's position that this shift from the absolute opens the way to 'a truly universal literature' or at least to the universal appeal of texts in an endless process of revisionary readings.[2] The creative possibilities of rereading are available to writers as well and Atwood's statement describes the space occupied by her own fictions which are all revisions of old texts written from the point of view of a Canadian woman writer. *Bodily Harm* and *The Handmaid's Tale* show Atwood in her most radical light, for here not only is she rewriting traditional literary genres like gothic romance and the utopias of science fiction but she is also attempting to revise the categories of 'Canadian' and 'female' through which her own identity is constituted.[3] Interestingly, her shifts of emphasis displace the boundaries of nationality and gender in a universalizing recognition of what it means to be a full human being.

In her seven novels published since 1969 Atwood has explored a wide range of the literary and social fictions through which women have inherited images of ourselves, though her novels insistently move beyond any narrowly defined feminist project to include her scrutiny of cultural myths about Canadianness and colonization and about structures of political power and oppression. A great deal of critical attention has been paid to *Surfacing* which is the novel where she engages most directly with the search for national and gender identity. It might be seen as the feminist complement to *Survival*, an attempt to identify the 'field markings' which would allow readers 'to distinguish the species of Canadian Literature from the other literatures with which it is often compared and confused.'[4] However, *Surfacing*, as a quest novel, is also a questioning of cultural myths so that it problematizes any definition of Canadian female identity and necessitates its redefinition. It is with problems of discrimination and necessary processes of revision that Atwood's fiction has continued to be concerned. As a Canadian woman writer she has moved through and beyond the primitivist myth of wilderness in her urban and international novels, though still retaining that distinctively Canadian female space. In *Bodily Harm* and *The Handmaid's Tale* the wilderness is still there as the 'subground, something that can't be seen but is nevertheless there', but its more important functions are in its transformations as cultural disorientation in *Bodily Harm* and as night in *The Handmaid's Tale.*

Like any other novelist Atwood writes within the language and literary forms available through her cultural inheritance, but she writes with an acute awareness of the multiple and often contradictory meanings encoded there. We might approach a discussion of Atwood's sensitivity to the language of fiction through Toril Moi's comments on a feminist analysis of language:

> We all use the same language but we have different interests . . . which intersect in the sign. The meaning of the sign is thrown open – the sign becomes 'polysemic' rather than univocal – and though it is true to say that the dominant power group at any time will dominate the intertextual production of meaning, this is not to suggest that the opposition has been reduced to total silence.[5]

For Atwood the main site of conflicting interests lies in inherited fictional forms, and these she insistently analyses and revises. She is not unlike Sally, her protagonist in the title story of *Bluebeard's Egg*, who is taking a course on 'Forms of narrative fiction' and discovering that story versions vary according to the point of view from which they are told. The main difference between her protagonist and herself is that Atwood would be teaching that course from which Sally still has so much to learn. Taking popular forms like gothic romances, ghost stories, spy thrillers, fairy-tales or science fiction, she exposes their inconsistencies in her attempt to disengage from the collective fantasies they simultaneously enshrine and mask.

She certainly writes about feminist issues like marginality, alienation and self-division; she takes up the traditional subjects of women's fiction which are love and marriage and domestic experience through which women have looked for their meaning and salvation; she explores romantic fantasy narratives where women see themselves as helpless victims in need of male protection and rescue. She is very aware of the stereotype images that women have of men as well as of themselves and of the kind of fictions through which such images are internalized. In her novels there is no enraged rejection of these fictions but rather an exasperated exploration of the ways that human beings have allowed themselves to be implicated in structures of victimization and oppression. Her protagonists are not innocent; instead they are shown to be collaborators in cultural myths shared by both women and men. For Atwood these myths are not confined to power relations between the sexes but form the basic assumptions for all patriarchal structures. It is a logical consequence of her vision that national and gender politics should mesh together in a colonial fiction like *Bodily Harm* or a dystopia like *The Handmaid's Tale*.

These novels have strong didactic elements which are both feminist and humanist. For Atwood the artist's major human duty is to bear witness as she says in 'Notes towards a poem that can never be written' (1981), and art does have a social function as the male porn artist declares in *Bodily Harm*: 'What art does, it takes what society deals out and makes it visible, right? So you can *see* it' (208). The importance of making things visible through writing about them is explicitly stated in *Bodily Harm* where the protagonist Rennie Wilford, a Toronto journalist doing a travel piece on lifestyles in the Caribbean, is exhorted to write about its hidden lifestyles by the one political idealist in the novel: 'Here, nothing is inconceivable . . . I wish you to write about it' (133). His plea is echoed later in the prison by her fellow victim Lora who says, 'When you get out . . . Tell someone I'm here . . . Tell someone what happened' (282). These are pleas for realistic reportage, but this still leaves space for other forms of narrative where alternative, unrealized possibilities may be canvassed. Believing as her Dr Minnow does that language is the agent through which social consciousness is changed, Atwood uses fiction to educate her readers. She made this point plainly in her essay on 'Witches' in 1980:

> When you are a fiction writer, you're confronted every day with the question that confronted, among others, George Eliot and Dostoevsky: what kind of world shall you describe for your readers? The one you can see around you, or the better one you can imagine? If only the latter, you'll be unrealistic; if only the former, despairing. But it is by the better world we can imagine that we judge the world we have. If we cease to judge this world, we may find ourselves, very quickly, in one which is infinitely worse.[6]

The narrator in *The Handmaid's Tale* is also a reporter, but by the time her report is heard her present time has become ancient history. Atwood uses the science fiction form of the Wellsian or Orwellian dystopia as a way of social inquiry, for although it is futurist it is actually a construct resisting principles and trends in present society. By making visible through writing their possible consequences, *The Handmaid's Tale* spells out a strong warning. As Atwood commented in her reading from the novel in London in March 1986: 'If you see someone walking toward a hole in the ground and you want them to fall into it, you don't *say* anything.'

These novels are ideologically and politically engaged but in no sense simplified; with their irrepressible verbal play and their challenging of traditional genre codes they are themselves duplicitous fictional discourses. Both *Bodily Harm* and *The Handmaid's Tale* are prison narratives with female subjects for whom marginality has become a condition of being. The traditional genres for such narratives are gothic romances and fairy-tales, and these are two of the models that Atwood uses in her resistant fictions. Having subjected women's victim fantasies to critical scrutiny in *Surfacing* and *Lady Oracle*, here Atwood carries her resistance several stages further. *Bodily Harm* for all its modern Toronto and Caribbean scenarios is traditional female gothic minimally transformed with its insistence on pervasive threats to the protagonist and her final incarceration, the dread of every gothic heroine. It is also an astute analysis of two of the main components of gothic fantasy, which are a heroine's fears of sexual assault and her hopes of rescue by a hero. While it bleakly confirms female dreads, it also exposes the damaging falsities of traditional gothic, for a third essential component of gothic assumes the premise that women are innocent and powerless to do anything to help themselves. It is, however, an interesting feature of Ann Radcliffe's gothic novels of the 1790s that her heroines who believed themselves to be so vulnerable always turned out to be invulnerable. Looking so defenceless, they were actually very manipulative of male power fantasies in order to protect themselves, and despite their fears they remained untouched by the violence around them.[7] Gothic heroines are solitary survivors in Radcliffe's fiction, and the same pattern is substantially true of nineteenth-century gothic novels like *Jane Eyre* or *Villette*. The gothic novel has female fear of male power at its centre, but often women are accomplices in male power fantasies. It would seem that there are several possible responses to this model: women may acquiesce in their victim role and so retain the fiction of their own innocence; they may reject the fiction entirely and so find within themselves the power to resist; or they may use the fiction of feminine innocence as a cloak to hide their own complicity and guilt. In *Bodily Harm* Atwood canvasses all these responses, exposing female gothic as a lie which damages women by limiting their perceptions of themselves as morally responsible human beings. *The Handmaid's Tale* offers a variant version of gothic, though the essential components of female fear and imprisonment remain. Patrick Parrinder in his review of the novel highlights these aspects of female fear and resistance which he sees encoded in the narrator's name, 'The real meaning of Offred, I believe, is Afraid; though since it is not her real name, she is also Not Afraid.'[8] In both novels the protagonists are forced to step out of their socially conditioned self images, and what they step into are hostile environments and uncertain futures.

Bodily Harm is about a woman's disorientation, for Rennie the Toronto journalist has to revise her image of herself as a middle-class Canadian exempt from the dangers that other people from other classes and other cultures have to face. As her securities are stripped from her, she has to look again at her cherished marginality as a guarantee of any kind of safety. 'Massive involvement, said Rennie. It's never been my thing' (34). By the end of the novel, in a Caribbean prison, Rennie has become marginal though she realizes that this no longer prevents 'massive involvement'. The narrative is told almost entirely in the third person, for there is a dramatic shift from the early Toronto section where Rennie speaks as 'I' in control of her own life to 'she' at the point where she leaves Toronto for the Caribbean island of St Antoine. Though she is still the subject, the shift in focalization indicates Rennie's growing recognition of her own powerlessness and the disjunction between herself and the outside world. We realize by the end that there is a total break between her story and what is actually going on, and that this is how the world feels to one woman arbitrarily caught up in power politics. As Atwood said, 'I was writing a spy story from the point of view of one of the ignorant peripherally involved women.'[9]

As in traditional gothic, images of female dread are pervasive. They radiate out from the coiled rope on Rennie's bed in Toronto and the absent faceless stranger who had put it there: 'In itself it was neutral, and useful too, you could use it for all kinds of things' (41). But Rennie sees the rope as a message and wonders what would happen if she pulled on it. 'What would come up? What was at the end, *the end*? A hand, then an arm, a shoulder, and finally a face. Everyone had a face, there was no such thing as a faceless stranger' (41). The narrative follows

Rennie's attempt to escape the threat of the faceless stranger, only to find that her sidestep from real life lands her in a truly unfamiliar place where she does discover what is at the end of the rope. As she looks out of her prison window to be confronted by the naked exercise of police power in the courtyard, she has one of those moments of uncanny insight so characteristic of gothic heroines:

> She's afraid of men and it's simple, it's rational, she's afraid of men because men are frightening. She's seen the man with the rope, now she knows what he looks like. She has been turned inside out, there's no longer a *here* and a *there*. Rennie understands for the first time that this is not necessarily a place she will get out of, ever. She is not exempt. Nobody is exempt from anything. (290)

As if to confirm this perception, the prison guards beat up Lora. All Rennie wishes is that someone would cover her eyes, something she achieves for herself through fantasizing about her own release from prison: 'This is what will happen' (293).

The rest of Rennie's story of her release and return to Toronto is, I suggest, fantasy, signalled in the text by the flickering of verb tenses between past, present and future. In this 'massive involvement' situation, only through fantasy can Rennie distance herself from her intolerable position. Yet it is in these unpropitious circumstances that she makes the one truly generous gesture of her life; she takes the injured Lora's hand and holds it with all her strength, willing her back to life: 'Surely if she can only try hard enough, something will move and live again, something will get born' (299). Very likely it is Rennie who is reborn (as her name would suggest), or at least she is struggling into a new awareness of herself as a morally responsible human being.[10] This seems to be confirmed by her resolution to write about the Caribbean situation, something she had earlier refused to do: 'In any case she is a subversive. She was not one once but now she is. A reporter. She will pick

her time; then she will report. For the first time in her life she
can't think of a title' (301). It is Rennie's new optimism which
dictates the ending:

> She will never be rescued. She has already been rescued. She
> is not exempt. Instead she is lucky, suddenly, finally, she's
> overflowing with luck, it's this luck holding her up. (301)

The dreadful irony is that maybe Rennie will never have the
chance to enact her new story about not being a victim, because
the power struggle has now expanded from a personal to an
impersonal political struggle where oppression and victimization have no sexual focus; dictatorships whether colonial or
postcolonial do not distinguish between women and men, and
she is still in prison.

To what extent is Rennie an unreliable narrator? It would
seem that for most of the novel she is caught like any traditional
gothic heroine in a female victim fantasy where she sees all the
men in her life as untrustworthy, threatening or sadistic. Her
lover Jake with his rapist fantasies, her doctor Daniel, so kind
and conscientious, who performed her mastectomy before the
action of this novel begins, and Paul, the American with whom
she has a brief affair in the Caribbean, all figure as failed
rescuers and therefore betrayers. However, like everything else
in this novel, they are double-sided, and they may also be seen
outside Rennie's disillusioned view as ordinary men with realistically limited powers. It is through Paul, the 'X factor' and
'the connection' that Rennie comes closest to making the
connections which would expose her own fantasizing. When
she is in prison Paul disappears, but whether this means
betrayal of Rennie or death to him she/we never know. 'He's
disappeared which could mean anything' (293). She does,
however, dream about him, and what the dream disturbingly
images is Paul as her own double:

> Rennie is dreaming about the man with the rope, again,
> again. He is the only man who is with her now, he's followed

her, he was here all along, he was waiting for her. Sometimes she thinks it's Jake . . . sometimes she thinks it's Daniel . . . But it's not either of them, it's not Paul . . . The face keeps changing, eluding her, he might as well be invisible, she can't see him, this is what is so terrifying, he isn't really there, he's only a shadow, anonymous, familiar, with silver eyes that twin and reflect her own. (287)

Rennie's story emerges as a warning against disabling female fantasies of innocence and victimization which displace women's recognition of the dangers of real life. Rennie is implicated; after all the first threat to her came from within herself with the cancer. Such a correspondence has all the characteristic Atwoodian doubleness, where external threats are not only paralleled but also prefigured by threats inside the self. The idea of women's complicity is mentioned by Judith McCoombs in her essay on Atwood's poetry: 'The Gothic terror and the Gothic horror, so divided and redoubled, take place in a hall of mirrors, where reality is constantly evaded and yet reflected, distorted and yet magnified.'[11] This comment comes close to Rennie's dream about the mirror sunglasses, though the fullest commentary on Rennie's attitudes is given in *True Stories*, the collection of poems which appeared the same year as *Bodily Harm*. Poems like 'Hotel', 'Postcard' or 'The Arrest of the Stockbroker' could have been written by Rennie herself – if she had written poetry or if she could have seen far enough into her own condition to gloss it so comprehensively.

The shift of emphasis signalled in Rennie's revised fantasy narrative at the end of *Bodily Harm* becomes a radical challenge to institutionalized patriarchal authority in *The Handmaid's Tale*. This novel is an exposure of power politics at their most basic – 'Who can do what to whom' as Offred the narrator says – and it deals in patterns of oppression and victimization based on sexual difference. As a woman's story of resistance *The Handmaid's Tale* is far more concerned with gender politics than with nationality, though Atwood's awareness of Canada's historical situation *vis-à-vis* the United States is written into the novel's Massachusetts setting and Offred's (former) American citizenship, for in this fiction Atwood returns to her own American past. As Catharine Stimpson points out in her review of *The Handmaid's Tale*, Atwood 'acknowledges that history in her dedication – to Mary Webster, a rebellious colonial American ancestor, and to Perry Miller, the professor who taught her to read national literatures when she was a student at Harvard'.[12] The dualistic patterns of traditionalism and resistance to tradition which are so characteristic of Canadian women's fiction are continued in this novel.

Atwood's double recognition of the power of patriarchal structures and of women's ability to evade these institutions by offering an alternative concept of power is the basis of this most subversive novel about a society which is in every sense fundamentalist. It is a science-fiction fable about the future, set around the second decade of the twenty-first century in the Puritan Republic of Gilead in what was formerly New England, which was also the area of the Salem Witch Hunts. History repeats itself with minimal variations and the major source of fear for the reader is that nothing in this futurist society is new. Gilead, whose doctrines of patriarchal domination derive ultimately from the thirtieth chapter of Genesis (which Atwood uses as one of her epigraphs together with a Sufi proverb and the most despairing sentence in Swift's *Modest Proposal*) represents a synthesis of already existing practices and ideologies. As a nightmare scenario it speaks to contemporary dreads about nuclear pollution, the spread of sexually transmitted diseases and possibilities of near-universal infertility. When survival of the race is at risk, human reproduction becomes the centre of social anxiety. In such a society women do have power, for they reproduce the species after all. However, the status of women depends on how a culture evaluates this power of procreation, and in Gilead a sharp distinction is drawn between the importance to the state of a woman's childbearing capacity and her worth as an individual. Fundamentalism is the distinguishing feature of Gilead, where the fundamental nature and interests of patriarchy are exposed: its institutions of oppression rest on the basic equation of 'male' with power and sexual potency and of 'female' with reproduction and submission. Here sex and gender are made to coincide completely, and as a consequence instabilities of gender difference are suppressed as deviations from nature's norm; lesbianism is ignored and homosexuality is a capital offence.

The Handmaid's Tale emphasises the dangers of thinking by sexual analogy when humanness is oversimplified to the point where individual identity is erased. In a world of male/female functionality everyone is exchangeable and nobody has value. As Offred says, her identity as a Handmaid in Gilead is constructed entirely in terms of her sexuality; 'blood defines us' (18) when women are seen and treated as 'two-legged wombs' (146). Offred's narrative does not, however, possess such diagrammatic simplicity. Her account of the daily working of Gileadean society reveals a complex range of women's responses to their predicament, from acquiescence in the system to active collaboration at one extreme and decisive rejection at the other. Perhaps the most disturbing feature of this dystopia is the power exercised over women, not by men (whose spy rings and terrorist activities are fairly predictable) but by one group of women over others. These are the older women beyond childbearing age whom the system has assimilated as 'Aunts'. It is the Aunts who organise the Rachel and Leah Re-Education Centre, acting in collusion with the male architects of Gilead to reinstate traditional gender roles for women and who have absolute power within their rigidly defined female world (the limits of which are prescribed by the patriarchy). Their role is actually a very traditional one within any colonizing situation, as the academic paper at the end makes plain:

> For this there were many historical precedents; in fact, no empire imposed by force or otherwise has ever been without

this feature: control of the indigenous by members of their own group. (320)

These absurdly terrifying figures with names 'derived from commercial products available to women in the immediate pre-Gilead period' (321) and whose speech is a bizarre combination of military metaphors, gender stereotypes and some of the catchphrases of feminism, could not be taken to constitute an antifeminist argument in the novel. There is a clear distinction to be drawn between the Aunts and feminists like Offred's mother who believed in women's economic and emotional independence and who ended up in the unspeakable Colonies to die of radiation disease. Yet the existence of the Aunts is a warning that some radical feminist positions run the risk of being appropriated by the dominant power group and then exploited as a new instrument for female oppression:

Mother, I think. Wherever you may be. Can you hear me? You wanted a women's culture. Well, now there is one. It isn't what you meant, but it exists. Be thankful for small mercies. (137)

What the Aunts' tyranny demonstrates is the danger that patriarchal authority may merely be delegated to become matriarchal authority if the psychology of power politics with its traditional patterns of domination and submission remains unchanged.[13] Far from being an antifeminist novel, *The Handmaid's Tale* may be read as an argument that feminism has not been radical enough to effect a change in either men's or women's traditional gender attitudes. By postulating a crisis scenario, it focuses on the vulnerability of the present moment in the western process of social change where gender roles are being revised. The question the novel addresses is whether the revisionary process has yet gone far enough to change human behaviour if the race were under threat of extinction. The answer would seem to be in the negative, for the power elites of

Gilead (male and female) are shown to be unreconstructed traditionalists.

Such a vision of the future would be bleak indeed if there were no dissenting voices, but of course there is the narrator herself. It is her refusal to believe in biological reductionism as an adequate definition of humanness that gives her the power to resist Gileadean ideology. Not unnaturally in her role as Hand-maid, she is peculiarly sensitive to the colour red, and looking at red tulips while thinking of blood she makes an effort to preserve distinctions that her culture would elide:

> The red is the same but there is no connection. The tulips are not tulips of blood, the red smiles are not flowers, neither thing makes a comment on the other. The tulip is not a reason for disbelief in the hanged man, or vice versa. Each thing is valid and really there . . . I put a lot of effort into making such distinctions. I need to make them. I need to be very clear in my own mind. (43)

In entirely unpropitious circumstances, Offred insists on believing that individuals are significant. Of the men in her life she says:

> Each one remains unique. There is no way of joining them together. They cannot be exchanged one for the other. They cannot replace each other. (201–2)

Her resistance is evident in her determination to tell her story, which is recorded on tape while she is in the process of escaping from Gilead via the Underground Femaleroad to Canada. Speaking out of a condition of enforced silence, she states her belief that the system can be evaded and that there is still a world outside Gilead:

> I keep on going with this sad and hungry and sordid, this limping and mutilated story, because after all I want you to

hear it . . . By telling you anything at all I'm at least believing in you, I believe you into being. Because I'm telling you this story I will your existence. I tell, therefore you are. (279)

By the time the reader receives the story two hundred years later when it is unearthed and translated by archaeologists, Offred's present has become history. What remains are fragments and voices only; there are spaces and gaps that may not be decipherable. As dystopia, historical novel and satiric comment on contemporary North American society, *The Handmaid's Tale* does face 'problems of authentication' (p. 312) (as the scholarly pedant points out in the Historical Notes) for however realistic it may look, this fictive world has no real existence and occupies only the space of writing.

What comes across most strongly is the novel's subversiveness. Offred watches vigilantly for those moments of instability through which human feelings at variance with the system are glimpsed. She calls them 'tiny peepholes' (31), an image reminiscent of E. M. Forster's 'breathing-holes for the human spirit' which he used in his essay written against fascism in 1938.[14] No power structure can ever operate entirely consistently with its principles, simply because it is composed of human beings. The stereotype of male power embodied in Offred's Commander 'Fred' deconstructs itself as he reveals his own vulnerability and desires. What he really wants of his Handmaid is not the serviceable monthly sex for which she has been allotted to him, but something much more surprising: he invites her to play an illicit game of Scrabble with him of an evening and asks her to kiss him 'as if she meant it' (150). He wants friendship and intimacy, feelings which work against the fear and terror on which the Gileadean regime is based. It is interesting that the recurrent section title of this novel is 'Night', the time for private exchanges when arbitrary distinctions are dissolved. This is the time when Offred remembers her past life before Gilead; it is also the time when she regularly meets her Commander in his study 'after hours', and later when she meets his chauffeur Nick 'time after time, on my own' (280). The novel is surprisingly lyrical and erotic, for there are women's whisperings and secret alliances; there are Offred's memories of falling in love and of her lost husband and daughter; there are gardens bursting with bloom in summer; there are the Commander's out-of-date women's magazines like *Vogue* and *Ms.* filled with promises of adventure and immortality; then there is the 'arrangement' between Offred and the Commander and the illicit love relationship between Offred and Nick. Even in such a well-regulated social system breakdowns do occur, like Offred's friend Moira's escape from the care of the Aunts, or Offred's night out with the Commander when they go to the forbidden nightclub, or finally her escape with Nick's help in the Black Van kept to cart dissidents away. It is a novel filled with desire and the fragrance of persistent hope, showing up the limits of tyranny and its costs to the oppressors as well as to the victims. Contradiction defines the conditions of possibility for this narrative, providing the spaces through which alternatives may be glimpsed:

> Maybe none of this is about control. Maybe it isn't really about who can own whom, who can do what to whom and get away with it, even as far as death. Maybe it isn't about who can sit and who has to kneel or stand or lie down, legs spread open. Maybe it's about who can do what to whom and be forgiven for it. Never tell me it amounts to the same thing. (144–5)

Forgiveness, love and trust are the alternative kinds of power which are offered by Offred. Such values would transform the concept of power from 'having power over' to 'having power to' as Marilyn French remarked.[15] The reader never knows what happened to Offred or whether she managed to escape to Canada or to England. As a part of history she is elusive: 'she slips from our grasp and flees' (324). What is left is her story as witness and exposure of the limits of Gilead's patriarchal system. By focusing on the powerful human needs which Gilead neglects, Offred's narrative demonstrates that 'the human heart remains a factor' (323).

> What did we overlook? [the Commander asks Offred]
> Love,   I said.
> Love?   said the Commander.   What kind of love?
> Falling in love,   I said. (231–2)

Heterosexual love is the excess term which the system can neither accommodate nor suppress. Its stubborn survival continually subverts the regime's claims to absolute authority, creating imaginative spaces within the system and finally the very means of Offred's escape from Gilead.

The supplementary Historical Notes delivered at a Symposium on Gileadean Studies in the year 2195 asserts that Gilead (like Orwell's *Nineteen Eighty-Four*) has become a thing of the past. History has proved that it was not invulnerable, so that there is a shadowed optimism built into the fiction. However, although these Notes comfortably manage to relegate Gilead to the status of failed social experiment, the final question to readers refuses to do so. After the the audience applause when the Director of Twentieth and Twenty-First Century Archives from Cambridge University, England has given his paper, comes the signal for opening up discussion:

> Are there any questions? (324)

Indeed there are. The novel ends not as academic speculation on the past but as a challenge to its readers in the present.

Offred's story offers itself to be read with the same ambiguous gesture of trust in its unknown readers as Offred herself makes her exit, 'I have given myself over into the hands of strangers, because it can't be helped' (307). Paradoxically, the condition of helplessness is the one that Atwood argues from and against throughout her fiction, scrutinizing both the damaging victim fantasies and the gestures of moral responsibility that perceptions of helplessness generate. Despite their increasingly bleak scenarios, her novels may be read as celebrations of the human spirit and demonstrations of the necessity for a politics of survival, based (unlike Gilead's) on a recognition of the mutuality within multiple human interests. As Atwood wrote in 1982:

If writing novels – and reading them – have any redeeming social value, it's probably that they force you to imagine what it's like to be somebody else.
Which, increasingly, is something we all need to know.[16]

4

Alice Munro
LIVES OF GIRLS AND WOMEN,
THE BEGGAR MAID

There I come back again and again to the center of my fantasy, to the moment when you give yourself up, give yourself over to the assault which is guaranteed to finish off everything you've been before. A stubborn virgin's belief, this belief in perfect mastery; any broken-down wife could tell you there is no such thing.

(Alice Munro, 'Bardon Bus'[1])

Everybody knows what a house does, how it encloses space and makes connections between one enclosed space and another and presents what is outside in a new way. This is the nearest I can come to explaining what a story does for me, and what I want my stories to do for other people.

(Alice Munro, 'What is real?'[2])

These two statements look as if they are about very different topics, for the first one is about female sexual fantasy and the second about writing short stories. Actually they are not so far apart for they are both concerned with making fictional structures, whether private like the 'belief in perfect mastery' or public like story-telling in print. There is an everyday quality about them as if Munro is addressing readers to whom these remarks will be obvious, a kind of beguiling ordinariness which is characteristic of all her writing. None of this should blind us to the extraordinary clarity of her insights into women's experiences nor the artifice of her stories, for like houses they are constructs where the details of real life are rearranged so that ordinariness is transformed and narrators and readers are able to see things that were previously invisible inside and outside the house. This is the art of fiction which as Munro reminds us, is a shaping of reality in a different notation: 'You can't write the way people really talk, and have anything worth reading to show for it.'[3] What her stories do is 'make connections' between separate events and different perceptions of reality enclosing disparity and contradiction within the same fictional space, while always recognizing that there is an 'outside' which resists the accommodation her fictions offer. How to find a narrative form which adequately acknowledges multiplicity is the challenge that Munro has faced since her earliest stories in the 1960s and there have been shifts and changes in her story-telling methods as she has experimented with different fictional designs and perceived the limits of truthfulness in them all: 'It is a shock, when you have dealt so cunningly, powerfully, with reality, to come back and find it still there' (*Lives of Girls and Women*, 247). Paradoxically, it is an awareness of the incompleteness if not outright falsity of any fictional structure that animates the efforts of her narrators to tell their own and other people's stories, with their constant tendency to revise and supplement, always recognizing that 'the hope of accuracy we bring to such tasks is crazy, heartbreaking' (249). Perhaps the most important thing Munro's stories do for her readers is to heighten our consciousness of the coexistence of strangeness and ordinariness, so that everything is at the same time both 'touchable and mysterious'.[4]

Munro's fictions are set in Canada, usually in small towns in south-western Ontario with names like Jubilee and West Hanratty, and like Laurence's Manawaka they are presented with all the scrupulosity of a documentary photograph, 'every last thing, every layer of speech and thought, stroke of light on bark or walls, every smell, and pothole' (249).[5] How different are these small Canadian towns from English country towns or villages, and is a non-Canadian reader interested in them for the ways in which they are different or the ways in which they are familiar? Certainly Jubilee and West Hanratty are very like small English communities in attitude, where everybody knows everybody else's secrets and where people have long memories so that there is always the same place to go back to though, as Munro's protagonists disturbingly find, it is 'the same but never at all the same' (*Lives*, 26). The physical details of these towns on the other hand differ from English ones for they have wide roads instead of lanes, houses with open verandas, swamps or open country on the edges of town, just as their hot summers and freezing winters are different – altogether a more 'heroic climate' than anything to be encountered in England or Australia or Toronto. This comparison made by the inhabitants of Jubilee in *Lives* is interesting, for Jubilee is so self-enclosed that anywhere else seems far away and alien. With that strong sense of location goes a kind of confidence in shared social values which is possible only in a small isolated community; but again these are points of similarity between small towns and villages anywhere, and when Del Jordan talks about people's lives and the feelings of girls and women in those places any reader finds the appeal of shared experience, for 'people's lives, in Jubilee as elsewhere, were dull, simple, amazing and unfathomable – deep caves paved with kitchen linoleum' (249).

What is more startling here than the familiarity and realistic documentation, however, is the image conjured out of it of domestic surfaces stretched over deep caves, for the one covers the other which is at the same time threatening to collapse it. This image directs the reader to the most distinctive characteristic of Munro's fiction, which is the way it contains the familiar and the unfamiliar within the same narrative structure, insisting that both components need to be recognized and that neither is more important than the other. The 'kitchen linoleum' might be taken as a sign of realism and the 'deep caves' as a sign of fantasy, and these are the two terms I shall use in describing Munro's split-level narratives (to go back to her own house image)[6] where her curious blend of photographic realism and the projections of fantasy continually unsettle the modest expectations aroused by story titles like 'The Flats Road', 'Baptising', or 'The Beggar Maid'. Though Munro is not a fantasy writer, her stories expose the limitations of realism by working within these conventions and then collapsing them by shifts into different fictional codes so that the storyline is continually open to question. Whereas realism works on the assumption that the world is describable and intelligible rather than alien, fantasy challenges that assumption by creating a different design focusing instead on subjective fears and desires, making visible what is usually unsaid/unseen in the acknowledged order of daily life.[7] Both realism and fantasy are constructs imposed on reality, each leaving out something the other includes and so inevitably disrupting the other's designs. Where neither realism nor fantasy is the privileged discourse, both ways of ordering coexist though they do not necessarily connect, and these stories insist on entertaining both possibilities in their resistance to any final narrative solutions.

Fantasy may be a way of escaping the restrictions of convention or it may be used as a way of gaining the necessary inner space to remake images of the self and to renegotiate connections between oneself and the outside world. It is a devious discourse full of secrets and silences and sublimations, and those very strategies of evasion have made it such a useful literary form for female writers for it allows for the expression of a range of feelings traditionally forbidden to women while at the same time preserving the decorum of women's fiction. Indeed the fantasizing of Munro's protagonists operates within this tradition for their fantasies belong to their inner lives which they do not share with any other characters. So these women maintain their surface of silence; they do not say their differences of view, but they think them and often they write them down. In Munro's fiction fantasizing coexists with a character's normal everyday living for the possibilities envisaged by the fantasist do not lie outside reality, rather are they hidden within it. Her language of fantasy is no different from the language of realism, for fantasy works on the same materials, merely stepping aside into one of the spaces within the text, another room of the house where its contents are rearranged. Fantasy and realism may discredit each other but they are supplementary, two kinds of discourse whose discontinuities make up a fictional text which is still less than the complexity of reality itself.

Lives of Girls and Women as its title suggests contains the stories of many women's lives, chronicled by Del Jordan as she writes her own life story of growing up in Jubilee to the point where, like so many adolescent protagonists in Canadian women's fiction, she decides to leave her hometown. These stories are of the 'infinitely obscure lives' that Virginia Woolf glances at in *A Room of One's Own* and they represent the 'experience of the mass behind the single voice'[8] which is that of the narrator as heroine of her own story forging her own identity through the multiple narratives which she has inherited. These stories or fragments are all about women's secret resistance to the maxims of a male-dominated culture; often they are about emotional wreckage and frustrated ambition and invariably they are stories of failure, but all of them reveal woman's stance as alien and critical of traditional structures of authority – like Del's unmarried aunts who 'respected man's work beyond anything; they also laughed at it' (*Lives*, 32). Del in *Lives* and Rose in *The Beggar Maid* are the inheritors of this tradition of repression and guerrilla warfare practised within the bounds of social conformity, but their difference is that through their intelligence and educational opportunities they have the chance to deviate openly from gender stereotypes, resisting not only the maxims of the masculine tradition but also of feminine cultural traditions, imagining newer and more ambitious plots for their own life stories. Ironically, it is through resistance to her mother that Del can begin to find the way to confirm her mother's optimistic prediction from which the title of the novel is taken:[9]

> There is a change coming I think in the lives of girls and women. Yes. But it is up to us to make it come. All women have had up till now has been their connection with men. All we have had. No more lives of our own, really, than domestic animals. (173)

Del's stories like Munro's other narratives interweave the voices of tradition and the voices of contemporary inheritors, showing by their intricate patterns of counterpoint the irreconcilable elements that have to be rearranged in writing new versions of old stories and revealing just how problematic women's relations to their cultural heritage really are.

Women writers like Del are also aware of a literary heritage which is female as well as male and which may entail as many resistances to literary mothers as to mothers in real life. Munro's stories share that ambivalent relation to realistic fiction so characteristic of women's texts since eighteenth-century gothic novels. Not surprisingly the gothic is a favourite fantasy form for her as for Atwood, though with both these writers it is gothic critically scrutinized and revised while still retaining its original charge of menace, mystery and malignity. Munro's fictional landscape is unmistakably Ontario gothic for it exists within the small Canadian towns where her heroines have grown up. In *Lives* there are unplumbed holes in the Wawanash River which the narrator Del Jordan has known since her childhood, and gothic villains who work on silver-fox farms or in the local lumber yard, while terrors of assault, rape and murder are the staple of local gossip and the newspapers. Gothic romance with its sado-masochistic plots is an important component in the fantasizings of Munro's characters, though it is an interesting difference between her and Atwood that since *Lives* (where Del tried unsuccessfully to write a gothic novel about Jubilee) Munro has come increasingly to see gothic as an 'unreliable structure', finding other ways for talking about the strange and the grotesque while Atwood continues to explore gothic possibilities in *Murder in the Dark*, *Bluebeard's Egg* and *The Handmaid's Tale*. Del's dissatisfaction with traditional gothic stems from her perceptions of what it neglects, for not only does it leave out ordinariness but more importantly for her it leaves out women's sexuality. Gothic fiction is obsessed with sex, but stories of heroines fleeing male predators elaborately displace female knowledge into fictions of feminine fear and innocence, refusing to recognize physical desire as a strong component in women's sexual fantasies. Barbara Godard in her essay on intertextual encounters in Munro's fiction mentions her revisions of gothic, though oddly she does not characterize gothic as a distinctively female tradition:

> Writing from the senses, from the reality of her female body, she tries to bridge the gap between experience and a literary tradition which has objectified or effaced her sexuality.[10]

Del's resistance to the very tradition within which she is writing seems to be yet another of her attempts to rewrite her female inheritance. What is evident in both Munro's and Atwood's revisions is that the world of gothic fantasy coexists with everyday reality and that fantasy and realism, which may be separate genres in fiction, blur into each other in real life.

It would of course be much simpler if Munro presented fantasizing as an exclusively female accomplishment but she does not. There are men who fantasize in these stories as well, and indeed the most accomplished fantasist in *Lives* is male. He is the subject of the first story, and though Del is the narrator it is clearly Del's father's hired man Uncle Benny ('He was not our uncle, or anybody's') (1) who is the steadfast eccentric. Del sees him as a sweetly sadistic gothic villain with his 'delicate predatory face' (2) and his wonderful house on the edge of town, so shabby and ordinary outside but pure gothic inside with its wealth of wrecked furniture and its odours of disintegration, 'a

rich dark rotting mess' (4) as Del describes it. It could only be at
Uncle Benny's house that she would read a pile of newspapers
full of sensational crimes with their 'versatility and horrific
playfulness', but this is a secret world. Why was it that the
nearer Del got to home the 'more doubtful it should seem that a
woman would really send her husband's torso, wrapped up in
Christmas paper, by mail to his girl-friend in South Carolina?'
(5). Uncle Benny's world really is wild and strange – like the girl
he marries through answering a newspaper advertisement – and
his account of his unsuccessful trip from Jubilee to Toronto to
find her when she unpredictably leaves him insists that we
recognize the ways in which bizarre worlds may also be necessary to the mind which inhabits them. What Uncle Benny sees is
an altogether sinister Toronto:

> So, lying alongside our world was Uncle Benny's world like a
> troubling distorted reflection, the same but never at all the
> same. In that world people could go down in quicksand, be
> vanquished by ghosts or terrible ordinary cities; luck and
> wickedness were gigantic and unpredictable; nothing was
> deserved, anything might happen; defeats were met with
> crazy satisfaction. It was his triumph, that he couldn't know
> about, to make us see. (*Lives*, 26)

It is the triumph of Del's narrative art to make the reader
see that frightening alternative world which is shared by the
repressed and disadvantaged of both sexes.

The presence of Uncle Benny raises an important question
about fantasy: is there anything about the content or the form of
fantasizing which is distinctively female? Certainly Munro's
stories stay closer to women's fantasies, though signals scattered
through the stories suggest that male fantasizing operates in the
same areas of sex and power but that it creates different designs.
As Del remarks of her lover, Garnet French: 'Perhaps I
successfully hid from him what I was like. More likely, he
rearranged me, took just what he needed, to suit himself. I did
that with him' (217). Again gender boundaries are blurred, for

fantasizing is a shared human activity though men and women approach it from radically different points of view, having different stereotype images and different objects of desire. What I am mainly concerned with here are the fictional forms that girls' and women's fantasies take and the ways they relate to female desires and deprivations. Both Del and Rose grow up with dual visions of themselves as exiles or spies in their hometowns, resisting the social and gender constraints imposed on them and needing to invent more glorious possibilities than their ordinary lives seem to promise. It is only through fantasy that they can recreate the world and themselves; they endlessly make and unmake imaginative worlds which are exotic and theatrical, usually with the transformed self as heroine. Not surprisingly, Del's favourite retreat from ordinary Saturday afternoons in Jubilee is listening to the Metropolitan Opera 'singing in my head with their voices on the radio' and imagining herself as Carmen hissing 'Et laissez moi passer!'

I was shaken, imagining the other surrender, more tempting, more gorgeous even than the surrender to sex – the hero's, the patriot's, Carmen's surrender to the final importance of gesture, image, self-created self. (181)

It is with a similar surrender to operatic gesture and image that *The Beggar Maid* opens. The first paragraph of 'Royal Beatings' is a riot of verbal fantasy created by Rose who is at the time 'nine, ten, eleven, twelve':

Royal Beating. That was Flo's promise. You are going to get one Royal Beating.

The word Royal lolled on Flo's tongue, took on trappings, Rose had a need to picture things, to pursue absurdities, that was stronger than the need to stay out of trouble, and instead of taking this threat to heart she pondered: how is a beating royal? She came up with a tree-lined avenue, a crowd of formal spectators, some white horses and black slaves. Someone knelt, and the blood came leaping out like banners. An occasion both savage and splendid. In real life they didn't approach such dignity, and it was only Flo who tried to supply the event with some high air of necessity and regret. Rose and her father soon got beyond anything presentable. Her father was king of the royal beatings. (3)

It is this same quirk of mind that has got Rose into trouble in the first place with her repetition of the nonsense rhyme:

> 'Two Vancouvers fried in snot! / Two pickled arseholes tied in a knot . . .'
> Rose couldn't stop herself. She hummed it tenderly . . . It was not just the words snot and arsehole that gave her pleasure, though of course they did. It was the pickling and tying and the unimaginable Vancouvers . . . The tumble of reason; the spark and spit of craziness. (14)

The tumble of reason brings Rose's moments of insight into the contradictory nature of reality, into that treachery 'on the other side of dailiness', and though discourse holds her double perceptions together between them 'only a formal connection could be made' (10). It is not surprising that one of these girls becomes a novelist and the other an actress, though it is also predictable that both are always aware of the fragility of these created worlds and the limits of their control, like Rose:

> The thing she was ashamed of, in acting, was that she might have been paying attention to the wrong things, reporting antics, when there was always something further, a tone, a depth, a light, that she couldn't get and wouldn't get. (209)

The power of fantasy to create alternative worlds whose design conforms more closely to desire is keenly scrutinized in the central female fantasy of falling in love. This romantic fantasy and its ending recurs in remarkably similar forms in at least three of Munro's stories in three different collections: Del's experiences in 'Baptising' (*Lives*), Rose's in 'Simon's

Luck' (*Beggar Maid*), and the unnamed narrator's in 'Bardon
Bus' (*The Moons of Jupiter*). As plot configurations they accord
with Nancy K. Miller's suggestion that there is a distinctive
female erotics which structures the plots of women's fiction, the
main elements of which are the heroine's longing to be overwhelmed by the exquisite currents of sexual desire, only to be
followed by her awakening into resistance and then renunciation. As Miller remarks, 'Perhaps this renunciation, this choice
to go beyond love, beyond erotic longing, is the figure that the
ambitious wishes of women writers take?'[11] Though Munro's
protagonists do not all take the initiative in renouncing love,
they all share that sense of self-possession that comes when love
is over. They crave the self-abandonment of falling in love,
crossing over into a world 'where everything we did seemed to
take place outside the range of other people, of ordinary
consequences' (*Lives*, 228). However, they all recognize such
loving as a kind of suspension of their real lives in a dream from
which they will inevitably awaken.

It is in 'Baptising', Del's story of falling in love in her last year
at high school, that the whole romantic paradox in its pristine
form is explored from a female point of view. Her love affair
with Garnet French has to be seen in the context of her
developing sense of herself and her multiple resistances as an
adolescent to images of femaleness offered her by society. It
may be seen as her reformulation of the question asked by the
New York psychiatrist in the magazine she reads: What is the
basic difference between male and female habits of thought?
While she resists his crude sexist stereotyping, she also resists
her mother's version of separatist feminism as too asexual and
intellectual, just as she rejects her friend Naomi's 'normal life'
(191) story of dances and hope chests and shotgun weddings.
Del feels trapped into a binary opposition when she is herself
hostile to such divisions: 'There was no other way. And I was
not going to be able to do it. No. Better Charlotte Brontë' (191).
Only her relation with Jerry Storey gives her any release, for as
the 'Brains Trust' (191) in their class they are at least able to

share their hopes and ambitions and together they evolve a
self-protective parodic relation to male and female stereotypes.
Yet even in this relationship masculine superiority is encoded in
Jerry's comparative estimate of women's intelligence, so that
Del has to resist his view of women too:

> I took his judgment like a soldier, because I did not believe it.
> That is, I knew it was all true, but I still felt powerful enough,
> in areas that I thought he could not see, where his ways of
> judging could not reach. The gymnastics of his mind I did
> not admire. (193)

So speaks Del Jordan and the woman writer, eluding masculine
classification.

Within this realistic narrative of Del's dissatisfactions is
hidden her sexual fantasy and just when she asserts, 'My need
for love had gone underground, like a canny toothache' (205),
she goes to the revival meeting at the Town Hall and the
rhythms of the story change completely. Del's scenarios for
romantic love, derived from reading novels and listening to
operas, find their real life enactment in her love affair with
Garnet French, the boy who comes over to stand by her during
the hymn singing 'like a recognition in an opera, or some bad,
sentimental, deeply stirring song' (207). Garnet comes from a
poor farm, he has already served a prison sentence for violence
and he is Del's gothic hero-villain come to life:

> His dark, wary, stubborn face. His face contained for me all
> possibilities of fierceness and sweetness, pride and sub-
> missiveness, violence, self-containment. I never saw more in
> it than I had when I saw it first, because I saw everything
> then. The whole thing in him that I was going to love, and
> never catch or explain. (211)

Garnet's combination of mystery and sex represents for Del a
'solid intrusion of the legendary into the real world' (211), and
with him she goes to the centre of that fantasy quoted at the

beginning of this chapter, 'that moment of assault which is guaranteed to finish off everything you've been before' ('Bardon Bus', 111). In the truck they go down Monday nights to the banks of the Wawanash river to make love. This is Del's wilderness experience, the impossible place of self-discovery where she and Garnet enact a primitivist fantasy of living in a world of pure sensation: 'The world I saw with Garnet was something not far from what I thought animals must see, the world without names' (218). Garnet's gifts to Del are the gifts of physical love, and through him she comes to a new awareness of self-surrender:

> Sex seemed to me all surrender – not the woman's to the man but the person's to the body, an act of pure faith, freedom in humility. (215)

This is the transformation at the centre of Del's sexual fantasy, but like her orgasm it does not obliterate herself but enhances it:

> I was amazed to undergo it in company, so to speak; it did seem almost too private, even lonely a thing, to find at the heart of love. (226)

Though the love affair shifts the emphasis in Del's life, her desire to be ravished and transformed is always contending with her double recognition of her independent self. Even as she craves self-abandonment she realizes it is only a dream from which she must escape – and she does escape Garnet at the peril of her life in this story so innocently called 'Baptising' where his playful attempt to baptize her by immersion becomes physical violence as he tries to subdue her by drowning her. At the point where he threatens her romantic fantasy by offering to marry her, Del realizes the unbridgeable gap between his fantasies and her own:

> I felt amazement . . . that anybody could have made such a mistake, to think he had real power over me . . . it seemed to

me impossible that he should not understand that all the
powers I granted him were in play, that he himself was – in
play, that I meant to keep him sewed up in his golden lover's
skin for ever, even if five minutes before I had talked about
marrying him. (234)

Spluttering, and resisting what she sees as a 'possibly fatal
game', she surfaces determinedly and walks 'slowly, safely out
of the water' and goes home alone.

Unlike most of Del's stories with their inconclusiveness and
uncertainties, this one does have an ending of 'absolute serious-
ness and finality' (236). Having escaped from that fantasy
world, she resumes possession of the real world and of herself in
the language of realistic discourse:

Unconnected to the life of love, uncolored by love, the world
resumes its own, its natural and callous importance. This is
first a blow, then an odd consolation. And already I felt my
old self – my old devious, ironic, isolated self. (236–7)

Through her own experience Del has disproved that old romantic plot of a woman's transformation through sex. The assault
does not finish off everything she was before, and at the end she
is planning a future 'without love or scholarships'. All of which
is not to deny the contradictions with which the story ends, nor
the pain involved for a woman in trying to revise the old plots:

Garnet French, Garnet French, Garnet French.
Real life. (238)

Munro is very interested in erotic fantasies as an urgent part
of sexual experience for women as well as for men, and in the
shadowy areas where male and female fantasies, though they
may appear to mesh together, actually contradict each other.
She is also interested in women's vacillations between complicity with and resistance to those fantasies, just as Rose in

'The Beggar Maid' allows herself to be coerced into marriage at the same time as she retains her double vision:

> She had always thought this would happen, that somebody would look at her and love her totally and helplessly . . . She would look at herself in the glass and think: wife, sweetheart. Those mild lovely words. How could they apply to her? It was a miracle; it was a mistake. It was what she had dreamed of; it was not what she wanted.
>
> (*The Beggar Maid*, 81)

The contradictions show Rose's recognition of both the banality and the power of fantasy, which remains a central fact of female consciousness little affected by ageing or by experience. After a disastrous marriage, Rose in her late thirties falls in love with a man called Simon and though her fantasies are never so lyrical as young Del's they follow a similar pattern, modified only by her mature chagrined realization that her fantasies are self-created:

> She had done it all herself, it seemed she never learned any lessons at all. (171)

But it is the awakening from fantasy to actuality that is emphasized here in language very similar to Del's:

> It was those dishes that told her of her changed state . . . All she could have said was that she saw them in a way that wouldn't be possible to a person in any stage of love. She felt their solidity with a convalescent gratitude . . . She thought how love removes the world for you . . . It seemed to her it might not be the disappointment, the losses, the dissolution, she had been running from, any more than the opposite of those things: the celebration and shock of love, the dazzling alteration. Even if that was safe, she couldn't accept it. Either way you were robbed of something – a private balance spring, a little dry kernel of probity. So she thought. (175)

What Rose registers as she readjusts to life is that she has been creating for herself beguiling romantic fantasies of feminine helplessness, first as a woman in love and then as a woman deserted by her lover. In a time shift at the end the emphasis shifts again, for a year or so later Rose learns that Simon had died suddenly:

> Simon's dying struck Rose as that kind of disarrangement. It was preposterous, it was unfair, that such a chunk of information should have been left out, and that Rose even at this late date should have thought herself the only person who could seriously lack power. (177)

The notion of love as displacement is one that Munro returns to in 'Bardon Bus', a recent critical scrutiny of the 'belief in perfect mastery . . . any broken-down wife could tell you there is no such thing.' Of course such knowledge does not prevent either the narrator or her friends from falling in love time and again and then having to undergo the process of recovery. It is in the letting go of romantic fantasy that the narrator moves to a recognition of the contradictions within reality itself, contradictions that love has over-simplified:

> The lightness is something to think about. It isn't just relief. There's a queer kind of pleasure in it . . . It's an uncalled-for pleasure in seeing how the design wouldn't fit and the structure wouldn't stand, a pleasure in taking into account, all over again, everything that is contradictory and persistent and unaccommodating about life. I think so. I think there's something in us wanting to be reassured about all that, right alongside – and at war with – whatever there is that wants permanent vistas and a lot of fine talk.
>
> (*The Moons of Jupiter*, 127–8)

The distrust of fantasy which has become so explicit here is an elaboration of Del's youthful perception in the epilogue to *Lives* where she rejects her gothic novel about Jubilee as an 'unreliable structure' which cannot accommodate the multiple resistance of contingent reality. Fantasies conforming as they do to patterns of desire are shown to be as incomplete as the discourse of realism. In either case there is always something in addition which disarranges any fictional structure however carefully it is created. If all fictions are incomplete and artificial, the question arises whether Munro's house analogy for the short story stands or falls. No fictional structure would be able to accommodate everything, 'every last thing . . . held still and held together' as Del wants when she writes about Jubilee. Rose, with her acting, fears that artifice may focus on the wrong things while leaving out the essential truths, and one of the narrators in *The Moons of Jupiter* states that she no longer believes that people's feelings can be reliably deciphered and their true stories told. In 'The Progress of Love' (1985) where 'missing the point' is the point of the story, Phemie the narrator remembers her mother's stories:

> Phemie had a feeling, with her mother's talk and stories, of something swelling out behind. Like a cloud you couldn't see through or get to the end of. (11)

Any structure leaves something out, so the question is how fiction might register the unaccommodating remainders of reality. What Munro's stories suggest is that some of the unexplained bits can be signalled as gaps within the narrative like the deep holes in the Wawanash river, but still something remains 'outside' towards which any story can only gesture. There are mysteries both ways as Munro shows in the last story in *The Moons of Jupiter*, where the narrator goes to visit her father in hospital and sees the diagram of his heartbeat on the screen at the foot of his bed. This diagram is the perfect image of the transference from inside to outside, though as the narrator realizes it does not explain the workings of her father's heart. His heart would have to be opened up to do that and the danger of such exposure is that the heart would stop. This image of mysteries inside is balanced in the same story by several images of mysteries outside: the 'shoreless seas' of Tennyson's 'Ulysses' which her father has been trying to recall and the 'horrible immensities' of outer space that she glimpses when she visits the Toronto Planetarium. All one can do is gesture towards this outside by making a simulacrum with words (like the poem) or with visual images (like the Planetarium), but neither is the real thing, any more than the diagram of the heartbeat contains the mystery of the human heart; while there remains the disturbing possibility that such exposure of secrets is a kind of treachery against the real world (see p. 31).

Reality is infinitely recessional. All a writer can do is to build a house of fiction while being aware of its 'structural treacheries' like the holes under the kitchen linoleum or the 'horrible immensities' outside. Any fictional structure is precarious yet necessary, like a house which encloses space within which we can view the operations of contingency and arbitrariness. Munro's protagonists may be comforted by 'walls of printed pages, evidence of so many created worlds' while at the same time they know that there are always gaps between fiction and reality for 'such questions persist, in spite of novels'. There is always something more – 'a letter, or a whole word, in an alphabet I did not know',[13] or feelings that can never be stated directly but only 'spoken of in translation',[14] or the tremendous mysteries of the human heartbeat and the intergalactic immensities of 'The Moons of Jupiter'. Munro's stories are enclosed textual spaces which always throw their windows open onto 'inappropriate and unforgettable scenery' ('Simon's Luck', *The Beggar Maid*, 177) which threatens dissolution of her ordered structures. Indeed her fictional order includes such acknowledgements of disorder, but the structure of a Munro story is like a house which contains its secret labyrinths within it and does not collapse into a fragmented postmodernist mode. The framework remains realistic while at the same time her shifts of emphasis into fantasy narrative challenge realism as an authoritative account of reality in an awareness shared by readers and narrators of the incompleteness and partial truth of all fictional structures.

5

Mavis Gallant *HOME TRUTHS*

> I suppose that a Canadian is someone who has a logical reason
> to think he is one. My logical reason is that I have never been
> anything else, nor has it occurred to me that I might be.
>
> (Mavis Gallant, Introduction to *Home Truths*[1])

Mavis Gallant is an oddity on the Canadian literary scene, a
truly cosmopolitan writer and not really 'on' the Canadian scene
at all until quite recently.[2] Since 1960 she has been living in
Paris writing short stories for *The New Yorker* and novels which
have been published in the United States and England but not
in Canada till 1974. (Her first book to be published in Canada
was the New Canadian Library volume *The End of the World
and Other Stories*.) She is a writer Canadians have not identified or identified with as Canadian until *From the Fifteenth
District* (1979) and *Home Truths* (1981). In November 1981
Mavis Gallant returned to do a cross-country tour to promote
her first collection of Canadian stories and was back as writer in
residence at the University of Toronto 1983–4. She has since
returned to Paris. Hers is certainly Canadian fiction with a
difference, interesting to readers outside Canada precisely
because she is a Canadian expatriate, but not 'expatriot' as she

insists in her introduction to *Home Truths*. The cliché title of this Canadian collection alerts us to her approach. Though no story in the volume is called 'Home Truths' yet 'telling a few home truths' is what it is about, for she takes a very critical look at 'Canadian' and its usefulness as a descriptive term just as she scrutinizes Canadian ideals of nationalism, cultural heritage, multi-ethnicity and the idea of 'home' itself. She attacks clichés, or as Wordsworth once put it, 'those arbitrary connections of feelings and ideas with particular words or phrases from which no man can altogether protect himself',[3] in the interests of lucid understanding and discriminating judgement.

Mavis Gallant is one of the few Canadian writers whose craft of fiction critics discuss rather than its content, partly because of the way she writes but also because she eludes normal Canadian categories. Yet she is Canadian and speaks some strong words on the matter of national identity in her *Home Truths* introduction; she is a Canadian citizen whose formative years were spent in bilingual Montreal and briefly in English-speaking Ontario. Speaking as an insider and as someone who has lived outside the country for a long time, her view of Canada is always seen from a distance, as Canada remembered somewhere else. She does not invariably write about Canadians (roughly a third of her stories are Canadian, while others are about Australians, South Africans, Americans, English abroad, Europeans displaced by the war) but *Home Truths* is entirely made up of Canadian stories. It is as a short-story writer that she is best known, though like so many of these writers her output includes work in other genres as well. As a regular contributor to *The New Yorker* since the 1950s (her first short story to appear there was 'Madeline's Birthday' in September 1951), she has had over a hundred stories published, as well as two novellas, two novels and a play.[4]

We might describe Mavis Gallant as a writer of fictions of displacement or of exile to be compared with Katherine Mansfield, Jean Rhys or Doris Lessing, for she always writes about people who are dislocated in some way, either in place or in time; her characters are outsiders, detached from the people among whom they happen to be living.[5] In *Home Truths* she writes about Canadians 'Abroad', with their problems of speaking across national boundaries, and draws a parallel with the experience of Canadians 'At home' in communities fissured by cultural and language differences (here Montreal is her archetype), also in families split by emotional differences where the reassuring concept of home is deconstructed before our eyes.

Her characters perpetually find themselves in situations of living 'temporarily' in rented apartments or furnished rooms or as guests in other people's houses, and travelling light. So her stories are never about belonging but about discreet/discrete encounters in places that are both real and unreal, with people who are seen but not really seen, speaking across gaps in words that are heard but not understood.

This anxious sense of dislocation is characteristic of expatriate fiction and it may be a reflection of Mavis Gallant's own condition, but there is another kind of displacement in her stories which is related to the way they are written as much as to the experiences they record. These stories seem much more like stories from the 1920s than anything later, for their perceptions and language belong with the modernism of post-World War I. Indeed, often when Mavis Gallant writes about the war and post-war experiences in Europe or Montreal we forget that it is World War II to which she is referring and think of it as World War I. Arguably her experience of displacement is modernist and metaphysical quite as much as it is Canadian and expatriate in its registration of the fragmented self split by trauma, repression and disorientation, just as the exaggerated roleplaying experiments of her characters, who wander as refugees through the shattered remains of European culture, have affinities with T. S. Eliot and D. H. Lawrence. What she records in her random encounters are the 'delicate and evanescent moments' of heightened perception and insight which Joyce called his epiphanies and Virginia Woolf her moments of being, and like Joyce's stories Gallant's offer no privileged point of view from which to judge what we have been reading. There are no authoritative interpreters, least of all the narrators of the stories. That pose of narrative detachment which has been described by A. J. Gurr as 'the clearest hallmark of the exile'[6] is also a characteristically modernist stance shared by Eliot and Joyce. It is with Joyce as a modernist who was also an expatriate and an exile that Gallant seems to have close literary affinities, for *Home Truths* and *Dubliners* raise similar problems for their readers over the questions of detachment and uncertain distance between the narrator and characters in a story. A recent comment by Patrick Parrinder on Joyce would also serve as a clarification of Mavis Gallant's narrative stance:

> The air of impersonality in the narration is itself a mask, and *Dubliners* uses a richly complex technique to convey a set of strongly ambivalent feelings towards Dublin life and people.[7]

If we substitute 'Canadian' for 'Dublin' with Gallant, we come close to the experience of reading *Home Truths*.

Just as modernism is an important feature in Gallant's fictions of displacement so there is yet another sense of displacement in time in the attitudes towards Europe in her stories. Set as most of them are in the period between the late 1920s and the 1950s, they reflect the attitudes of past generations like Morley Callaghan and Scott Fitzgerald, based on what used to be called a 'colonial' conviction of the cultural superiority of Europe. Her Canadians abroad have the desire to know Europe from the inside but also a sturdy resistance to being assimilated, a double attitude which generates complex ambivalences towards both North American and European cultures. The shifting designation of 'home' (Where is it? In Europe or in Canada?) and the attendant anxieties about homelessness and the impossibility of going back suggest the dimensions of the European challenge to her Canadian characters.

The settings for her stories may be Montreal or Paris, the

Riviera or post-war Germany, but they are always about things incompletely understood, about failures in communication, about the fallibility of memory, about ghosts and secrets. Perhaps what the stories are really about is the entire disparity between social conventions of order and decorum and the individual's private sense of truth, 'which is no reliable counter-event' as one of her women characters in a story called 'The Moslem Wife' realises,[8] and therefore best forgotten in order to survive. Having said that, we can see more clearly how her definitions of Canadianness become at the same time so problematical and yet so emblematic of a wider human condition. As Gallant says rather irritably in her *Home Truths* introduction, 'A Canadian who did not know what it was to be Canadian would not know anything else; he would have to be told his own name' (xiii). The national sense of self depends on the frames of geographical and cultural reference with which anyone grows up:

> The accident of birth does not give rise to a national consciousness, but I think the first years of schooling are indelible. They provide our center of gravity, our initial view of the world, the seed of our sense of culture.

To this Gallant adds a further layer:

> A deeper culture is contained in memory. Memory is something that cannot be subsidized or ordained. It can, however, be destroyed; and it is inseparable from language. (xv)

This is not unlike what Margaret Laurence says about memory and childhood places; it is just that Gallant and Laurence are talking about very different places, different childhood experiences, different frames of reference. But they share a common feature of Canadianness, which is itself a form of the problem that confronts us all, that of defining and maintaining our own sense of identity. How as frames of reference change do we retain our individuality, our independent sense of self? Gallant explores this psychological and social problem in many stories that are not about Canadians, but in *Home Truths* she looks at it in a specifically national context. The most disturbing home truth of all is that the condition of being dispossessed is as common at home in Canada as it is among Canadians abroad. All this leads back to her point about memory and language being inseparable, for 'one needs a strong, complete language, fully understood, to anchor one's understanding' (xvii) – of oneself, of one's own culture, of other individuals and of other cultures. Many of these stories, especially the ones set in Montreal, are about the human casualties in a bilingual culture like Canada's and about the kinds of emotional crippling or 'intellectual maiming' as she calls it that result from arbitrarily imposed switches of language which constitute a form of banishment from one's childhood. Actually that kind of exile is shown at its most traumatic in the 'At home' stories, whereas in the expatriate fiction the linguistic dimension is blurred by being only one of the complexities of confrontation with recognizably foreign cultures.

'The Ice Wagon Going Down the Street' is a story about Canadian expatriates for whom 'expatriate' has become a way of life and a state of mind where optimistic dreams of living in the future balance against a condition of being permanently lost.[9] Peter and Sheilah Frazier who wandered away from Toronto to Paris in the early 1950s on the last of his inherited family money are back in Toronto from the Far East in the 1960s with their two daughters, staying as guests in Peter's sister's house:

> 'Everybody else did well in the international thing except us.'
> 'You have to be crooked,' he tells her.
> 'Or smart. Pity we weren't.' (107)

It is a story where 'nothing happens' but in the process of telling about this 'nothing' the layerings of dream and pretence and loss under the Fraziers' faded glamorous international image are successively revealed.

What first strikes us as odd in this story about dilettantish expatriates is the title, which obviously belongs to an old-fashioned provincial world far removed it would seem from the Fraziers' mode of living. Yet as Peter and his wife Sheilah sit drinking coffee on a Sunday morning in Toronto dressed 'like peacocks' in their silk dressing-gowns from Hong Kong, the morning dissolves into Peter's memory of someone else's remembered morning, a different kind of Canadian morning where a girl from a poor immigrant family in Saskatchewan had watched 'an ice wagon and a trail of ice water in a morning invented for her' (134). Peter's memory of that girl, Agnes Brusen, and their discreet encounter in Geneva is the one secret he keeps from his wife and the image of the ice wagon has lodged in his mind as the sign of a precious fleeting moment of shared recognition between them. Of course Agnes was mislaid when the Fraziers moved on once again from Geneva to Ceylon, but by a kind of Proustian association the memory Agnes had entrusted to him surfaces on another morning in a different place years later, to detonate slowly in Peter's vision of his own failure and loss. After all, 'What can Peter do with the start of a summer day?' (134). The story ends on a delicate counterpoise between his 'true Sunday morning with his wife in Toronto' and his sense of dereliction:

No, begin at the beginning. Peter lost Agnes. Agnes says to herself somewhere, Peter is lost. (134)

Made up of disparate memories, this story is structured on a powerful opposition between two images: the ice wagon of Agnes's secret life and the Balenciaga dress which belongs to Sheilah; there is nothing at all that belongs to Peter. These images by their recurrence and their strongly contrastive patterns of association assume the status of symbols in an otherwise naturalistic text, with the ice wagon suggesting the freshness and promise of a prairie morning for a young girl and the black Balenciaga afternoon dress becoming an increasingly soiled relic of a glamorous past. Taken a stage further, the ice-wagon might be seen to suggest the values of 'home' in contrast to the Balenciaga, the symbol of European *haute couture* and of the Fraziers' failed aspirations. Caught as he is between two cultural value-systems, Peter is indeed lost, an exile inside his oriental silk dressing-gown.

The phrase 'dislocated forever' occurs in another story of Canadians abroad, 'Virus X', which is about two girls from Winnipeg who come to Europe in 1952.[10] Whereas Lottie Benz comes honourably as a student on a Royal Society scholarship to work for a short time on her sociology thesis on 'the integration of minority groups without a loss of ethnic characteristics' (178) the other girl, Vera Rodna, has been 'shipped abroad to an exile without glamour' (176) because she was pregnant. The story shows two different kinds of Canadian response to Europe, with Lottie Benz, assured of her certain certainties, resisting the challenges it offers and in the end going home to Winnipeg, while Vera Rodna makes the more romantic gesture of choosing to stay in France. Such an account certainly obscures the picture in the diagram, for the story articulates a very complex structure of elusive moments in the experiences of both these women, working through the juxtaposition of different frames of social and moral reference towards a point of harmony between them which is then destroyed as they choose to go off in different directions. This story serves to illustrate perfectly Gallant's 'voix particulière' with its creation of double perspectives and its resistance to simple formulations of meaning or of value and finally perhaps its resistance to analysis.[11]

Beginning with a clear contrast between Lottie Benz, like one of Margaret Atwood's 'sweet Canadians' in her innocently narrow provincialism, and Vera Rodna, who is a more marginal figure altogether with her immigrant background and her flamboyant risk-taking, the narrative gradually erodes those differences between them to the point where new choices are possible for them both. But then Lottie makes a gesture of denial, reaffirming the original contrast in which neither of the women any longer believes. In choosing a safe return to married life in Canada, she turns her back on what she and we the readers have come to recognize as her only chance of self-realization. So the story ends in betrayal of friendship and betrayal of self; Lottie will have to forget so much in order to go home again that there is no certainty that her reassimilation will be completely successful.

What has happened to Lottie as she and Vera spend their Christmas and New Year holidays together travelling from Paris to Strasbourg and Colmar on the German border is signalled directly but decisively in her attack of illness in Strasbourg from the mysterious 'Virus X'. Illness and damaging occur so often in Gallant's stories of Canadians abroad that physical symptoms come to look like indices of psychological or emotional crisis for the characters. This seems to be true for Lottie, whose high fever generates her clearest flashes of insight. Only in that state does she realize that her thesis is worthless because no sociological theory can truly account for the complex variety of human interrelationships, and only in a fever can she know the extent to which her experiences in Europe have radically changed her: 'She was dislocated, perhaps forever, like the clock [in Strasbourg Cathedral]' (204). Hallucinations though they may be, these moments connect eerily with an earlier unsettling experience in Strasbourg when travelling to meet Vera, for it was there that Lottie had her first experience of speaking German in public, the 'secret language' of her own family and her childhood memories so defensively hidden under her image of Canadian respectability. Instead of dread, what those German words release are 'certain warm memories' of 'home – not of Winnipeg but of a vestigial ceremony, never mentioned as German, never confirmed as Canadian' (189). But Lottie keeps all this secret from Vera for 'none of this was Vera's business' (190). It seems as if all Lottie's most crucial realizations are enclosed in mental parentheses – like the revelations of real experiences in her imaginary letters to her fiancé in Winnipeg or her view across the plain of the Rhine, that ancestral place 'she loathed and craved, and never mentioned' (195). All her authentic life of feeling is situated in the private spaces beyond the margins of her cherished respectability, so that even Vera's recklessness can only stimulate a momentary response in Lottie. Their high point together is their celebration of Vera's twenty-first birthday at a café in Strasbourg from which they return 'drunk on friendship' and kümmel to be confronted by Lottie's fiancé waiting for them in their hotel lobby 'with his habitual patience'. For a flash Lottie knows what their future will be like:

> One day, she would become accustomed to Kevin, Lottie said to herself; stop seeing him, as she had nearly grown used to mountains. (211)

But being too insecure and too frightened to refuse the promise of security that Kevin offers, she makes her choice by telling a lie:

> What I would like, Kevin – I don't know if you'll think it's a good idea – would be to go back with you. If I stay here I'll get pneumonia. It's a good thing you came. Vera was killing me. (213)

The dimensions of betrayal and self-betrayal become clear in the visit the three make across the border into Germany where, hooded again, Lottie sees nothing:

> If that was Germany, there was nothing to wait for, expect, or return to. She had not crossed a frontier but come up to another limit. (215)

When Vera packs her bags and leaves for Paris, there is nothing for Lottie to do but to get ready to go home with Kevin.

The spaces for adventure and risk have almost closed up for Lottie, but she does two odd things before she leaves. She 'made a list not of what she was taking but of what she was leaving behind: food, wilted anemones, medicine, all Vera's residue as well as her own' (216). Her farewell gesture to Strasbourg is her last imaginary letter to Kevin, but 'it was not a letter to anyone. There was no sense to what she was doing. She would never do it again. That was the first of many changes' (216).[12] Lottie is carrying out her original determination stated to herself on her arrival in Paris:

> She intended to profit from this winter of opportunities . . .
> but in no sense did she desire to change or begin a new life.
> (175)

However, as the narrative slips at the end from indirect interior monologue to the voice of the omniscient narrator in the last sentence, there is a curious undermining of such certainties. 'Many changes'? (216) Lottie had desired none at all when she arrived, but perhaps for someone as dislocated as she has become changes will never cease. 'There was no sense to what she was doing' is intriguingly ambiguous. Does it refer (as she thinks it does) to her writing of the imaginary letter, or does it refer to her departure (as the list-making and the letter might suggest)? The language holds together Lottie's reductive ideal of social decency and her life of feeling in an uncomfortable paradox. Her malaise is, after all, unnameable and possibly incurable.

One does not need to go to Europe to be 'dislocated forever'; it can happen at home in Montreal too, as 'Orphans' Progress' suggests.[13] In this bleak story about growing up, Gallant tells the history of the two Collier sisters, Cathie and Mildred: as orphans in Montreal, taken away from their French-Canadian mother at the ages of six and ten because she was deemed by social workers to be unfit to care for them, they are shuttled first to their father's mother in Ontario, then to their cousins in

Montreal, then to a convent, and finally Mildred is adopted by another aunt and her name is changed. When the sisters meet again at the ages of fifteen and nineteen they feel no sense of connection and do not know what to say to each other, locked as each is inside herself and incapable of any emotional initiatives whatsoever. This is a frightening record of repression and alienation, where 'not knowing' changes from being the happy condition of childhood innocence shared by the sisters to the emotional paralysis of the two young women irreparably damaged by their upbringing. The story ends with Mildred's point of view as she looks at the garage where she and her sister had lived so happily with their mother:

> Mildred glanced up and then back at her book. She had no reason to believe she had seen it before, or would ever again. (62)

What should be the *éclaircissement* becomes its puzzle: why do the girls forget their childhood so completely? In trying to locate the source of a sense of damage we have to engage with the complex and contradictory signals offered by the story. Michel Fabre's analysis of how Gallant articulates the double perspective of the 'doxa' (the public voice of received opinion) and the 'individual personal vision' offers us a way in to reading the girls' history as a painful one of silent resistance, trauma and final refusal. However, it would seem that of the many signs of emotional censorship imposed on these girls the most obvious is the language change involved in their 'helpless migrations' from Montreal to Ontario and back to Montreal again. Whereas in their grandmother's house 'French was an inferior kind of speech', back in Montreal

> Language was black, until they forgot their English. Until they spoke French, nothing but French, the family pretended not to understand them, and stared as if they were peering in the dark. They very soon forgot their English. (60)

The result of such a linguistic quandary is not only the separation between words and their meanings but also a split within the self and 'forgetting'. As Gallant says in her introduction, 'Memory is something that cannot be . . . ordained. It can however be destroyed, and it is inseparable from language' (xv). While it would not be true to say that the story is 'about language' for it is surely about another variety of exile, language does offer important clues through this labyrinth of the sisters' psychic dislocation where silence and forgetting become the only ways to survive.

'Another variety of exile' and a child's 'helpless migration' occur in another group of Gallant's stories about solitary survival, a sequence written in the 1970s centred on a character called Linnet Muir and set in Montreal between the wars. Told as first-person narratives they certainly have autobiographical elements, for the Montreal of these stories is the image of Gallant's own childhood place remembered, but she refuses to allow us to make any direct correspondences between life and art:

> Behind this image [of Montreal remembered] was a fictional structure of several stories which became the Linnet Muir sequence. (xxii)

These stories are 'about a self, a city, a way of life irrevocably engulfed in time past' to borrow George Woodcock's Proustian description,[14] just as they may be seen as a portrait of the artist as a young woman if we think of analogies with Laurence or Munro; in either case it is the artifice of narrative and not artless self-revelation which is important. Told by an older Linnet Muir, these stories of a girl determined to make her own way of life apart from others independently of her upbringing hint as much at the limits of the young Linnet's understanding as they endorse her youthful optimism, so that we see again the characteristic Gallant double perspective structured this time through social situation and personalized narrative.

One of these stories, 'The Doctor',[15] is particularly interesting. It tells about Linnet's childhood doctor in Montreal and
about a late Victorian picture called The Doctor.[16] It is also a
piece of Canadian social history reflecting the isolationism and
the fissions of Montreal society at the time of Linnet's youth
where the obvious division between English and French could
be complicated still further by internationally-minded liberals
like her parents and their 'mixed' social circle of English and
French – but where the language of cultural exchange was
'usually English'. This cat's cradle of overlapping cultures is
also a tangle of individual desires and secrets, some of which the
child intuits but many of which she does not. Her vivid recall of
this vanished lifestyle is measured against a context eleven years
later, when Linnet, now twenty years old, reads the three
obituaries to her doctor in the Montreal French papers, all
recording his life under different forms of his name in three
different roles: as family man, as doctor, and most shockingly as
'the poet R. É. Chauchard' (313). Shockingly because Linnet
suddenly realizes that her understanding of her doctor is full of
gaps, just as a story she hears even later about one of her parents'
friends reveals other gaps in her knowledge of that social circle
and its dynamics of feeling. The true dimensions of Linnet's
isolation begin to emerge as she glimpses incompletely and too
late what she should have been able to hear as a child in the
secret unspoken words of her parents' generation:

> I ought to have heard it when I was still under ten and had all
> my wits about me. (310)

The story ends not with revelation but with Linnet's heightened awareness of being an outsider in her own home and her
realization of possibilities of knowledge now forever vanished,
for the stars are already 'burned out' and the play has ended.
There is no 'Truth with a Capital T' (which is the title of
the next Linnet Muir story) but only fictions, all of them
incomplete.

Though 'The Doctor' may be read as social history or fictionalized autobiography, it may also be read as being about language and art and interpretation, a kind of metafictional discourse made into a short story, as Gallant's meditation on the relation between art and life, or her indirect commentary on her own fictions. The point about Gallant's stories is that they are not reducible to a single meaning; they are not imitative of reality, though we do recognize states of mind and feeling and characters and situations. Instead, they offer significant moments:

> This is what fiction is about – that something is taking place and that nothing lasts. Against the sustained tick of a watch, fiction takes the measure of a life, a season, a look exchanged, the turning point, desire as brief as a dream, the grief and terror that after childhood we cease to express. The lie, the look, the grief are without permanence, the watch continues to tick where the story stops.[17]

What these stories register is both the moment in time and the jarring of incompatible frames of reference, so that the reader is led not outside the text but back into it, into its interplay of differences, its juxtapositions, and to an appreciation of her art of fiction:

> It is not a naturalistic fiction, but it is a fiction of enhanced reality, in which life is reshaped by artifice, but not distorted; part of the artifice is in fact to give this imaginative reshaping of existence a verisimilitude more self consistent than that of existence itself.[18]

Gallant is keenly aware of cultural codes (of Montreal, of Winnipeg, of Toronto, of European cities like Paris) and the clash of cultures, of language as the repository of cultural and social history, and of public language and private inner language. The stories are structured through the interrelations of

these different codes, the codes being spoken by different voices
– different characters' voices, or the voice of the same character
at different times, or the narrator's voice – not one of which may
be taken to represent completely the way things really are.
Gallant denies the possibility of fiction ever fully represent-
ing reality, and one of her best jokes in *Home Truths* is about the
problems of representation. In 'The Doctor' Linnet comments
on some photographs of Paris which she sees in the waiting-
room:

> The sitting-room-converted-to-waiting-room had on display
> landmarks of Paris, identified in two languages:
>
> > Le Petit Palais – The Petit Palais
> > Place Vendôme – Place Vendôme
> > Rue de la Paix – Rue de la Paix
>
> as if the engraver had known they would find their way to a
> wall in Montreal. (299)

The pictures are not real but copies of a real place, the captions
explain neither the image nor each other, and they clarify
nothing in Quebec; reality recedes before the forms of its
representation. This joke is central to what the story is about:
the elusiveness of reality, the multiple possible readings of any
art object, and the lack of authority of any reading. If this is true
of pictures, it is even truer of one person's reading of someone
else, for we never see people as they really are but only through
our own limited ways of seeing (limited by age, language,
culture, gender, just by not being that other person). While the
problem is highlighted here by the narrator's being Linnet Muir
at different ages, it is true of all Gallant's narrators.

In this sense isolation is the human condition; discrete
moments are all we have and they signify what is missing, what
is 'beyond our capacities'.[19] Doubtless there are origins in real
life for these stories, but their interest is not in representation;
rather it is in the way each story interweaves different codes and

how the way of telling resists any final single meaning by articulating irreconcilable differences. What the stories do reveal is Gallant's genuine interest in modes of signification and her awareness that 'making sense' involves silence and forgetting, perceptions of loss and limits of understanding. If dislocation is a way of life for her characters, it is also a feature of her fictional method.

Any discussion of Gallant is bound to involve close attention to language manipulation and shifts of emphasis which are related to changes of place as well as changes in narrative focus. Her expatriate perspective might be seen as an extraordinarily clear demonstration of that fissured pluralistic view of reality so characteristic of Canadian writing. She is an acquired taste and one well worth acquiring for those who are fascinated by the craft of fiction and by its possible land-mines as well as its revelations:

> He thinks there is more than meets the eye, and in a sense he is right: fiction, like painting, consists entirely of more than meets the eye, otherwise it is not worth a second's consideration. (xii)

6

Marian Engel   *BEAR*
Joy Kogawa   *OBASAN*
Janette Turner Hospital
THE IVORY SWING

> Always another place and/or another time is superimposing
> itself on the present, like two slides jammed in the same
> projector and thrown simultaneously onto the screen.
>
> (Jannette Turner Hospital, Interview[1])

Janette Turner Hospital's inescapable doubleness of vision,
recalling as it does Atwood's description of Susanna Moodie's
state of mind, may serve to focus the connections between these
three novels and nineteenth-century Canadian women's writ-
ings, for they all belong to the central tradition of wilderness
fiction in its feminized versions. As I have argued, the wilderness has provided a textual space for women writers' exploration of female difference and a site of resistance to traditional
structures of patriarchy and imperialism. These three novels set
variously in Ontario, the prairies and the Indian sub-continent
demonstrate the continuing presence of wilderness as landscape
and metaphor in contemporary Canadian women's fiction.
Wilderness is the space outside ordered enclosures and so
possesses all the doubleness of fascination and danger that
being 'off limits' connotes. Promises of freedom are linked to
an awareness of transgression, for boundaries assume a new

importance when they have to be crossed, and dislocation with its attendant doubleness of vision is always a feature of wilderness narratives. The wilderness assumes multiple images in these novels with their shifts from realistic conventions of landscape presentation into romance, fantasy and dream. In *Bear* it becomes the impossible space of female desire, while in *Obasan* wandering through the wilderness is the painful preparation for a new future, and *The Ivory Swing* teeters on the borderland without ever venturing over into forbidden wilderness territory. What they have in common is their ambivalent relation to cultural and literary traditions and their attempts to revise those traditions in more adequate recognition of the woman's angle on experience through narrative.

Bear signals its ambivalent relation to the tradition of wilderness writing by its shifts between pastoral, porn and myth, where the Canadian dream of communion with the natural world and its creatures is explored through the mode of female sexual fantasy. In the process, gaps between past and present, like those between reality and fantasy, are shown to be unbridgeable except through the transfigurations of imagination and myth. *Obasan* belongs to the capacious genre of prairie historical fiction which has documented the wilderness wanderings of numerous dispossessed ethnic groups, though it eludes this classification by being also a female quest narrative and a ghost story. The prairie is both a real place and also unreal, a space of 'angry air', for the Japanese-Canadian child uprooted from her home in Vancouver. To the waking nightmare of arbitrariness and homelessness runs the silent counterpoint of dreams which form an intricately interwoven sub-text of unspoken connections linking childhood memories to an eventual adult recognition of continuities. The narrative web blurs the boundaries between past and present, even between life and death as it leads out of the wilderness into promises for the future. *The Ivory Swing*, which might be described as a flirtation with wilderness, has all the eclecticism of women's popular romance superimposing traditional elements of fairy-tale over features of the realistic travel narrative. Situated on the borderlines between western and Indian culture, it swings between those two worlds as Hospital writes about characters 'who straddle cultures and countries (or subcultures within countries), who live with a constant sense of dislocation',[2] though the wilderness of southern India remains alien territory to her Canadian protagonists. This novel is in many ways the revival of an older romance tradition where wilderness is allegorized as the forbidden dangerous place, for despite its modern trappings it is closer in spirit to Spenser's *Faerie Queene* than it is to Modie's *Roughing It In The Bush*. However, similarities in narrative method are my main concern here: all these writers use a mixture of genre codes superimposing one upon another, which results in a doubleness of vision and a characteristically feminine recognition of the provisional nature of story-telling.

Marian Engel BEAR

Sure, they're women's books, because they're about women and written by a woman . . . Remember that glorious song from *The Music Man*, 'The Sadder but Wiser Girl for Me?' That's what I call a woman – and when I get letters and phone calls from intelligent women, I don't think the term 'woman's writer' is pejorative, not at all. Who's afraid of women's books?

(Marian Engel, interview with Graeme Gibson in
Eleven Canadian Novelists[3])

Bear is a Canadian pastoral about landscape and wilderness, about a quest, about a bear, about the relation between civiliz-ation and savage nature.[4] Like *Surfacing* it is a pastoral written by a woman offering even more radical alternatives to the conventions of pastoral and animal stories, for what *Bear* does is attempt to inscribe female sexuality on the wilderness. A curious mixture of tradition and innovation, *Bear* erects a complex structure of pastoral, pornography and myth in its exploration of desire and our unattainable dreams of communion and transcendence through sex, through wild nature, through mystic vision. Inevitably dreams have to confront real possibilities of limits and transgression and in the end have their fulfilment only in fantasy and myth. This is the territory of *Bear* as it traces a woman's experiences on an island in Northern Ontario in the late 1970s.

The story can be simply told: it is about a woman and a bear. The woman, Lou, a librarian from the Historical Institute in Toronto, has a summer assignment to catalogue the resources of the Cary Estate on an island off the north shore of Lake Huron which has been bequeathed to the Institute. It is only when she arrives on the island that her prospects change, and a familiar academic job of investigating early settlement in the area becomes an unfamiliar journey into the wilderness of Lou's own psyche as well as of the Canadian place itself. There has always been a bear on the estate; bears are part of the Cary family's history, for the first Colonel Cary had a tame bear (following the model of Lord Byron whom he had met at Malta) and there is a bear there still. It is this bear whose massive presence comes to pervade the novel, taking possession first of the house and then of Lou's consciousness and her fantasy life. The story develops as a summer idyll of her love affair with the bear, which is for Lou a regenerative experience releasing imaginative energies and allowing her to make vital connections with her own hidden nature and with the natural world outside herself. It might be seen as a process of 'decreation' where Lou gets rid of her socially acquired persona and pushes to the very demarcation line between humanity and nature or animality.[5] But with the end of the summer comes the end of the idyll: Lou's work is finished, the bear obeying its natural rhythms is getting ready to hibernate, and finally the bear draws the demarcation line between them and shows her what is forbidden by natural law. As Lou approaches, ready to copulate with him, the bear reaches out one paw and rips the skin on her back from shoulder to buttock. Only then does she realize the gap between the animal and the human and retreats to her side of the line, dismissing the bear and waving a burning stick at him. She gets ready to leave; the bear is taken away by an old Indian woman, and having made her farewells Lou starts her drive back to Toronto at night. She is the same yet not the same, her old self but 'at last human', in transition between the wilderness and the city, between old patterns and new possibilities, and comforted as she drives by the constellation of the Great Bear in the sky.

Bear has its place in a long Canadian tradition of writing about the wilderness and its creatures (either Indians or animals) and civilization's attitudes towards them.[6] The vastness of landscape seems to have affected the Canadians' imagination differently from their American neighbours' for there is much less of the challenge of frontier experience and far more of the feeling of 'wilderness', disorientation, and a sense of human inadequacy in Canadian literature – just as there is a stronger awareness in modern Canadian writing of the regenerative powers of landscape and the possibilities it offers for psychic and spiritual renewal. The penumbra of allusions to nineteenth-century wilderness literature like Major John Richardson's *Wacousta*, *The Journals of Susanna Moodie* and the animal stories of Jack London, E. Thompson Seton, and Sir Charles G. D. Roberts (who also wrote a novel about a bear, *The Heart of the Ancient Wood*) plainly signal the context within which *Bear* will spell out its differences, for though it too is a response to the strangeness of Canadian landscape it is finally not about hostility and victims but about the inviolability of natural order and the healing corrective power of nature to save us from ourselves. The novel also carries a strong sense of the alienness of the landscape with which human beings have to come to terms in order to go on living in Canada. The brownness of the bear is of a different quality from the whiteness of the whale in *Moby Dick*, for even if the bear is a blank to human

beings his colour makes him a part of the landscape with its dark
forests and curiously dark, clear lakes. The bear's otherness,
something that D. H. Lawrence would have appreciated if he
had gone to Canada as well as to Australia and Mexico, is a sign
of the mystery of the natural world that remains outside human
comprehension. Jay Macpherson spells out the literary response to this perception of affinity between the creatures and
the wilderness:

> In Canadian writing as a whole, the ambiguity of the animal
> and of our relation to it, its passivity in suffering, its inability
> to speak, balanced by the occasional power to make itself felt
> in destruction, make it embody the imaginative essence of life
> in this [Canadian] setting.[7]

The behaviour of the bear in this story presents the same
enigma, with its indifference to the woman's initiatives and its
final assertion of power as it tears her skin in an indecipherable
gesture which she is free to interpret as she pleases. She can see
the gash as a way of making the relationship more equal, for if
the bear strikes back it removes her feeling of guilt at exploitation (the rape of the countryside surely hovers behind this
version), just as it reminds her of her transgressions and
restores her to sanity. But the bear's action is as neutral as a
flood or a snowstorm, and next day it retains no memory of the
previous night. It is this moral neutrality which cleanses the
woman of guilt so that finally she chooses to read the indifference of nature as benign. However, that is her response and it
reflects more about herself as a reader of nature than about the
bear or the landscape.

I said earlier that this was a version of pastoral, and it has
many of the traditional signs of that genre with its emphasis on
seasonal imagery highlighted in the Canadian context by the
real difference between Canadians' lives in winter and summer;
it draws sharp contrasts between life in the city with its
overheated basements and gas fumes and life in the country

with its smell of water and trees; it also suggests the oddly ambiguous quality of the pastoral world as a separate, enclosed place wherein the artificial and the natural coexist, for Cary's nineteenth-century colonial house with its European library and its lawns is set on an otherwise uninhabited island – uninhabited that is, except for the bear. This is a Canadian translation of the world of Shakespeare's comedies and late romances, with the woman sharing the values of both worlds and finally returning to the cultured world from which she came, rehabilitated and perhaps redefined by her wilderness experiences. Again, like every pastoral, this novel is ultimately elegiac, celebrating while at the same time mourning a world of lost innocence, 'thinking herself into a rugged, pastoral past that it was too late to grasp' (*Bear*, 130). Only the vestiges remain in memory or in dream, available to be transformed into myth.

I have written at some length about the pastoral wilderness aspect, realizing I am in danger of falling into the very trap that Lou envisages for herself in one of her bookish similes:

> She felt like some French novelist who, having discarded plot and character, was left to build an abstract structure, and was too tradition-bound to do so. (84)

However, this way of proceeding is intended as a counterbalance to my discussion of sex in this novel and what I see as its rehabilitation of pornography for women readers. This seems to me a decidedly female narrative about sexuality and sexual fantasy explored with a lack of inhibition which makes it very unusual. I want to call it 'pornographic' rather than 'erotic' for several reasons, first because of its highly charged atmosphere of sexuality, then because of its desire to transgress or transcend limits within the self. In her very interesting essay, 'Mass market romance: pornography for women is different', Anne Barr Snitow defines the essence of pornography in ways that are directly applicable to *Bear*:

Pornography is not about personality, but about the explosion of the boundaries of the self. It is a fantasy of an extreme state in which all social constraints are overwhelmed by a flood of sexual energy. . . . Class, age, custom – all are deliciously sacrificed, dissolved by sex.[8]

It is in this sense that *Bear* may be called pornographic – soft porn certainly, but arguably close to pornography for women as Snitow characterizes this in relation to the Harlequin romances which are her subject. These romances treat sex from the 'respectable' woman's point of view where sex, love and marriage are explicitly linked, whatever the provocations to transgress these codes. In the end it is 'sex as social drama' (Snitow's phrase) where the heroine successfully domesticates male feelings to accommodate her own desires. What is perhaps most interesting about these romances are the contradictory undercurrents within female fantasy. On the one hand there are the elements which are very similar to the standard elements of male pornography like the fascination with wild men or wolf men ('under-socialized heroes' as Snitow calls them) and the heroine's fantasies of violation, while always working against this is the 'push for power in female fantasy' where the hero is brought into submission through love.[9] *Bear* seizes on these contradictions which are interwoven in Harlequin or Mills & Boon narratives and highlights them. The 'under-socialized hero' becomes a bear and the heroine recognizes that to be ravished is a consummation as devoutly to be wished as to be feared; at the same time, it is she who assumes the dominant role in the sexual scenarios. Not only does this novel expose the hidden dynamics of women's romantic fiction, it also turns upside-down the power fantasies of conventional male-oriented pornography, for here it is not the woman who is tamed and transformed into a sex object, it is the bear: 'It was indubitably male, she saw, and its hindquarters were matted with dirt' (35). She has the attributes normally given to the hero in popular romances; she takes all the initiatives, asserting her own wishes and instructing the bear in ways to give her sexual pleasure with his licking and later his dancing. It is always her gratification which comes first, for she continually emphasizes the bear's indifference and passive sexuality in this story about the transfer of power from male to female. As she says, 'He served her' (118). The animal with his own vitality gives the woman something she needs: the free expression of her sexuality uninhibited by any male expectations of what a woman should be.[10] Yet Lou is not entirely cavalier in her demands. Porn for women *is* different, one of the main differences being, as Snitow and Coward both remark, the necessity for strong personal feeling as an ingredient in women's sexual pleasure, whether this be romantic intensity or strands of maternal caring.[11] Lou's 'love' for the bear, as she repeatedly calls it, represents that combination of eroticism, motherliness and sexual domination which is the strongest argument for this novel as a feminized version of power fantasies about sex.

Though the novel has a realistic setting it is actually closer to fantasy, for Lou's summer experiences on the island constitute her own private odyssey and have no direct connection with her real life in society. Indeed it is the bear's otherness that she enjoys so much, for like the wilderness itself he is a blank screen on to which she can project any images and fantasies that she likes:

> She had discovered she could paint any face on him that she wanted, while his actual range of expression was a mystery. (72)

So the bear undergoes a variety of transformations which are an index of Lou's own needs and desires. He can be 'solid as a sofa, domestic, a rug of a bear' (70) or 'a strange fat mesomorphic mannikin' (113); he can be a male lover on to whom she projects her impossible fantasies of rescue:

Bear, take me to the bottom of the ocean with you, bear, swim with me, bear, put your arms around me, enclose me, swim, down, down, down with me. (112)

And at the end when summer is over and the bear is being taken away in the Indian's boat he can be feminized into 'a fat dignified old woman' in a fur coat (138).[12] These are imaginative transformations of course, counterpointed by the woman's sane recognition that the bear is always a bear and ultimately invulnerable:

There was a depth in him she could not reach, could not probe and with her intellectual fingers destroy. (119)

The bear is her ideal fantasy object, malleable to her imagination yet unreachable in reality, a partner in the woman's dream journey as it tracks through unexplored forbidden territory allowing her to discover her own repressed primitive self and to make connections with the natural world outside.

Fantasy here has the violent ending so characteristic of pornography where the male inflicts physical damage on the female during a sexual encounter, but here it is not rape which is enacted but its opposite. The sexual consummation wished by the woman is transformed by the bear's gashing her into something entirely different as the frame of reference suddenly shifts from male/female to animal/human. In this displacement of the sexual context, what is written in blood is the line that cannot be crossed between the woman and the bear. Only now does she recognize the impossibility of her dream of communion with wild nature and the important category mistake she has been in danger of making. Sexual difference becomes a sign of basic differences in kind, for the bear's action scarifies her into recognition of herself as human, of him as an animal, and of the inviolability of the natural order. When being 'wanted' by the bear becomes the possibility of being 'eaten' rather than 'loved', Lou assumes control as a human being by threatening the bear and ordering him to leave – which he does. Her wounding is as far from being the mark of Cain as it is from a love bite, for instead it inscribes a natural taboo line and it saves her from bestiality. Then follows a necessary movement beyond her fantasy of their 'high whistling communion' of summer back to the ordered world of social relationships again, the safety of which is imaged most reassuringly in Lou's last evening with the bear. Back in his place beside the fire as a domestic pet, he licks her hand while she sits at her desk reading *Times Literary Supplements* and looking for another archivist's job. When the bear is taken away the next day, he licks her hand again then settles into the boat: 'He did not look back. She did not expect him to' (138). This is no happy folk-tale ending of the kind we get in 'Song of Bear' in Anne Cameron's *Daughters of Copper Woman*, where we are shown 'the wonder of a woman and a bear livin' together and bein' happy' – but in that story it is a female bear, and besides that story belongs to a different genre.[13] Lou and the bear belong to different worlds and she has to leave the island to go back to the city when summer is over. What she takes with her are two books about landscape, her memories of the bear and the wound on her back which had 'healed guilt' (166). Clearly the bear has only been the medium through which she has been able to make her psychic journey through the wilderness, just as pornography has provided the appropriate language for telling some of the asocial primitive elements in female sexuality which are hidden within our own consciousness as within our writing.

Though the novel modulates back into real life with the car drive to Toronto at the end, its final image is not realistic but mythic:

> It was a brilliant night, all star-shine, and overhead the Great Bear and his thirty-seven virgins kept her company. (141)

So the bear has undergone another transformation, this time into a constellation of stars. Such metamorphoses have a long literary history stretching back to Ovid and Catullus, through Chaucer and Pope's 'Rape of the Lock' up to Irving Layton's glorious snake in the sky at the end of 'A Tall Man Executes a Jig'.[14] In every case it celebrates the power of the imagination to transform life into art – a very literary process, which reminds us that *Bear* is actually a very literary fantasy. Where else (besides in pornography) do we find couplings between beasts and women except in legends, myths and fairy-tales? Indeed the legends about bears are written into this novel, and Lou is led into her strange summer fantasy life through her work as a librarian. It is while cataloguing the Cary books that she finds handwritten slips of paper about bear legends and mythology which fall out of the books like clues leading from her familiar world of the printed text into a labyrinth more primitively inscribed, first by hand and finally by the bear's claw. Her love affair may be seen as a transformation of her usual professional activities as a reader of narratives, for the whole time she is on the island she is not neglecting her work, and her comment when initially faced with the unknowability of the bear is not entirely facetious: 'Book, book. Always, when these things happen, pick up a book' (64). She continues to seek clues lodged in books to explain and sustain her fantasy life with the bear. The problem is that such clues have to be interpreted; though on one level they may be read as encouragement with their fragmentary accounts of bears as gods and the heroic offspring engendered by women and bears, on another level they insist on the unreal dimensions of such encounters. On the two occasions when Lou's fantasies threaten to assume the proportions of myth and she tries to couple with the bear, she is brought up against practical physiological limitations. At her first attempt on 'the night of the falling stars' she realizes that the mythic conjunction between herself and the bear is impossible, for like the stars it is 'always out of reach' (122). However, the tormenting possibility that 'the trouble with you Ontario girls is you never acquire any kind of sophistication' (124) is not entirely true, for Lou's poetic language in this episode signals her temporary shift beyond sexual fantasy into the mysteries of dream and desire. Transcendence of human limits is impossible and no stars will ever fall into her grasp, a truth underlined in her second sexual attempt with/on the bear, when he inscribes the prohibition on her back in the primitive language of blood. Such failure would be truly forlorn if it were not for the redeeming power of Lou's imagination and the transfigurations of myth.

In the end Lou does have her revelation when she sees the Great Bear there in the sky, out of reach of course but part of a natural order which may be read as benign, at least on a clear night. The end leads back to the epigraph of the novel, chosen from Kenneth Clark's *Landscape into Art* :

> Facts become art through love, which unifies them and lifts them to a higher plane of reality; and in landscape, this all-embracing love is expressed by light.

In this final transformation sexual longing dissolves in the light of the stars into a vision which is close to mystical communion. *Bear* emerges as a feminized version of the Canadian wilderness myth, a quest for unity of being through loving connection between the human and the natural worlds. Such desires have their realization only in fantasy or myth, though as Jay Macpherson remarks, 'the power to dream is not mere passivity or escape, but is creative and transforming, a kind of Art.'[15]

Joy Kogawa *OBASAN*

> I'm not really at home in either world. But I feel more Canadian. I have this ability to read gestures and subtle intonations – anyone who grew up in a non-verbal culture has that. But one of the distinguishing features of Japanese culture is this process of things going on internally which is never exposed. I'm not like that. I'm more inclined to want to tell everything.
>
> (Joy Kogawa, interview 1983[16])

Obasan presents a very different view of Canadianness from any of the other novels discussed, for Joy Kogawa is a Japanese-Canadian born in Vancouver into two cultures utterly different from each other in customs, language and frames of reference. This is a novel which questions the benevolent Canadian social myth of multiculturalism by suggesting that dual inheritance may be a split inheritance rather than a double one, at least for those whose citizenship is Canadian and whose race is Japanese. It is a historical novel written nearly forty years after the events it reports; it is also a woman's fictive autobiography where she writes about the experience of being an 'other' in Canada. Through language she struggles with the conflicting intermingled voices within herself in an attempt to rehabilitate herself as a speaking subject in a slow progress from alienation to belonging. Written by a woman, told by a female narrator, the title referring to a Japanese woman's domestic role as Aunt, the novel is about the lives of girls and women. There are stories about the narrator Naomi Nakane born in Vancouver to a second-generation Japanese family and raised a Christian who grows up to be a prairie school teacher, about her Japanese-Canadian mother who died in Japan after the Nagasaki bombings in 1945, about her two aunts Emily and Obasan, who maintains a home in western Canada for Naomi and her brother through all the troubles of the war and who is still living there at the time this story is told in 1972. All the themes of women's fiction are here – marginality, lack of political power, patterns of submission, enforced silence, but the story Kogawa tells necessitates a very different treatment for these themes are all transposed beyond individual experience to include that of a racial community, the Japanese-Canadians of British Columbia at the time of the Second World War. In the telling a very different image of Canada emerges, as a place where it is not nature which is indifferent and hostile but the white society of wartime Canada where for some Canadian citizens one's native land becomes alien territory.

Obasan is very much part of the late twentieth-century

Canadian effort to revise and rewrite the official history of the
nation, to fill in some of the gaps in the documentary record by
making known other versions of historical events told not from
the point of view of the authorities but from that of the people
whose lives and deaths were directly involved. In this respect
Obasan is like Rudy Wiebe's novels which chronicle the history
of the prairie Indians and the Métis at the time of colonization
one hundred years ago, or like Laurence's *Diviners* in its
concern for oppressed peoples. It is also a war novel yet not to
be compared with Timothy Findley's *The Wars* for this is war
domesticated showing how it affects families, opposing the vast
irrationality and cruelty of war to the more delicate irration-
alities of love. The methodology in all these novels is similar in
the combination of documentary and fictional supplement. In
Obasan there are the records of real historical events in the
evidence of newspaper clippings and Acts of Parliament, public
and private letters, photos and personal diaries. All this material is shaped by the narrative imagination which transforms the
chaos of fact into art and creates new possibilities for the future.
T. S. Eliot's question in 'Gerontion', 'After such knowledge,
what forgiveness?' is turned inside out here for *Obasan* asks a
subtly different question, 'After such knowledge, what else
except forgiveness?' The novel insists on mutual forgiveness
which can only be achieved after knowledge as a possible way
forward out of the past.

Obasan is about a crisis point in Canada's history during
World War II and the situation of Japanese-Canadians after the
Japanese bombing of Pearl Harbor in 1941. Kogawa tells the
story of the dispossession and dispersal of the West Coast
Japanese community through those war-years and beyond up to
April 1949 when restrictions on Japanese-Canadian citizens
were finally removed. By this time irreparable damage had been
done to the Japanese community which was scattered and
destroyed, and the remaining individuals were displaced persons in their own country. This is the heritage out of which the
novel is written and in consequence it is a rewriting of Canadian

multiculturalism from a different angle, and not this time from the English-French perspective. As Kogawa said in the *Globe and Mail* interview quoted at the beginning:

I think that multiculturalism should be viewed within the English issue. It may be a sub-issue for Québécois, but it is no use to create a policy of multiculturalism as a means of confusing, or defusing the fundamental problem of this country. Each situation is unique. The Japanese-Canadian situation is unique. The dispersal policy was an official policy that was systematic and tragically effective. It should be addressed on its own terms.

We hear a very different version of 'O Canada' from the optimistic official anthem:

Where do any of us come from in this cold country? O Canada, whether it is admitted or not, we come from you, we come from you. From the same soil, the slugs and slime and bogs and twigs and roots. We come from the country that plucks its people out like weeds and flings them into the roadside . . . We come from Canada, this land that is like every land, filled with the wise, the fearful, the compassionate, the corrupt.

(Obasan, 226[17])

This novel is subversive in its exposure of the prejudices hidden behind official Security Acts in time of war, revealing what the dispersal policy felt like as a tragedy of dispossession and the fragmentation of a culture. This history of a vanished people and its damaged survivors constitutes the documentary thrust of the narrative. It is the story that had not been told before, creating voices out of the silence of nearly forty years in an attempt to free Canadians from their own past history. 'Unless the stone bursts with telling' (as Kogawa's narrator says in her Prelude) there can be no possibility of integration. In seeking to

make audible what has been forcibly silenced and conveniently
forgotten, Kogawa's novel is a historical engagement on behalf
of an oppressed minority. History is retold as 'herstory' for it is
Naomi Nakane's story about her quest for her mother who went
back to Japan to visit her grandmother in 1942 when Naomi was
six, and who then vanished. It is the story of a mother's absence
and a daughter's waiting and longing, a ghost story whose
substance is childhood memory and dreams. Eventually it does
have an ending in the revelation of that mother's agony in the
bombing of Nagasaki in August 1945 and her survival in Japan
for a few years, silently masking her damaged life from her
children in Canada. Through that painful knowledge comes
forgiveness and the transformation through love into hope for
the future, so that Naomi's story ends as fragile promise. It may
also be read as feminist in its celebration of women's strength
and endurance and love, as in its demonstration of the woman
artist's power to use language as a creative force freeing the
subject from the deadening silence of the past:

> Unless the stone bursts with telling, unless the seed flowers
> with speech, there is in my life no living word . . . If I could
> follow the stream down and down to the hidden voice, would
> I come at last to the freeing word? I ask the night sky but the
> silence is steadfast. There is no reply. (Prelude)

The vast silence of the sky in this prelude is answered by the
questioner herself, and her answer is the novel.

In its narrative method *Obasan* interweaves many strands of
the Japanese tradition Kogawa has inherited with elements that
are commonly associated in western culture with femininity.
These would include its obliqueness and lack of assertiveness,
its celebration of intuition and imagination, its decorous side-
stepping of enshrined authority, and its belief in the redeeming
power of countless loving acts by which individuals and communities are nurtured. Naomi Nakane is a very different kind of
narrator from the narrator in Maxine Hong Kingston's *The*

Woman Warrior, which tells of the experiences of a Chinese-American girl growing up in California.[18] True, they both spend their childhoods among ghosts, but Hong Kingston's quest is different in its attempt to understand her Chinese heritage when she is born and brought up in an American culture. She has a confidence in 'solid America' which is entirely lacking in Kogawa's account of the fogs and mists and 'place of angry air' which is the Canada of her childhood, and Hong Kingston sees herself heroically as a woman warrior avenging her people's wrongs through her writing whereas Kogawa's method is more oblique. The differences between them are emblematized in the ideographs they use: whereas *The Woman Warrior* quotes the Chinese ideograph of 'Revenge' (53), *Obasan*'s ideograph is for 'Love' (228). Hong Kingston's narrator is overflowing with words engraved on her back, into her psyche:

> The reportage is the vengeance – not the beheading, not the gutting, but the words. And I have so many words – 'Chink' words and 'gook' words too – that they do not fit on my skin.
> (*The Woman Warrior*, 53)

By contrast, Naomi Nakane resists telling the story of herself and her people preferring to let past wrongs stay buried in silence, for it is perhaps less painful to bear wrongs than to lay them bare. Much of the early part of the novel is concerned with the narrator's acts of avoidance and the tension between the impulse to tell urged by her Aunt Emily (who is a woman warrior) versus the temptation of silence embodied in Obasan. Naomi's self-division is clearly exemplified in her two aunts as in her double readings of the dust that swarms in Obasan's attic:

> Everything, I suppose, turns to dust eventually. A man's memories end up in some attic or in a Salvation Army bin. His name becomes a fleeting statistic and his face is lost in fading photographs, the clothing quaint, the anecdotes gone.
> (*Obasan*, 25)

But dust is also substantial and so is memory:

> Potent and pervasive as a prairie dust storm, memories and
> dreams seep and mingle through cracks, settling on furniture
> and into upholstery. Our attics and living-rooms encroach on
> each other, deep into their invisible places. (*Obasan*, 25)

'Seep' is the operative word here, and almost without knowing it
Naomi starts making connections between the present and the
past as she sits in Obasan's silent house in Alberta in the week
after her uncle's death, surrounded by shadows and memories.
Indeed both her aunts act as guides on her quest, Aunt Emily
placing history and facts at her disposal in a large bulky package
of documents, and Obasan leading Naomi indirectly and gently
into the story about her mother – at the heart of which is a time
bomb. The explosive knowledge of her mother's fate is contained in the two Japanese letters written on 'slippery blue
pages' preserved by Aunt Emily in a grey cardboard folder and
left lying on the sofa by Obasan to be read by the old Japanese
pastor to Naomi and her brother at her uncle's wake. The two
old women are the guardians of Naomi's past and together they
lead her into the knowledge of her inheritance.

The novel is about memory, a child's memories of confusion
and absence as she is separated from her parents and their
beautiful home in Vancouver with its music and its goldfish and
its delicate harmonizing of eastern and western culture, all the
things that 'do not bear remembering'. Then gradually 'the
fragments of fragments' and the 'segments of stories' begin to
mesh together into a web of memories, the child's in the years of
the Japanese-Canadians' dispersal to the ghost towns in the
mountains of British Columbia and later when she is ten to the
sugarbeet fields of southern Alberta, her 'sleepwalk years of late
childhood' when she is buried under sadness 'like a long winter
storm' (200). The child's perspective of anxious unknowing is
counterpointed by the adult view of racial antagonism and
persecution contained in the long quotations from Aunt Emily's

documents, but even they do not solve the riddle of her mother's disappearance. The daughter's incessant questioning runs on in the silent counterpoint of dreams under the processes of daily living. She grows up to become a schoolteacher, staying on the prairies near Obasan and her uncle, while her brother adopts the opposite course of separation as a way of dealing with the pain of his childhood. As a talented musician, he flees to Toronto and then to Europe rarely coming back and 'always uncomfortable when anything is too Japanese' (217). It is only the occasion of her uncle's funeral which brings the vestiges of the family together: Obasan and Naomi, Aunt Emily and Stephen, the old pastor Nakayana-sensei. This is the time of revelation swarming with dust and dreams when the full burden of the past is laid on Naomi and the letters about her mother are read out. Only through her knowledge of the past can she find the power of healing her own fragmented psyche.

The novel ends where it began with Naomi standing alone out on the Alberta coulee where she had gone for twenty years with her uncle, on the spot where 'the underground stream seeps through the earth' (247) and smelling the faint perfume of the wild roses. There is no outrush of optimism here and indeed we are made far more aware of the difficulties of telling than of any sense of accomplishment. The novel ends elusively, for like her uncle's favourite fugue this is 'a light piece, more sad than happy, but quiet and dignified, as Uncle was, as Mother was' (244). But the stone has burst, the seed has flowered into speech in the words of the novel and Naomi is freed from the burden of silence.

It is with words that I am concerned in this last section, for much of the novel's power lies not in its historical indictment nor in the story of Naomi's private quest but in the lyric intensity of its vision. This is an invented world of art whose surface of daily living is often chaotic but under that surface is an intricately structured web of interconnecting threads binding together the present and the past, the living and the dead by feeling, intuition and dream. Joy Kogawa is a poet who has also written this one novel so she is acutely aware of the multiple possibilities within language, of its power to distort and lie which is matched only by its power to create texts of subtly interwoven images which shadow the life of the psyche.

Virginia Woolf's woman artist figure in *To the Lighthouse* wanted her picture to be 'beautiful and bright on the surface, feathery and evanescent, one colour melting into another like the colours on a butterfly's wing; but underneath the fabric must be clamped together with bolts of iron.'[19] Kogawa's narrative method is subtler and more flexible, for instead of clamping together she weaves together her images into a net like the fishing nets her uncle used to make in Japan and then in British Columbia: 'Fish swimming through the gaps in the net, passing shadows' (21). Nets and webs are images of narrative and psychological process here as they bind together through the mesh of language disparate places and events and feelings, creating patterns and connections hidden from the narrator's consciousness. Images of childhood mesh with those of adult life, creating a continuity in the psyche which has been deliberately numbed and can only be released by revealing those hidden connections. From the child's world come those images of organic growth – grass and flowers and trees which link the daughter's life to her mother's and which persist in dreams as evidence of deep longing and hope. However, these are counterpointed by more sinister images of defenceless victims damaged and killed – yellow chickens killed by a white hen or by hawks, drowning insects, smashed butterflies, an abandoned kitten – all of which point to dimensions of fear hinting at horrors which are seldom made explicit though they may be sometimes:

> There's something called an order-in-council that sails like a giant hawk across a chicken yard, and after the first shock there's a flapping squawking lunge for safety. One swoop and the first thousand are on ships sailing for disaster. (188).

The nets are strongest in the passing shadows of dream. Naomi has always been haunted by dreams, and her telling them in the text together with her attempts to interpret them provide the clearest evidence of her own life and growth buried under her surface of silence. It is in dreams that 'seepage' occurs most visibly, for the past and the present encroach on each other in the dream-life where nothing vanishes. Dreams are more than repositories here for they give access to an 'underground stream' of communal psychic life flowing out of what the narrator calls, in her prelude, 'that amniotic deep'. It is the strongly maternal image here which alerts us to Naomi's deepest need and to the visionary quality in her dreams about her mother. She has two remarkable dreams, one as a child in 1945 and another one twenty-seven years later after her uncle's death – and they are both nightmares. In the first dream she is visited by the ghost of her mother which reaches out to her as 'her hair falls and falls and falls from her head like streamers of paper rain' (167), and the child knows that 'something is happening but I do not know what it is' (167). She does not find out till many years later when she hears about her mother's agony in the Nagasaki bombings:

> Martyr mother, you pilot your powerful voicelessness over the ocean and across the mountain, straight as a missile to a hut on the edge of a sugarbeet field. You wish to protect us with lies, but the camouflage does not hide your cries . . . Young mother at Nagasaki, am I not also there? (241–2)

That knowledge can only be attained after the revelation of the letters, and before that comes the narrator's second nightmare during the week of mourning for her uncle. In that dream-collection of surreal images Naomi sees her mother dancing in a Japanese flower ceremony holding in her mouth a rose 'red as a heart' on a twisted stem as a cloud falls to earth 'heavy and full of rain', while the air becomes 'a formless hair vest' (227–8) and a black Inquisitor appears who tries to pry open her mother's mouth. As an adult the narrator tries to interpret her terrible dream using for a clue the ideograph for 'love':

> Once I came across two ideographs for the word 'love'. The first contained the root words 'heart' and 'hand' and 'action' – love as hands and heart in action together. The other ideograph, for 'passionate love', was formed of 'heart', 'to tell', and 'a long thread'. (228)

Guided by this, she comes to see the dream as a 'slow courtly telling' of her mother's love and for the first time she wonders whether her insistent questions about her mother's disappearance are 'unseemly' and 'blameable'. Only when Naomi learns to acquiesce in her mother's absence and silence can she see beyond her own grief: 'My mother hid her love, but hidden in life does she speak through dream?' (228). The riddle of her mother may be solved by the slippery blue pages of the letters about the Nagasaki bombings, but Naomi's own quest to find her mother and to hear her dream-speech is not complete until she tunnels back through her childhood and comes to recognize that both she and her mother share the guilt of mutual silence: 'Gentle Mother, we were lost together in our silence. Our wordlessness was our mutual destruction' (243). Old Nakayama-sensei's words: 'Teach us to see Love's presence in our abandonment. Teach us to forgive' (243) guide Naomi on the final stages of her quest to embrace the mystery of her mother's absence, and her recognition ends in love: 'Love flows through the roots of the trees by our graves' (243).

A strong indictment of women's silence and the silence of two cultures, the novel insists that forgiveness and hope for the future depend on speech, on the telling of suffering and injustice as the only way to heal wounds in the psyche. The novel reaches a point of optimism when the story of private and communal suffering has been told, in a characteristically elegiac movement away from grief towards transcendence of loss and back into life:

This body of grief is not fit for human habitation. Let there be flesh. The story of mourning is not a lifelong song. (246)

At the end as Naomi stands on the coulee in the early prairie dawn, the delicately interwoven images of the wild rose bushes, the underground stream and the moon's reflection on the river make a 'quiet ballet, soundless as breath' which combines with the memory of her uncle's words: 'Umi no yo,' he always said. 'It's like the sea' (247). There is the quiet suggestion that transformation has already occurred and that the narrator is freed from the blank of 'white sound' into 'the living word', for 'The Perfume on the air is sweet and faint. If I hold my head a certain way, I can smell them from where I am' (247). The images suggest those connections that the conscious mind is slower to make as they net the fragments of an individual life and a broken culture into a fabric of words which is the created artefact of the novel. Joy Kogawa has obeyed her Canadian impulse 'to want to tell everything' and she has done it in a way which keeps faith with her Japanese inheritance, echoed in the image of the craftsman using his tools:

There is a fundamental difference in Japanese workmanship to pull with control rather than push with force. (24)

Janette Turner Hospital *THE IVORY SWING*

She bent over the curry paste again and closed her eyes, imagining herself and Yashoda side by side on the ivory swing, their vacillations preserved as art.
(Janette Turner Hospital, *The Ivory Swing*[20])

Months later, all we had to do was to say 'Latakia.' . . . It became a private metaphor for any situation in which, for whatever reason, you were in over your head.
(Audrey Thomas, *Latakia*[21])

This section is about *The Ivory Swing* which is set in India and not about *Latakia* set in Crete which I shall discuss later. However, I begin with these two quotations because they both focus on very similar responses to what is unfamiliar and on how the imagination copes with strangeness. It does so in ways that are informative about the process of fiction-writing itself and about our reactions as readers. What we see in the first quotation are eyes 'closed' to the external world while the imagination selects and projects its own images and in the second quotation the dissolution of an exotic place-name into a metaphor for state of mind. Such transforming of real life into the order of art and language is the distinctive feature of narrative, just as seeing through our own frames of reference is characteristic of how we read a novel. The problem of the cultural baggage we bring with us and the extent to which we can perceive our limits and then make connections through imaginative effort is one which seems especially relevant in novels like these two or *Bodily Harm*, for all of them are stories about outsiders confronting cultures other than their own, fascinated by difference and in the end led through their very awareness of difference to new insights into themselves. I am not talking about assimilating the traditions and viewpoints of another culture, but rather about how being somewhere unfamiliar calls in question our habitual certainties as well as offering us variants of ourselves, 'transposed identities' as they are called in *The Ivory Swing*, through whose lives we envisage other possibilities and are enabled to make new choices for the future.

This kind of imaginative engagement is as important for us as readers as it is for the characters in *The Ivory Swing*. The novel offers us the exoticism of India, the strangeness of the place and its customs, the sense of living in a dream or a fairy-tale – all of which is an outsider's response and no less appealing for being that. But it is all under western eyes, India seen through an imagination preoccupied with the values of western culture, so that what is unfamiliar assumes an illusory quality as India becomes a screen on to which are projected magnified images of the observing western self. In this novel the outsiders are Canadians, though 'Canadian' is less significant than 'western' in this experience of the clash between two cultures. The main narrating consciousness is a woman's point of view. The only difference is that now the scenario has moved outside Canada, but it remains her story about contradictions and desires and in the end 'India' does become rather like 'Latakia', an evocative metaphor for a state of mind.

The blurb on the paperback advertises *The Ivory Swing* as 'Ripe . . . vivid. . . . It will be widely read and enjoyed.' This is the description of a bestseller and it is as popular fiction that we can appropriately treat this novel. The most sensitive discussion of bestsellers and how they appeal to us as readers has appeared in a paper given by Professor Elizabeth Waterston of Guelph University.[22] She reminds us that bestsellers offer hooks on which to hang our own desires, 'they offer encoded messages, messages related to the reader's needs and sense of identity'. Now, what are these codes to which we respond? I quote from Waterston's paper:

> A fuller study of the whole series of best-sellers by Canadian women writers would show a tight interlocking of motifs offered to readers, as variations and inversions on motifs of duality, alienation, and dominance. But even so brief a reprise suggests what journeys they offer to readers: journeys into undiscovered or unadmitted selves. For women readers, the journey is often into what Elaine Showalter calls a 'shadowed self,' into a female space, a wilderness shadowed or repressed by the world's values.

A book like *The Ivory Swing* offers vicarious experiences which are fascinating to decode and interesting to relate to; actually it offers the reader the same kind of screen for self-projection as India offers the female protagonist in the novel. As we read we are drawn into an exotic environment which looks more or less realistic as an outsider's view of India, while at the same time we

are enmeshed in a world closer to fairy-tale with its images of
forests and birds of paradise and sandalwood figurines of Indian
gods and goddesses. This is wilderness territory between reality
and dreaming, the space for fantasy, and it is in the passage into
this fantasy world, the risks encountered there and the insights
gained from such encounters that *The Ivory Swing* engages
us imaginatively. Waterston comments on the appeal of this
fairy-tale element in bestsellers:

> As readers we face terrible possibilities, emerge into reassur-
> ing endurances and move through the mythic crisis . . . to be
> restored at the end of our reading, to ordinary waking life.
> (10)

A brief glance at the story will make clearer this double appeal
of the exotic and the familiar, the realistic surface and the
fairy-tale sub-text. The novel opens with the strangeness of
domestic life in a South Indian village for Juliet who has come
from Canada with her husband David and their two children on
his sabbatical research trip. It feels odd to be living in a house in
a coconut grove beside paddy fields that border on jungle and to
have for a servant an Indian boy the same age as her son, who is
also a cowherd and a flute player. In this place Juliet is isolated
in the woman's role as wife and mother, not sharing the same
adventures of cultural discovery as her husband but having time
instead to explore the wilderness of her own contradictory self.
Reflecting on what she was in Canada as a young woman and
what she has become after twelve years of marriage and whether
she wants anything different in the future, Juliet discovers areas
of uncertainty in herself which are fed by memories and fanned
by the frustrations of daily living, and then she finds correspon-
dent images in the figures and situations she encounters in
India. The most provocative figure is the beautiful young
Indian woman Yashoda, who first appears beside Juliet in the
confusion of the Indian market and then one day walks past her
house, appearing and disappearing swiftly and insubstantially

as an illusion. Though Yashoda has an existence in the real world as their landlord's niece and though she has her own history of western education followed by Indian marriage and widowhood, her rebelliousness against the constraints of Indian tradition also make her an ideal shadow-self for Juliet, who sees her own contradictory desires mirrored in this woman. It is their friendship and what happens to Yashoda which are the core of the narrative. In the end Yashoda is murdered and it is Juliet and her husband who find her body. They discover that they are at the same time implicated in the murder yet outside the cultural traditions which sanctioned it, protected from danger by their westernness while being rejected as intruders. The novel ends quietly with a conversation between Juliet and David: 'When the children were asleep they stood together in the cool night air beneath the palms' (251). They are planning to leave India and return to Canada, but whether their marriage will survive is presented as an open question:

'How can I know?' she murmured.
They held each other, frail beneath the moon and palms, and kissed timidly, as frightened children do. (252)

Here is another tentative ending to a woman's novel, though I cannot help feeling that Juliet is insisting on a measure of free choice in which she no longer believes. Yashoda's story with its disruptions and violation has enabled Juliet to pound out some answers to her own dilemma just as she has pounded curry while calculating 'which cluster of losses was the more death-dealing' (251). After her Indian experiences, or rather through watching Yashoda's experiences, Juliet has begun to make her choice for the future, and possibly it is the sign of her choice that the novel ends with 'a vast tenderness' (252).

It is instructive to compare *The Ivory Swing* with a novel of Indian domestic life written by an Indian woman, Anita Desai's *Clear Light of Day*[23] being an obvious comparison. The story of a Hindu middle-class family in Old Delhi, it tells what happens

to the sisters and brothers of the Das family from their adolesc-
ence at the time of the Partition riots of 1947 up to the 1970s. By
contrast with *The Ivory Swing* this is a novel about Indian
interiors, the view of a culture from inside Indian homes and
Indian minds. Situated within Hindu traditions, it offers different and much more varied responses to the same elements of
Indian culture that Hospital's characters notice. The response
to the lassitude of India would be one example, for there is the
same desire in Desai's Indian adolescents for a life 'rich and
vibrant with possibilities' (*Clear Light*, 120) but not the same
impatience that Juliet feels nor anything of the manic-
depressive behaviour of Yashoda. Two members of the Das
family do escape, the elder brother by marriage into a Muslim
family and the younger sister by marriage to an Indian diplomat, so that there is the sense of changes occurring through
time, new ways being assimilated without shock and disruption. The same kind of interiorization occurs in the treatment of
violence in these two novels. Certainly there are the 1947 riots
in *Clear Light of Day* which are more widespread than the
Malayan market riots in *The Ivory Swing*, but for Desai actual
violence is held at a distance and it is the repercussions in the
characters' psyches which are important, whereas physical
violence is directly experienced in *The Ivory Swing* in the
accident of an overturned bus. Yet the Canadians escape the
worst effects of the chaos they witness because they are outsiders. Questions of women's independence and women as
scapegoats are treated very differently as well. Instead of the
melodrama of Yashoda's punishment and death, in *Clear Light
of Day* we have the story of the widowed aunt Mira with her
sense of inferiority which finds its expression in her alcoholism,
yet always this is balanced by her service inside her sister's
family and her assimilation into cultural patterns. Similarly the
independent-minded sister Bim finds her place as wage-earner
and head of the family all within the traditional Indian system
which can actually absorb a surprising range of dissent and
variation. Dominated by tradition where 'Nothing's *over*, ever'

(Clear Light, 174), the novel ends with the creation of a complex harmony out of confusion and multiplicity in a musical party under the stars in the garden of a house in Old Delhi, where though the guru and his pupil are not even singing about the same things yet the two can coexist within one ancient school of music.[24] There is established a deep continuity of things underneath their seeming contradictions all drawing from 'the same soil, the same secret darkness' (Clear Light, 182). This Indian sense of the value of tradition is what Hospital's characters do not see at all. Instead of assimilation, The Ivory Swing is about confrontations which disrupt the cultural system where 'someone had broken dharma' (218) and transgressions have to be punished, all very much India seen through western eyes. The fairy-tale quality of the story and its strong mythic typologies where Yashoda can be seen as an image of the goddess Radha or a demonic Yakshi living in a forbidden forest, where the young Indian servant is identified with Krishna and a sandalwood figurine, is a measure of the simplifications that are only possible when a culture is unfamiliar. What the narrative actually demonstrates is the 'gap between divine allegory and social practice' (The Ivory Swing, 151) which David's academic mind had intuited in his visit to a Hindu temple.

The focus is really on Juliet and her conflicting desires for independence and domestic security, problems that women readers may recognize as familiar. All India does is to highlight the uncertainties Juliet brings with her as she finds shadowy parallels for her own condition in Yashoda and in the mythic figure of Radha for ever suspended on her swing. To someone who has already seen her life in Canada as a 'balancing act' there is a strong appeal in the image of Radha on her ivory swing (balançoire in French), while Yashoda's elusive rebelliousness makes her the flesh and blood equivalent for the mythic figure. Though Yashoda does not have quite the convenient blankness of Marian Engel's bear her foreignness permits very different interpretations of her behaviour so that while Juliet sees her as a shadow-self, from David's point of view Yashoda is the vulnerable female of his power fantasies. She is something else again for the Indian men in the story where she figures as the Yakshi, the evil temptress who has to be destroyed in a ritual of purgation.

However, it is Juliet's sense of affinity with her which is perhaps most interesting, for she sees in Yashoda's self-division between western modernism and Indian tradition a parallel with her own conflicts between different ideologies of woman-hood. As a woman 'born on the cusp between eras', she had 'evolved wings her mother never had, but not the free flight patterns of her younger sister Annie' (*The Ivory Swing*, 19). Juliet's pervasive image of dread is of herself plummeting like a wounded bird and then being forced to live wingless in a cage. Later she uses the same images to describe Yashoda:

> She seemed to see a confusion of blood and mangled feathers, an inevitable wounding, a bird of Paradise plummeting past the stares of small Canadian towns and Indian villages alike. Flamboyance will not be tolerated. (110)

So strong is Juliet's sense of their identification that she inter-prets Yashoda's response to the social constraints of her widow-hood in the way she would have felt them herself as a denial of basic human rights: 'I won't let them do this! It frightens me. It threatens me. It threatens *me*!' Juliet said. (99) This insistence on the connections between them is emblematized in the image of them both together on the ivory swing:

> Yashoda and I, she thought, we want everything. We swing between worlds, always in conflict, always looking for impossible resolutions, destined to uncertainty and dis-satisfaction. (207)

So Yashoda becomes for Juliet a 'transposed identity' who enacts one of her possible choices, that of rebellion, and carries it all the way to death. It is as if like Lou in *Bear* Juliet has to be shown what is forbidden, has to experience what 'decreation' means. This comes in her nightmare after Yashoda's murder when she sees them both clinging desperately to the ivory swing and to each other, then plummeting down one after the other, 'the bird of Paradise mangled on the rocks':

> Then impact. A ballet of fragments, pieces of her own body, her own life, floated before her eyes like atoms in space. She clutched at them, frantic to prevent the dispersal. (250)

The difference is that Juliet survives whereas Yashoda does not, and arguably there are far greater differences between them and their internal frames of reference than those of which Juliet has been aware. Yashoda is for Juliet the shadow-self who has crossed the borderline into forbidden territory, while she remains on the right side of the line doing her balancing act; Yashoda has been a scapegoat for her too. Juliet's dream-self is actually wiser than her waking self, for her dreams alert her to the dangers of transgression and show her the need to find other less extreme answers to her dilemmas. In the end she does, the most important sign of which is the shift in Juliet's use of the swing image in her conversation with her husband at the end:

> We are like trapeze artists who swing away from each other, she thought. It is a delicate act, full of balance and hazard. For such a long time we have been skilful, never falling though never certain. Will we touch on the next inward arc? Or will we miss? (252)

No longer is it Yashoda or Radha on the swing nor is it Juliet in her wild careening between worlds, but instead the swing becomes the site of a delicate balancing act between Juliet and David. This has its attendant risks certainly but there is also the reassurance of skill gained through practice, together with Juliet's recognition of what they share as well as the gaps between them:

All we have between us is more shared years than I can remember, two children, a tragedy, an aching sense of the terrible limits of knowledge and understanding, and this vast tenderness. Just these few things. (252)

Juliet faces a future in Canada beyond Yashoda's shadow-world which will be different because of Yashoda's story, though there is a sense in which she has always misread Yashoda just as she has misread India through the lens of her own cultural conditioning. She does not quite escape her former lover's accusation made earlier in Montreal: 'Jeremy raised a sardonic eyebrow. "The illusion of risk," he said. "That's all you want, the *illusion* of risk" (19). Perhaps that is all the reader of such a romantic novel wants too – hooks on which to hang desires, images of alternative selves, and a final safe return from the strangeness of fiction to the ordinary world, where the giddy sensations of the ivory swing may be transformed into art and where 'Latakia' with all its confused emotions is reduced to 'private metaphor'.

7

Audrey Thomas *LATAKIA*
Joan Barfoot *DANCING IN THE DARK*

Thomas and Barfoot have both written novels with specifically
Canadian locations in British Columbia and Ontario, but in the
interests of a realistically plural definition of Canadian writing it
is worthwhile resisting the 'Made in Canada' / 'Fait au Canada'
label as too restrictive and too colonial for a postcolonial
literature. Neither *Latakia* nor *Dancing in the Dark* is concerned with nationality though both may be seen to be concerned with colonialization in its gender sense and with the
damaging effects of sexual power politics on women's lives.
Like so many of the narratives in this book, these novels
question women's relation to their cultural inheritance and
social fictions of femininity. As stories of resistance and rebellion they are problematized by their narrators' recognition that
they are determined in their resistance by their cultural conditioning, so that narratives and narrators are divided against
themselves in an exposure of the limits of fiction and the failure
of fiction and real life to coincide. If Thomas's novel shows how
a woman's attempt to revise old stories entails a deal of painful
unwriting of her own internalized narrative, then *Dancing in
the Dark* takes this dilemma several stages further by focusing
on a woman who does not want to revise the old stories but who

would prefer to remain within the shelter of romantic fantasy. However, the narrative does not allow her to do so and her fantasy is exposed as a dangerous illusion.

Though they are postmodernist narratives which shift between flashbacks, memories of the past and moments in the present, the disrupted story-telling methods produce very different effects, with *Latakia* insisting on multiplicity and inclusiveness and *Dancing in the Dark* attempting to sever connections and to create an enclosed space for the narrator. These differences which are clearly a sign of personality differences between two women should not, however, obscure the similarities between two novels. Both of them explore through first-person narratives the possibilities of writing as a creative displacement of reality, and end up exposing the duplicity of language, for the activity of writing draws attention to the discrepancies between orderly surfaces of written words and personal pain and longing. Both narrators write themselves into freedom which is fraught with paradox; Barfoot's remains confined in a mental hospital and Thomas's letter-writer finds her freedom only through a language which cannot hide her sense of loneliness and loss.

As stories of women's lives they have much in common with the autobiographical fictions of Laurence, Munro or Kogawa, though the extreme fragmentation of these two narratives suggests that women's resistance to traditional structures of authority may take on new iconoclastic dimensions when writing fiction changes from revision to revenge.

Audrey Thomas *LATAKIA*

'Women have been shanghaied,' Alice said, 'and now we are waking up and rubbing our eyes and murmuring, "Where are we?"'

'What's the answer then?'

'Some kind of mutiny, I suppose. Unless we can talk the captain into letting us go.'

'But that's where your argument falls down,' Stella said. 'We don't want to be "let go".'

(Audrey Thomas, *Intertidal Life*[1])

This dialogue is emblematic of the contradictoriness in women's feelings that Audrey Thomas writes about, on the one hand the urge towards independence and on the other the desire for attachment. Again and again in her novels and short stories Thomas presents versions of women as self-divided, always in dialogue with themselves and with others. *Latakia* is a woman's story about herself and her love affair with a man who has now left her; written out of anger and resentment and longing it is also a celebration of freedom and independence, and because the narrator is herself a novelist it is a story that draws attention to the ways a woman can write about herself and her feelings. It is presented not as a novel but as a break from writing a novel, in the form of a letter from Rachel to her former lover Michael. But is it a letter ('the longest love letter ever written') or is it, as Rachel wonders, an 'imaginary monologue'? These two very different descriptions suggest the conditions of instability out of which she writes. To what extent is this a shared communication and to what extent is it all an effort towards understanding for herself alone? Yet Rachel's need to write a letter to Michael signifies her lack of him; writing is her way of recreating his presence and alleviating at least temporarily her own pervasive sense of loss and loneliness.

Writing a letter to a person is not the same as being with him for words are only substitutes for lived experience as Rachel knows. Her letter is about their two-year-long love affair, from when they first met at a creative-writing class in Vancouver until the present when she is sitting alone in her flat in Crete after Michael has gone to Africa to rejoin his wife. As a successful novelist and divorcee with three daughters, Rachel writes as much about self-division and the multiple demands of her life as she does about love. After a year fraught with tensions when Michael lived with Rachel and her family, her daughters

go to join their father while she and Michael embark on a voyage
out to Europe, thinking that this will mean a new life of writing
and loving but soon finding that old patterns reassert themselves – Michael's need for his wife and Rachel's double need for
independence and her maternal role. When it all goes wrong
Michael leaves Rachel and goes back to his wife who is teaching
in Dar es Salaam. So Rachel is left alone, having finished the
first draft of her sixth novel and waiting for her daughters to
come to spend their summer holidays with her in Crete. This
letter which is her reply to one from him five months after their
separation weaves together snatches of present experience
with memories of their shared past in a 'collage technique'
characteristic of Thomas's writing,[2] dissolving linear time
arrangement in the narrative as memory and desire are
intermingled.

The postmodernist form with its fragmentation and self-
referentiality reflects Rachel's own inner divisions, torn as she is
between her desire to create an ordered world through the art of
writing and her desire for the chaos of daily living. It rehearses
the shapes of possible stories for women as wives, mothers
and lovers, and registers the difficulty of telling new stories
about a woman's life even when the old stories are no longer
authentic accounts of one's personal experience.[3] Rachel's
narrative is not one of self-discovery for as a mature woman she
already has her identity and she knows in what her definition
consists: instead she scrutinizes the layers of self-delusion
which protect her from the knowledge of her strength in
opposition to the favourite female fictions of weakness and
dependence.

What she discovers is that the old patterns of female narratives are ingrained in her body and in her psyche, as permanently with her as her children.[4] Just as she did not cease to be a
mother when she became a novelist, so she could not cease to be
a mother and a writer when she got divorced or when she
became Michael's lover:

You said it was my 'life experience' that made me so attractive to you. But it was precisely the result of that life experience that you hated so much: my children, my books (the fact of their publication).[5]

Any new role is in addition to her former roles and exerts a strong force against radical change: 'Of course this reverence for established order is not unique with the Egyptians. All human beings tend to keep to the old ways even when they are adding the new' (Oscar Ogg, 'The 26 Letters', one of the epigraphs to *Latakia*). Certainly Rachel would like to displace love and sex from the centre of her narrative and to write about other kinds of experience which are significant for herself alone as writer and solitary observer:

> But there's Crete and this village and this street and all that seems much more interesting than the story of how I fell in love with you and all the complications of the affair. . . . Lovers in a landscape, perhaps, but the lovers are just *part* of the landscape. (30)

Yet this is what she cannot manage to do, caught as she is in the old romantic fantasy-narrative of falling in love and needing a man. She criticizes that old story and sees through it, 'It's almost as though we have some kind of prefrontal lobotomy when we women fall in love. Eros' flaming arrow is really a scalpel which severs one part of ourself from another' (109), yet she continues to see through this frame of reference and any new story she tries to tell about herself is disrupted by the old one. She is haunted as much by her longings as by her memories, and perhaps this fragmented narrative does reflect the reality of her life.

What we have in *Latakia* is not Rachel's novel, the first draft of which is already finished (69), but her letter (or maybe her monologue?) where her efforts to impose order are continually undermined by the intrusion of her feelings and self-contradictions, diagrammatically presented as an irresolvable problem like the Cretan Lie in logic:

I HATE YOU

I LOVE YOU

_____

EVERYTHING ABOVE THIS

LINE IS TRUE.

It's all so bloody complicated, isn't it? (29)[6]

Because this is a letter the focus falls on Rachel herself as remembering, feeling subject, allowing her to take an insistently double view by being both inside and outside the story she is telling, less distanced from the narrative than one assumes she would be if she were writing one of her novels. The letter form images instability in its registration of process which undermines any attempt at closure or certainty so that when her story looks as if it has reached a stable point near the end, we realize this is only an illusion. Real feelings continue to eddy chaotically underneath carefully constructed verbal resolutions, refusing the order that the writer wishes to impose through her language. No words can contain the details of lived experience and Rachel's very act of writing a letter draws attention to the fact that Michael is absent and she is alone, creating her own fictive world which emphasizes even as it displaces her loneliness. Her letter ends as a celebration of writing but at the same time it generates a deep unease, for Rachel knows the difference between metaphor and real life just as she knows that writing is a reduction if not a betrayal of living. It may be a means of clarification but it is also a fabrication and Rachel is left to celebrate alone. In the end her story of desertion for all its modern variations is as old as the myths of Greece and Crete.

Rachel's fascination with words – her own words, Michael's spoken and written words, the foreign words she hears in Syria and Greece and Crete – directs our attention towards the central preoccupation of this novel. It is as much about language and writing as it is about story-telling, for the story of Rachel and Michael's relationship is also a story about writing novels or trying to write them. Having met on a creative-writing course, their conversations are about the novels Rachel has written and the one that Michael is writing, and when they decide to go away together it is in order to write. (Indeed, Michael's wife lets him go because she claims it will be beneficial to his art!) They live together in Europe as writers and lovers and crises occur when the two roles get confused. Taking up a feminist line of argument (one of the few pieces of programmatic feminism in the book) Rachel argues for the differences in priorities between a man and a woman: 'A man's first love is never his woman, but his work. That is what he has been taught; that is how he defines himself . . . A "wife" was not supposed to be like that' (85). However, it is equally true that Rachel's priorities are really the same; the centre of her life is her work, her writing, which generates her own double sense of needing but not needing Michael:

> Although I love you in some very real way, I do not miss you. You – or our relationship – got in my way . . . I can't afford that kind of involvement. (21)

Yet when the relationship ceases to get in her way, Rachel feels forlorn. All she has left is words, and her own determined optimism at the end of the letter is undercut by her earlier remark about one of Michael's wife's letters:

> Brave words, but I didn't believe them. What else can one say – it's a matter of pride. I could have taught her a few more phrases. (66)

The doubleness of language, both its inadequacy to net the complications of life and its necessity for human communication, runs like an obsession through this novel. While Rachel wishes that language was a transparent window on to reality she knows that it isn't, and as a professional novelist she is very aware of the limits of language:

> It is very hard, with tools as worn as words, to capture the way the street looks in early morning, mid-afternoon, beneath the moon. It is like trying to write legibly with worn-down pencils. I have always longed to be a painter . . . I want a palette, not a pen. I have to say that such and such is *like* something else – I have to take the long way round when what I really want to do is dip my brush directly into the ocean, the sky, the sun . . . I pace my study in frustration. (60–1)

Her frustration comes very close to Bernard's *cri de coeur* in Virginia Woolf's *The Waves*, '"Like" and "like" and "like" – but what is the thing that lies beneath the semblance of the thing?'[7] Whether words are written or spoken, they can never substitute exactly for things.

Rachel has always perceived this lack of equivalence between Michael's words and meanings, also his wily exploitation of such gaps: 'Every time I heard you talk about "sparing Someone's feelings", I knew you were afraid to tell Someone the truth' (135). Truth disappears into a mysterious space as surely as the boat which she watches every night from her rooftop in Crete:

> The white boat starts out . . . and at one point it is as though the horizon simply raises itself, like a window, and there is a gap between earth and sky into which the boat suddenly disappears. (17)

It is this disappearance of meaning and the futility of words that Rachel realizes acutely while living in a foreign country where she cannot understand the language or even decode the alphabet. Her crisis of despair over failures in communication occurs at Latakia, the Syrian port where she is confronted with indecipherable Arabic:

> 'Oh, the whole question of language, of communication, it's impossible. Why didn't we just stick to gestures and grunts?'
> 'I'm surprised at you, of all people.'
> 'Trying to make things clear. We invent alphabets and language systems in order to make things *clear*. But it doesn't really help. Once you get beyond letters, into words, into emotions and ideas, it doesn't help at all.'
> 'That's nonsense.'
> 'Is it? Nothing ever changes. . . . And people who speak the same language don't even speak the same language. You. Me. All of us.' (171)

Yet it is out of this dilemma over phonology and semantics that Rachel writes her letter. It is no wonder that she is uncertain whether she is writing a letter or a monologue. With 'Latakia', that place of revelation, Rachel brings her letter to an end, when she redefines it not as place but as metaphor:

> Months later, all we had to do was to say, 'Latakia', and we'd both start laughing hysterically . . . It became a private metaphor for any situation in which, for whatever reasons, you were in over your head. In the end, it became a metaphor for you and me. (167)

('Goodbye, Rachel. I love you. It was a Latakia.') (171)

'Latakia' has become a shared private joke where a word substitutes for feelings in ways that are both reductive and evocative of lost intimacy. It is emblematic of the crosscurrents which pervade this narrative of a woman's effort to impose order on a mass of memories and feelings that resist literary restructuring. The same effort is there in Rachel's last words when she says goodbye in her letter and looks out over the sea, 'as smooth and grey as a skating rink':

> Life calls. Goodbye, Michael. I love you, my dear. I'm
> going skating. And remember, the best revenge is writing
> well. (172)

The novel ends in metaphor with the narrator knowing full well that skating is not the same as swimming, just as writing is not the same as talking or making love. It is all a displacement from living into language. Though she manages to end with the phrase 'writing well' she cannot avoid drawing attention to her motive of revenge, which is arguably a transformation and an abuse of former intimacy. In a curious way she takes her revenge on Michael by rewriting their love story better than he could. Just as their relationship was always haunted by the letters and significant absences of his wife and her children, so she hopes that her letter will now haunt him with her loss. Yet such revenge is double-sided, for writing the letter has also refocused Rachel's attention on her loss of Michael. Contradictions of feeling and viewpoint are interwoven through this novel with all the intricacy of Greek traditional dance in continually reforming stylized patterns. Words shift and perspectives change for language holds no resolutions. Yet for all its artificiality and ambiguity, writing is necessary to the narrator and so is the illusory order imposed by art. As Rachel says on one occasion:

> I think you write with your whole body, that it's more a
> question of 'balance' than you realise. (I do not mean mental
> stability by the way.) (124)

But the balance is precarious and Rachel is alone:

> You made me bloom again, Michael, and you taught me just
> how strong a woman I really am. I do not *need* to be 'looked
> after' or 'defined', even if I might want it. (108)

And 'want it' she still does.

Joan Barfoot *DANCING IN THE DARK*

> What good are pages and pages of neat, precise letters
> spiralling into tidy words and paragraphs, if they only look
> good? Underneath it is a mess.
>
> (Joan Barfoot, *Dancing in the Dark*[8])

In *Dancing in the Dark* the 'Angel in the House' murders her
husband with a tomato knife after twenty years of happy
marriage, destroying her own life as well as his as she cuts her
way out of a self-imprisoning fantasy of domestic bliss. Like so
many of the novels discussed in this book, Barfoot's is a product
of the raised feminist consciousness since the 1960s in its
exposure of the consequences of sexual power politics and its
resistance to traditional realistic conventions of narrative. It is
another story about women's revision of their inheritance but it
questions inheritance from a different angle, focusing not on
strategies of male domination but exposing women's own self-
enslavement to inherited gender images and romantic fantasies.
The closest parallel to *Dancing in the Dark* would be Atwood's
coolly sensitive analyses in *Surfacing*, *Bodily Harm* and
Bluebeard's Egg, but Barfoot's novel is both angrier and simpler in its indictments. Like feminist revisions of fairy-tales,
this confessional novel is a strong protest against stereotyping
and the social fictions that condition the ways women think
about themselves and their relationships. Mrs Edna Cormick's
story, told to her notebooks as she sits confined in a mental
hospital three years after the murder, exposes what lies behind
her silence and the multiplicity of unstated feelings below the
surfaces of social and fictional decorum.

Female revenge fantasies are surprisingly uncommon in
women's fiction, and the *crime passionel* is usually regarded as a
male response to infidelity. On the face of it Edna Cormick
would seem to be the most unlikely murderess in fiction; she
would also appear to be the most unlikely narrator of a novel of
feminist protest, for she is an old-fashioned 'feminine' woman

who always preferred to live within the shelter of inherited fantasy structures. Brought up in the first post-war generation, she has willingly allowed her life to be created for her through the fictions offered by 1950s magazines with their romantic images of desirable women as lovers, brides and wives in happy marriages and glossy homes. Her modern domestic fairy-tale with herself in the role of little woman adoring her strong, successful husband provided the script for twenty years of marriage to Harry. As a fairy-tale it depended on maintaining an enclosed space wherein she and her husband were flattened into stereotypes in a deliberate reduction of complexity and contingency. Only when Edna's fantasy is threatened by self-doubts on her fortieth birthday and then radically challenged by a report of Harry's infidelity does Edna surface as a 'betrayed woman' who takes her revenge by stabbing her husband to death in the kitchen.

As a 'true romance' plot it is not far removed from the clichés of Edna's magazine fiction, and the reader's interest is really not in the plot but in the story-telling method. Told entirely from Edna's point of view it is a story ceaselessly at odds with itself. Presented as a woman's story of her perfect marriage, it is also the story of a failed marriage told from the other side of her collapsed fantasy; described as 'a simple, ordinary, domestic failure' (219), it recounts a murder where the 'Angel in the House' is a liar and a killer. Begun as a narrative designed to sever connections between the past and the present and to create a solipsistic enclosure for the narrator, it becomes the means through which vital connections are made in a process of self-rehabilitation. A narrative which has its origin in the writer's search for perfect order is continually disrupted by remembered details which resist and contradict that order so that finally it is exposed as 'lies and lies and lies' (167).

This is really a story about the making and unmaking of fictions where a woman creates and then destroys her domestic fantasy, killing 'her husband and herself in another life' (183), and then reinvents herself in the secret life of fiction. As she tells the story of the self she had repressed for twenty years she becomes increasingly aware that her life has become a text written in her secret notebooks, 'reduced to me, this pen, this notebook' (161). The narrator is interested in writing as a private activity but not as communication, for she will not let anyone in the mental hospital read what she has written and she records in her notebooks the questions her doctor asks her instead of replying to him. Her writing is a gesture of defence against the outside world and against herself:

> It was the doctor, not she, who brought me the first pure, perfect notebook. I don't know what I thought of when I first saw the one in the nurse's hands. A poem maybe. Or some other way to put events in place. Flatten them out with words, or straighten them, or look at them. Or just get rid of them. Put them some place where covers could be shut on them.
>
> They thought a notebook might be an opening? It has built a new wall instead. And this time it is just my wall, I don't have to share it. So no groping fingers are going to poke through this time. In either direction. (125)

Edna's obsession with orderly surfaces where she will 'not permit erasures, no blots or irregularities are allowed' (4) is a displacement and a continuation of her twenty years of house-keeping and incessant vacuum cleaning, all part of her rage for order against chaos.[9] Yet from the start her narrative effort is self-contradictory, for even the 'pure perfect notebook' has holes in the margins on every page which allow for speculation on other holes 'irregular and unspaced, made by a knife in a body' (1). Designed as a wall or a bandage ('I bind my wounds with paper'), this double-voiced narrative continually disrupts its own project so that the very process of retelling precipitates Edna's revelation of the central crisis of her life which has been hovering on the margins of her story:

All the blue covers, grey lines, pink margins, and even holes, filled with all the meticulous writing. All the vital letters of my life. And the paper no longer binds the wounds. Blood seeps between the pages, and oozes out the covers. (171)

Seepage is again a key word as it was in *Obasan*, and like *Obasan* this is a story which registers the narrator's resistance to its telling in a similarly disrupted narrative form. However, there is no underlying web image here but just the opposite, for the narrator actually unpicks her life story in her effort to find the flaw in her vanished illusion of perfection. Characters and action are presented in dismembered fragments which the narrator would prefer not to assimilate, especially the image of her dead husband: 'I don't see him whole, only bits and pieces. And of those bits and pieces his hands most clearly' (5). Throughout the text Harry's absence is signalled in his partial appearances as 'a handsome, well-known, well-loved face before me' (12) or as 'two long legs in front of me' (177). Similarly her narrative is continually threatened with dismemberment with her references to chasms and disasters, the phone call so obsessionally recalled, and the outbreaks of sweating which disrupt her silent composure. For all her attempts to transform the past, 'altering substances with words', Edna knows that she cannot uninvent it:

I would give anything to go back. To undo and do again, I am blinded by knowing it is not possible. It should be possible. I would be so much better, knowing what I know. I would be perfect. If I were perfect (I thought I was, but now perceive the cracks), would he not be also? And then all of this unnecessary. Unreal, impossible. (20)

Not only are there gaps in Edna's narrative method but her retelling of her life story reveals gaps and blanks there as well, for this is also the narrative of her own self-development which was interrupted by her meeting with Harry and their marriage:

I'm curious now if I might have seen my poem in that magazine and how I would have looked in a black sweater and if I might have been some other Edna. Instead, Harry came one day between the poem and the meeting and there was no need to long for anything again. The swan and the butterfly himself he was, not me. (39)

And a murder later:

What would my own rules have been? I can't imagine. It doesn't seem to have been my life at all; although it must have seemed like my life at the time. (170)

Edna prefers to exist within the artificially enclosed space of her marriage fantasy, concentrating on polished surfaces and forcing her husband and herself to disappear into her magazine stereotypes. Though she accuses her mother of being a witch who 'must have done something truly strange to make my father so invisible' (27), it is Edna herself who is adept at making all traces of the living vanish, whether making beds so that 'we were erased' (85), wiping surfaces 'where there might be Harry's fingerprints' (83), or incessantly vacuuming. Vacuum cleaning is the perfect symbol of the emptiness of this childless marriage, where Edna creates the vacuum into which she is finally sucked. When she murders Harry, the vacuum cleaner is appropriately enough still plugged in upstairs. Only when it is too late does she look from the other side of the chasm at her shattered fairy-tale to realize its dangerous reductiveness:

Real passion – how would that have been? What would it have been like to really feel Harry's skin, and my own, instead of turning it into something tougher, harder – protection? How would it have felt if there had been nothing between us? What if I had understood those hands, the body, all the words he spoke, were someone else, another person, a life?

I took the face he gave me and transformed it into something else.

I wiped myself off like a child at the blackboard and then both of us must have gone about writing on it something wrong. (169)

The script of such a fantasy will predictably contain a banal infidelity, which comes in Harry's affair with his secretary. This is reported to Edna (as she is vacuuming) in a phone call from an acquaintance who could not be regarded as a reliable witness. Yet this one report is enough to send Edna's precariously balanced structure collapsing about her ears, and when Harry arrives home twelve hours later she stabs him to death without a word. From hints in her story it may well be apparent to the reader that the marriage was hollow and that the vacuum was already there. To borrow Atwood's image of the vacuum in *Bodily Harm*, 'something had to come to fill it. Maybe the man with the rope hadn't so much broken into her apartment as been sucked in by the force of gravity. Which was one way of looking at it, thought Rennie' (39). Certainly this is not one of the ways that occurs to Edna, though it may occur to the reader. Edna finds herself inside the vacuum:

This was not a different atmosphere, however, but no atmosphere at all; the air sucked out, leaving me holding my breath. (173)

Caught in her airless fantasy, she is finally in danger of disappearing into it and can only turn to the reassurance of her gold-flecked wallpaper which she stares at for hours. Unlike Charlotte Perkins Gilman's protagonist, however, she resists dissolution, and when Harry's face, 'earnest and concerned' (177), blocks her view of the wall she stabs at him as an obstacle.

Edna cuts her way out of a self-imprisoning fantasy by cutting her way through Harry's body. The murder when she finally recounts it is a bizarre mixture of domestic detail, displaced violence and eroticism:

It does not go into him so far that it is necessary actually to touch him. The softness is pleasing and surprising, and I experiment with it again; several more times. It is a little like digging a trowel into soft earth in the spring to plant a flower. Once there is some hard impediment, like a root or a rock, but it's easy to twist around that, back into the softness.

It is the way I once thought making love would be: a soaring loss of consciousness, transcendence, and removal; I have gotten out of myself at last – so this was the way; and I am joined and free. This instant is wholly mine, and I am so free and light, tiny and light, a helium being. (179)

Edna achieves her one supreme moment of being in a revenge fantasy which has much in common with male fantasies like Gerald Crich's in Lawrence's *Women in Love* or Ionesco's professor in *La Leçon*. This time it is the woman who has the power to kill, and Edna's revision makes plain what passion it is that motivates a *crime passionel*: 'It was rage, not love, that gave the moment clarity and purity' (181).

This duplicitous narrative culminates in the impossible moment of Edna's celebratory dance. Having reinvented herself through her secret notebooks, she has also reincarnated Harry whom she sees in the last chapter as 'adding up to something' and a being separate from herself:

Poor man, poor stranger, poor Harry, whoever he was. I expect there was a time when he loved me, whatever that meant to him and whoever he thought I was. Poor me, poor stranger. (180)

The mirror is shattered and Edna is now faceless and free to dance all the missed connections in her life:

I feel muscles leaping, blood thundering, heart hammering. Like the dances, they want to leap from my body. Everything wants out to dance. Lost words too, all inside, clamouring like my lost children. I can dance and dance. (183)

Having written herself out of living into language, her last
dance occurs in the purely fictive dimension of the text. It is a
culmination of those earlier dances of Edna's when with eyes as
tightly shut to the outside world as Juliet's in *The Ivory Swing*
she had allowed her imagination to project its own images on
the screen behind her eyelids. As she releases the multitudes
contained within herself, she even projects a future and another
reincarnation:

> A whole pure future in which to sketch a whole new Edna, the
> singer and the dancer, the free woman in the narrow corridor,
> alone in a small white bed. (183)

This celebratory outburst at the triumph of imagination
collapses finally into contradiction as all Edna's other fictions
have done. Writing may be the way to a creative displacement of
reality, but Barfoot's narrator is as aware of its limits as
Thomas's Rachel or Munro's Del Jordan:

> It is a shock when you have dealt so cunningly, powerfully
> with reality, to come back and find it still there. (*Lives of
> Girls and Women*, 247)

Dancing in the Dark might aptly have been called *Whistling in
the Dark*, for its incarcerated protagonist has no possibility of
freedom except through imagination. As a revisionary effort
Edna's narrative exposing women's fantasies becomes self-
exposure where she is the 'lying angel' whose one authentic
moment was an act of violent rage. Unpicking the social fabric
into which she has allowed herself to be woven, Edna finds the
holes through which her frustration and resentment can be
made visible. Her story of revenge is an extreme expression of
the anger which fuels so much current women's writing. This
too is part of the female literary inheritance which Virginia
Woolf identified in her comments about Charlotte Brontë's
Jane Eyre.

8

Marie-Claire Blais
LES NUITS DE L'UNDERGROUND /
NIGHTS IN THE UNDERGROUND
Anne Hébert   *HÉLOÏSE*

It is difficult for an English-speaking reader to talk about contemporary women novelists in Quebec, for one feels doubly an outsider as a non-Canadian and a non-native French speaker. These Québécois novelists write out of a different literary tradition more closely related to French than to English as well as out of a different culture and in a different language which we are reading in translation. Yet the French Fact in Quebec is striking to people outside Canada, for we have the sense of two very different Canadas depending on whether the view is through English or through French. A possible way of approaching these novelists as part of the Canadian literary scene is through our recognition of the essentially regional nature of so much Canadian writing with its sense of particular places each with its own cultural ethos. We might see Quebec literature as another form of Canadian regionalism exacerbated by differences of cultural history and language to the point where it almost looks like a 'national' difference. It is true of course that Quebec presents another version of Canadian multi-culturalism – that same phenomenon that Joy Kogawa talked about in *Obasan* – and in many ways we find parallels in Quebec for her painful experience of difference. Whereas the markers were in her case racial, with the Québécois they are cultural and linguistic. Like Kogawa's, these women's novels treat the themes of women's desperation and pain and marginality projected on to the wider screen of an oppressed community where self-enclosure and silence have been the signs of resistance to domination for over two hundred years.

In order to understand Quebec's pervasive sense of being a colonized culture, one needs to know something of the province's history. It was colonized in the eighteenth century as part of New France and so was French-speaking from the beginning. Then there was General Wolfe's scaling of the Quebec Heights and his defeat of General Montcalm in 1759; in 1763 by the Treaty of Utrecht (at the end of another European war, the Seven Years' War) Quebec passed to English sovereignty. The Québécois call this 'La Cession' which nicely underlines the ambiguity of whether it was an English Conquest or a French Betrayal.[1] Quebec has been haunted by its history as its motto 'Je m'en souviens' suggests. Seeing this on all the car registration plates from the province, I have often wondered just what it is they are remembering and more importantly how they are remembering, for their history is still a source of anguish to them. Quebec has sturdily resisted Anglicization and when by the 1867 British North America Act it was created as a separate province within the Dominion of Canada, it retained the right to use the French language in the national and provincial parliaments, a pyrrhic victory in a way for the language difference inevitably encouraged Quebec's isolation from the rest of Canada and its inturned parochialism. But it did survive, and with the Quiet Revolution of the 1960s Quebec finally assumed a sense of its own 'national' identity. It was in the 1960s that 'Québécois' came to replace 'French-Canadian' as a descriptive name for the people of the province, and of course such definitions are ideologically weighted:

> In a period of world decolonization this instinct [to rid ourselves of traditional ideologies] makes us straightaway

universal. It is this which since 1960 has allowed us to be reborn to ourselves and the world; it is this intuition of a name – since it all began with a name – which has allowed us to rediscover, in all its reality, our true identity; an unambiguous name, a clear, transparent name, precise and hard, a name that concretely gives us back our sovereignty and reconciles us with ourselves: *Québécois*.[2]

Quebec is not officially bilingual like the rest of Canada, for in 1977 French was established as the only official language of Quebec. Language is indeed crucially important for Quebec's sense of its own separate identity within Canada; it has even been called Quebec's national neurosis, for 'anyone who has been brought up with constant language choices (home-language, school-language, hyper-correct international French, the foreign pressure of English and American) is bound to be sensitive to language's power to shape reality.'[3] It is this concern with language and its relation to cultural assumptions that currently engages the most radical Quebec feminist writers. I shall not be treating this *nouvelle écriture* here, though arguably it is the most subversive and innovative women's fiction being written in Canada at the present time, with its strong feminist urge towards deconstruction of patriarchal ideologies and literary conventions. I am not discussing this new writing here for the very good reason that not much of it has been translated into English and because these poststructuralist preoccupations are very French and not very English. There are currently some attempts to make this avant-garde feminist writing available to English readers, and the writers' names to be noted are those of Nicole Brossard, Madeleine Gagnon, Louky Bersianik.[4]

Though neither Anne Hébert nor Marie-Claire Blais is overtly concerned with the language question in the novels I shall discuss, they too, like the writers of *nouvelle écriture*, are concerned with marginality as an ideological issue. This brings us to the point of remarking on the importance of women in

Quebec's history. Quebec has always depended on women for its physical survival with its policy encouraged by the Roman Catholic church of the *revanche des berceaux* (the revenge of the cradle) and its large families, a tradition which was only broken in the 1960s. Since then, freed from their traditional sexual role as childbearers, women have celebrated their release during the 1970s and 1980s in forms of radical feminist writing which have no parallel in the rest of Canada.[5] Hébert's and Blais's relation to social history in their fiction is more oblique for both of them have evolved strategies of resistance that are not obviously polemical. The two novels I am treating both belong to the period following the Quiet Revolution and the election of the Parti Québécois as the government of Quebec in 1976. Neither novel takes up a politically engaged stance but both of them bear the traces of Quebec's alienation, and the same moral and cultural dilemmas are written into these women's texts as into the more radical feminist ones.

With Hébert and Blais it is a question of displacement into fictions of the underground life of self-enclosure and fantasy, as *Nights in the Underground* and *Héloïse* both show. As we might expect, both have strongly gothic elements, figuratively in Blais's novel while Hébert's *Héloïse* is gothic fantasy. I have chosen these two because the 'underground' is intuitively right as the image of Quebec culture with its haunted sense of precarious survival. Surrounded as it is by a sea of English language and pressurized by economic and cultural influences from the rest of Canada and the United States, it is always threatened with a 'collective cultural death by assimilation', to use R. Sarkonak's vivid phrase.[6] It is through such fictions as Blais's and Hébert's that Quebec sees the image of itself. At a conference on women and writing held in Montreal in 1975, Nicole Brossard asked in French:

How is it that women have played such an important part in our literature: Gabrielle Roy, Anne Hébert, Germaine Guèvrement, Marie-Claire Blais? How come, in particular, that their works were able to reach such a wide section of the Quebec public? With what collective schizophrenia did their own phantasms connect? On what oppression did they throw light?[7]

I suggest that part of the answer to this question of the appeal of Blais and Hébert lies in their use of the gothic mode which is both sublimation and displacement of Quebec's contemporary cultural dilemmas and in their celebration of hidden lives which flourish so violently and subversively underground.

Marie-Claire Blais LES NUITS DE L'UNDERGROUND / NIGHTS IN THE UNDERGROUND

> But the hunger of night was also a hunger for women, the taste of their desires, the joy of seeing them again, knowing them . . . Meanwhile, winter winds blew them in the direction of a ceremony they would share and celebrate underground, pushing them and their bodies, their coiffures, their separate souls united and vibrating to the tune of one verb: love . . .
>
> (Marie-Claire Blais, *Nights in the Underground*[8])

Nights in the Underground is not the best known of Blais's fifteen novels; her first one, *La Belle Bête/Mad Shadows* (1959) published when she was twenty, or *Une saison dans la vie d'Emmanuel/A Season in the Life of Emanuel* (1965) which won the *Prix Medici* and has been translated into fourteen languages, or *Le Sourd dans la ville/Deaf to the City* which won the Governor-General's Award in 1979 would better qualify for that distinction. However, *Nights in the Underground* aptly illustrates the hidden subversive impulses in women's fiction and Quebec women's fiction in particular. Though not as violent as the other novels I have mentioned, this one takes up Blais's characteristic themes of marginality and estrangement and her obsession with damaging and death. It is set, as so many of her novels are, in Montreal with its bars and its night-life, though it does not have the broad social convas of *Un Joualonais, sa joualonie/St Lawrence Blues* written two years earlier; instead it shows a very particular section of Montreal society in the hidden lives of lesbians.[9] It is the only novel about lesbianism I treat, though I would like to have discussed the lesbian fiction of Jane Rule and shall make several references to Rule's writing in this chapter.[10] I shall concentrate on lesbian images rather than Canadian or Québécois images here, but clearly the urge to find an adequate self-image is a problem for all colonized groups; lesbian and Québécois are only an exacerbated form of the struggles for identity that have been discussed all through this book.

Lesbian writing has a great deal in common with heterosexual women's writing with similar interest in images of female heroism and forms of female desire; the difference is that 'lesbian' has distinctive sexual connotations which push to extremes women's difference of view. Lesbianism is an important component of separatist feminism with a strongly ideological basis as well as emotional and sexual preferences. As a radical stance against patriarchal values it pushes female dissidence beyond the point of heterosexual feminism, for here women's resistance is codified into a total break with male culture.[11] Instead of the image of a woman alone modern lesbian writers prefer to tell stories about female communities, of alternative societies of women living together without men, stories of 'woman-identified experience' to use Bonnie Zimmerman's phrase.[12] Lesbian fiction presents strong arguments for female difference, though inevitably it carries within it the constant recognition of its own marginality in the knowledge that 'the self must function in a society that remains male defined, blind or hostile to lesbians, but it is also the world in which we live and work.'[13] The negative markers of such social status are written into every lesbian text, not any longer as the sense of transgression and guilt, but as signs of women's humiliation and their necessary survival strategies of secrecy and silence. *Nights in the Underground* presents lesbians' lives shut out from the light of day and hidden away; the three main characters in the novel are haunted by the sheer precariousness of living and threats of death, so making the novel gothic and rather desperate for all Blais's efforts to write a celebration of lesbianism.

Lesbian fiction presents more extreme versions of the feminist themes of women's silence and marginality and the devaluation of women's experiences. It also suggests new ways of understanding women by showing how women's refusals might take different forms – in their refusal to be silent for example, or their refusal to share in heterosexual love relationships. As the Quebec feminist writer Madeleine Gagnon powerfully suggests:

> Instead of denying our differences, repressing our desires and fantasies, ignoring our bodies and trying to integrate ourselves into the male myth and its values, we should assume our difference, as women, as fighters, as lovers, assume our diversity and our multiplicity in the framework of common struggles . . . I will participate in the struggles around me against capitalist exploitation, against national domination, against racism, but I want to tell about, to explore the silences of my mother, my aunts, my sisters and myself.[14]

Such a programme of writing points towards new ways of valuing ourselves as women by seeing female difference within an extended context of diverse kinds of social injustice. Certainly for Blais there are strong connections between lesbian experience and larger historical patterns of oppression, so that by the end of *Nights in the Underground* lesbianism begins to look like one particular example of marginality and idealism continually under threat from a barrage of hostile forces.

Yet the crucial difference with lesbianism lies in the recognition that women's sexuality may be defined not in relation to men but to women, and the scandal of lesbianism is its challenge to the traditional belief that femaleness/femininity functions as the complement to maleness/masculinity.[15] In its celebration of women's self-sufficiency and separateness lesbianism is indeed subversive of social and psychosexual structures as they are commonly assumed. As Adrienne Rich puts it, 'woman identification is not in the prescribed script of the heterosexual world.'[16]

It is in this territory outside the prescribed script that Blais situates her novel subtitled in its English edition 'an exploration of love'. Undeniably there is a certain polemical force about that subtitle, rather like Thomas Hardy's *Tess of the D'Urbervilles: A Pure Woman* which goes on to tell the story of someone who commits adultery and then murder. Blais directly engages with the social image of lesbianism as she does with the difficulties of finding new ways of speaking and writing about lesbian sensibility. How to find a language to describe women's passionate love of other women when erotic language is so strongly heterosexual? As an exploration of feeling and ways through which feeling is encoded in language, *Nights in the Underground* is especially interesting for it investigates the kinds of language already available – like the language of Lea's lesbian theatre, 'somewhat like an anatomy lesson inflamed with revolutionary fervour (187) ('une leçon d'anatomie enflammée de cette ardeur révolutionnaire', 251), or the silent language of seduction, 'when one woman put all her powers into play . . . just by the intensity of her eyes' (11) ('quand une femme exerçait auprès d'une autre . . . son pouvoir par l'intensité des regards', 23) while at the same time it tries to forge a subtler language through the story it tells about the female protagonist and her love affairs with two very different women. The focus is on one individual's search to find ways to recognize and articulate her own feelings, which is where Blais's project links up with other women's novels showing yet another way of writing about a woman's process of self-discovery.

The novel might be seen as an *éducation sentimentale* for the protagonist Geneviève Aurès. As other lives eddy around hers in the shifting locales of Montreal and Paris, it is she who remains at the centre, observing, questioning and changing. The novel traces Geneviève's progression from sexual ambivalence to confirmed lesbianism through her two relationships, first with the young Austrian immigrant Lali Dorman in Montreal and then with the fifty-year-old Françoise in Paris. In their different ways Geneviève, Lali and Françoise are all glamorous, exceptional women, for Geneviève is a sculptor, Lali is a doctor in a cancer ward, and Françoise is the former wife of a French diplomat who now runs an art gallery. When Geneviève first meets Lali Dorman at the Underground bar in Montreal, she has just returned from Paris and is coming to the end of a ten-year-long affair with a man called Jean. Her first response to Lali is primarily an aesthetic one as the first sentence in the novel suggests, 'Geneviève's love for Lali Dorman began as a passion for a work of art' (1) ('L'amour de Geneviève Aurès pour Lali Dorman naquit comme une passion pour une oeuvre d'art', 9). Though in time she realizes that such a view of another human being is illusory and incomplete, not only does it remain typical of Geneviève's responses to others (what she always notices first are women's faces) but there is through their relationship a characteristic doubleness in Geneviève's perception of this other woman as individual and as work of art:

> It wasn't Lali she loved, it was the beauty, the artistic perfection, she saw in her. But it devastated her to think how art was alive, everywhere, in the flesh, so that what she contemplated in the security of museums, safely and from a distance, lived and trembled right beside her, in her own life. Lali was exactly that kind of living work, vulnerable, a potential victim of violence, war, and stupidity, all those forces counter to love, life, and art. (9)[17]

With her beauty and her elusiveness Lali is the perfect object of desire for Geneviève, the focus of her artistic yearning while at the same time by the very fact of her humanness sharpening

Geneviève's sense of the threat of mortality. Surely this is the fascination of enigma, for Lali is always the unknowable outsider. Born of an Austrian Jewish family who came as post-war immigrants to America, and also a lesbian 'with a profound sexual idealism' (5) ('une affirmation profonde d'un idéal sexuel', 15), she maintains her separateness even in the Montreal bar. Irreparably damaged by her wartime experiences, Lali is haunted by nightmares, the central image of her life being a black hole remembered from her childhood:

> There was a big fireplace in the house and there was, how do you call it? *Un trou*, a gap in the chimney and I'd look at it for hours on end. Oh, it was terrifying . . . Maybe it was that wretched crack in the chimney, thought Geneviève, that was the focus of Lali's stare when she drank alone at the bar. Was there a whole world leaking out of it, as if from a tomb; a world of forgotten, faceless victims, refugees with bent backs and rag-wrapped feet who won't let you rest? Lali's entire childhood came and went through that apocalyptic fissure. (17)[18]

This gap through which memories of the dead insistently prey on the living shapes Lali's life as much as it affects Geneviève's perception of her, and it infects their love with the sense of mortality:

> Why this dry and bitter doubt reminding her that all love may be nothing but a gift, a miracle, but a gift we brand with the sign of its own madness and destruction? (47)[19]

Sexual love can be nothing but a 'song of desperate transitory happiness' (65) ('ce chant d'un bonheur un instant perdu et éperdu', 91) snatched always in defiance of circumstance. The difference is in their kinds of defiance, for while Geneviève's urge is to beat time (in its progress towards death?) by transforming bodies and feelings into static *objets d'art* of wood and stone, Lali's is a total immersion in the present moment as a mockery of time and a refusal of futures. The death-haunted quality of Lali is caught in a striking visual image of double exposure, one of the most perfect examples of figurative gothic in the novel, when Geneviève happens to glance at Lali's face on a car drive through the white frosted city of Montreal:

> Hitting Lali's face in that way, the rays of sunlight passed through the down on her cheeks (so unlike flesh) as if through a veil and made the fragile bone structure stand out, the ghost of another, lifeless face that Lali herself didn't seem to know was there. (69)[20]

Geneviève's language of eroticism always disperses the immediate experience of sensuality, as in this description of lovemaking where Lali's body is dissolved into the multiple voices of other women from the past:

> It was as if every woman who had ever loved Lali, multitudes of strangers . . . had invested Lali with all their heat, and the murmur of their voices, the warmth of their breath, passed through her voice and breath to celebrate her idea of the body. It was a very cerebral idea, but it could only free itself through her arduous and yet trembling flesh. (74)[21]

Here flesh ceases to exist, becoming instead a metaphorical space, 'un trou', through which issue a troupe of vanished women who fragmentarily re-enter the present. On a literal level, Lali opens the way for other women to enter Geneviève's life, for it is as a result of their relationship that Geneviève comes to a full recognition of her lesbianism as 'a consciousness of herself, of her value and the value of other women' (48) ('conscience tardive d'elle-même, de sa valeur, de la valeur des autres femmes', 69). This might be seen as Lali's gift to her, only to be wholly appreciated in Lali's absence after their affair has ended and only after Geneviève has reinvented Lali as an art object by transforming her into a sculptured figure:

> Lali had initiated Geneviève, through herself, to a whole throng of women belonging to the homosexual community . . . but now more than any other she abandoned Geneviève to that blessed innocence where she became her own mistress, threw off the rule of Lali's law and followed her own. (132)[22]

As a love affair it seems to have been a metaphysical as much as a physical initiation, and it is heartening to find that Geneviève's next affair with the ageing Françoise in Paris has much more tenderness and human caring about it. Françoise, a woman of an earlier generation, has disguised her lesbianism under an almost impeccable social surface as a diplomatic wife and mother, for hers has been a life of protective silences which Geneviève sees as a 'martyrdom' and a complicity 'in a kind of sexual racism' (142) ('une sorte d'un racisme sexuel', 192).[23] Yet for all its human warmth their love has its death hauntings: Geneviève sees it as her 'work of resurrection' and Françoise herself is obsessed not only by the past but by the future and the threat of her own death. Though the differences between Françoise and Lali are obvious, it is their similarities which are most striking to Geneviève when she notices a portrait of the older woman at sixteen which has the same defiant look as Lali's:

> In its completeness, the fulness of its youth and sensual audacity, it was the portrait of Lali as she progressed from Van Eyck's almost pink, unbearably sweet light into the brown violence of a face by Goya. (145)[24]

The image of one is superimposed on the other in her double vision of the painting where history and the future are simultaneously projected. It is also noteworthy that Françoise and

Lali are exiles, for Françoise is a Québécoise who has made her home in Paris; Geneviève shifts between the two but unlike them she has her homecoming to Quebec at the end. Through Françoise Geneviève also comes to see lesbianism as having a past history as well as a future, and the possible doubleness of that future which may well come to look like the past rather than something more open and optimistic as her Montreal friends believe. Both possibilities are shown to exist and both are there in the ending when Geneviève is back in Montreal with her friends, waiting for Françoise to come from Paris after a major surgical operation.

If reading the novel as a lesbian *éducation sentimentale* makes it sound schematic that would be an injustice, for this 'exploration of love' includes love in a social context, primarily the context of the Montreal lesbian community but also with clear recognitions of a wider human context. Not surprisingly most of that wider context provides evidence of heterosexual society's tyrannical enforcement of its codes on a group which it has branded as deviant, and there are some very hostile portraits of men as lovers, policemen and soldiers, thugs, rapists and murderers. Blais writes about 'lesbian existence' as Rich calls it, suggesting 'both the fact of the historical presence of lesbians and our continuing creation of the meaning of that existence' ('Compulsory heterosexuality', 227). The most vital community in the novel is shown to be the closed universe of the Underground bar 'where life was transformed into theatre' (5) ('où la vie devenait théâtre', 14) in the night world of women's dancing, drinking, talking and falling in love. As Geneviève remarks, 'How little was known about sexual attraction between women, since it's almost always seen from a man's point of view' (11) ('On sait si peu de choses de la sexualité des femmes entres elles, car presque toujours celle-ci est aperçue du point de vue de l'homme', 23). Rich in her essay offers a fascinating suggestion about female difference: 'As we delineate a lesbian continuum, we begin to discover the erotic in female terms: as that which is unconfined to any single part of the body or solely to the body itself, as an energy not only diffuse but, as Audre Lorde has described it, omnipresent in "the sharing of joy, whether physical, emotional, psychic"' (228). Blais fixes on the theatre as communal metaphor to describe life in the Montreal bars in a way that parallels the ideological gesture of one of her characters who combines a women's restaurant with lesbian theatrical performances. Theatre always gives life a heightened intensity, presenting a vivid and carnivalized world which is acknowledged as illusory but which dramatizes alternative possibilities for living. The women who swarm through these bars – working-class Québécoises with their Montreal slang, poets and intellectuals, students, a black model from New York, a Haitian-born hockey star, Big Yellow the marijuana addict and Cat Girl with her young son and her astrology – have the variety and glamour of a troupe of players in their passage through the text. What they offer is a challenge to barriers of class and race and positive lesbian images in a paradigm of female freedom which can only be fully expressed in the clandestine world of the Underground.

It would be impossible to see this lesbian society as entirely hedonistic, though there is a gaiety about these shared moments of irresponsibility that is immensely appealing. Many of these women have an active feminist engagement as well and their positive social resistance is also part of the story of lesbianism that the novel tells. We see them campaigning for change in social attitudes with their Committee for Lesbian Defence, we hear about the completion of a women's co-operative housing project in a village, just as we see women caring for one another and for the community as social workers and doctors. These women are not exempt from anything any more than Rennie in *Bodily Harm*, for they too can be attacked, like the actress Lea who learns about pity and fear through being raped by a Negro; they too can be murdered like the black model from New York; they too suffer from 'the relentless weight of violent destiny' (191) ('la fatalité de ce destin de violence', 256). This lesbian world is always aware that it is under threat of humiliation or worse, which undermines at the same time as it underlines their courage and idealism. Blais finely catches this double awareness in her ending. Having written her way through a Montreal winter into spring and then into summer, she ends with a celebration of 'women's radiant explosion' into the open air:

> Summer seemed to be triumphing over everything, even over Lali as she stepped out of the rough armor of her coat into a pair of boy's shorts . . . glowing with her own special kind of naïve, animal happiness, a happiness carrying so many illusions with it, especially on these crystal-clear days, that nobody could ever believe it might not last forever . . . And yet, beyond this certainty represented by Lali, so carefree today in her youthfulness, another person, Françoise, still lost in the shadows of the forest, was walking towards Geneviève. This other person was also made of beauties and doubts, and she was what Lali might become tomorrow, when her defiant smile was gone forever . . . (199)[25]

So shadowed in its final sentences, the ending is really a song of innocence sung by the voice of experience which knows that innocence is made of 'so many illusions' and that any assertion of freedom has to be stated in the knowledge of life's betrayals and the threat of mortality itself. Like the changes of the seasons, human beings are caught in patterns of recurrence and transformation which must be the conditions of loving and of art.[26]

I shall end this discussion of *Nights in the Underground* with a quotation from Jane Rule, for it brings into radiant focus the same preoccupations as Marie-Claire Blais's novel:

> A body we know is designed to die will never be a simple plaything, nor will the language we use to express our sexuality ever be without that irony . . . A language adequate to express our sexual experience must be able to describe

negotiations far more complex than the entrance of penis or finger into vagina, and it will arouse pity and terror as well as pleasure in its readers if it says anything real about that experience.[27]

Anne Hébert *HÉLOÏSE*

The epigraph of the book is an extract from a poem – 'The world is in order / The dead below / The living above' – which is to say that the world appears to be in order, but that a single small incident can overthrow everything. The world appears exceptionally in order for Christine and Bernard. They are young, they are good looking. They are well brought up. They come of good families and they have life ahead of them. But it only needs one encounter to overturn the whole structure. The world is never in order.

(Anne Hébert's comment on *Héloïse* in an interview with Donald Smith, 1983[28])

With Anne Hébert's novella *Héloïse* we come to the most subversive woman's story of all. It is a gothic tale about a female vampire and at first it looks as if it might subvert my account of Canadian women's writing. It is about a woman who is both *femme fatale* and victim, and its Canadianness is subliminal with Canada referred to only once as the place which the characters never manage to get to. To choose *Héloïse* might seem perverse when Hébert has written several identifiably Canadian novels, the best known of which, *Kamouraska* (1970), is utterly Québécois with its dark tormented figures and its violent images of blood on the snow. So why this tale set in modern Paris as my ending? The answer is partly because of my interest in discovering those hidden connections which are a mark of the feminine gender of women writers and critics. It is really not very difficult to see connections between *Héloïse* and the other novels discussed, for this is gothic fantasy dealing in the secret realms of the imaginary and the forbidden which Margaret Atwood and Alice Munro treated; it is about a woman's quest and her will to survive; it is about female violence; and like *Bodily Harm* and *Dancing in the Dark* it is a reminder not to trust surfaces. These are all recognizable characteristics of women's fiction, but the oddity here is that suddenly with a vampiric heroine like Héloïse we are forced to confront the shadow side of woman's power and the female inheritance, when the struggle toward self-possession becomes demonic possession and when sexual love and mothering are transformed into death-dealing, not life-giving, forces. There is a certain risk-taking here on Anne Hébert's part in telling such a threatening story, but arguably it is another of the stories that a woman might tell (like Sylvia Plath's 'Lady Lazarus') which murmur up from the dark depths of the female psyche.

Of course it is fantasy: Héloïse is 'unreal' as she pursues her predatory way underground travelling on the Paris Metro in her turn-of-the-century costumes, seducing the young man Bernard away from his fiancée and later slashing his throat in an erotic embrace on his marriage bed. The story ends down in the Metro at midnight on the platform of Père-Lachaise station, with Héloïse holding Bernard's body in an embrace that is both blasphemous and maternal, surrounded by milling crowds of ghosts. Fantastic yes, but set in a world which presses uncomfortably close to the real world. In true gothic tradition this story began according to Hébert as a dream (or more accurately as a 'reverie'):

In the Paris metro, I often thought about the period when the metro was built, of the first line [in 1900], of the women who wore long dresses and the men with their tall top hats. I saw them mingling with the people of our own modern world. *Héloïse* comes out of a long reverie that I had in the metro. It could have been something else; it could have been realistic, for sometimes we do meet very odd people in the metro, but it took the form of a fantasy.[29]

It is undeniably costume-gothic with its *fin-de-siècle* decor, still to be seen in the art nouveau decorations of Paris subway entrances and in the old buildings which exist as 'forgotten enclaves in the heart of the city' ('une sorte d'enclave oubliée, au coeur de la ville').[30] Hébert has caught the ambiguities of modern Paris and used them as her passageways between the real everyday world and the unreal fantastic world inhabited by the vampires. Paris is a historic city full of traces and fragments of its past and she makes her story out of the coexistence of these 'worlds alongside' (to use Alice Munro's phrase), moving from the literal underground of the Metro into the imaginary world of the dead through closed subway stations. It is all the result of going below, a fear of going down dark holes which Hébert herself expressed[31] and which Bernard the young man in the tale also feels. The French original with its words like 'trou', 'tomber', and 'perdue' catches the frisson of gothic horror more precisely than the English translation:

> An air pocket. Yes, that's it, that feeling of falling through space. My old dread of the metro comes back. I am sinking deeper into the earth. To its heart of fire and ice. The level of the dead. Gray walls slip past in the dark. The stations briefly light up the night. Then once more, dark gray walls, red and blue pipes. Occasionally, a Dubonnet poster, half-erased, like a vanished fresco. (20–1)[32]

Such a passage marks the transition from one world to another, from real to unreal, from present to past, from the world of the living to the world of the dead, always haunted by the old gothic fear that what is buried underground may not be dead at all.[33]

Gothic fiction has always had a strong and peculiar sense of history, which is arguably the expression of women's attitudes to history not as facts but as fragments of the past which are indecipherable until re-imagined and reconstituted as personal histories. This attitude has much in common with the Canadian impulse toward revisions of history which I have discussed earlier. But Anne Hébert's tale is not Canadian history at all; it is Parisian history and it is a story about a woman's undying desire. Hébert's Québécois sensitivity to the oppressive weight of history alerts her imagination to the tragic story of how the past survives by draining life out of the living, undergoing multiple transformations till it exists only as fiction while still retaining its power to fascinate and erode any impulse towards futures. The gothic tale with its celebration of hidden, subversive life which undermines existing social and psychological orders from within is the perfect deviant discourse for 'forging' connections with the past, for repossessing history/being repossessed by it as it articulates deep anxieties about the relation of the present to history. Being Québécois is perhaps only to be cast into an extreme form of the Canadian ambivalence towards its European past which we have seen in other novels, and being a Québécois woman writer is perhaps only to experience in exaggerated degree that marginal and resistant relation to history which characterises Canadian women's writing.

It is the title *Héloïse* which provides the all-important clue to this gothic tale. Though Héloïse never tells us her story and we see only one small segment of it enacted here, we know who she is (or who she was) almost as soon as we hear her strange song on the subway train which stops mysteriously at the closed Metro station of Cluny. When we see her accompanied by the wheezing old asthmatic figure of Xavier Bottereau, our suspicions are confirmed. Héloïse and Abelard, those legendary twelfth-century lovers are back again in the land of the living – or is it the land of the living? Is it the land of the dead or of the un-dead? Unlike the other women's stories we have been looking at, this is the opposite of an intimate story about the self for we are always held at a distance from Héloïse. Yet we know her history from other texts and from some very intimate letters which she wrote 'in another life' (hers was truly 'a medieval lifetime') and as readers we have supplementary information which Bernard does not have. Héloïse does not refer to her own past yet she is herself victim to that history of sexual passion and the whole story is dominated, swallowed up by the past.

We all know the story of Héloïse and Abelard in broad outline: how Héloïse was Abelard's student and how they fell in love, using the tutorial relationship as a disguise for their secret sexual relationship; how that was exposed, only to be followed by their clandestine marriage and then by the castration of Abelard at the hands of her uncle's minions. After that public shame the lovers separated, Héloïse going into a convent and Abelard retreating to a monastery in Brittany. But that was not the end of their story, for ten years later Héloïse became the Abbess of Abelard's former monastery and so he became her spiritual director. At this point their love story shifts into a different dimension being transformed from a physical to a spiritual love with Héloïse as the bride of Christ, but no less a transgression of order than before. In her fascinating book *Fictions of Feminine Desire: Disclosures of Heloise* (1982) to which I am much indebted, Peggy Kamuf gives a reading of that love story through their letters which suggests that it was Héloïse who resisted the religious laws of silence and who continued to insist on her erotic passion for Abelard regardless of his castration and her own spiritual vows. The persistence of her attachment to Abelard transgressing all limits of physical possibility and spiritual order comes close to blasphemy when she declares in one of her letters, 'I would have had no hesitation, God knows, in following you or going ahead at your bidding to the flames of Hell.'[34] The original Héloïse was a subversive too, a woman whose erotic desire transformed itself into a 'peculiar and magical game' (Alice Munro's phrase) of infinite deferrals and displacements without losing any of its original sexual charge. The impossible erotic encounter always desired and always out of reach becomes the condition of life for Héloïse shut up in her convent, and this in turn becomes the condition of being for Anne Hébert's Héloïse eight hundred years later. In her we see female desire stripped of the pleasure of sex and life itself, retaining only its insatiable, amoral thrust.

Héloïse's undying love takes a sinister turn when it survives her own death.

There is yet another aspect of the Héloïse and Abelard story which makes it peculiarly suitable for the kind of gothic confrontation between Eros and Thanatos which Hébert tells, for the history of their burials and reburials is quite as enthralling as their love story.[35] Peter Abelard died at the Abbey of Cluny in 1142, but six months afterwards his body was transferred clandestinely to Héloïse's convent and when she died twenty years later she was buried beside him. Then followed a history of repeated disinterments and reburials during the next six hundred years, and it was not until 1816 that the remains of them both were transferred to Père-Lachaise cemetery. In 1817 a mausoleum was erected to their memory and it is still there. As a story about the scattered fragments of personal history it is unsurpassed, for as Kamuf remarks, 'In this process, no last word, no final resting place, which does not leave something still to be said and exhumed' (xiv).

Hébert's story is situated within this provocative frame of reference, continuing Héloïse's history of transgression and hidden desire beyond the grave in more senses than one. She has now become a vampire, crossing the boundaries between life and death in her quest for blood as easily as she moves from the station platform at Père-Lachaise back through fissures in the brick wall and underground passageways to her vault in the cemetery. Always accompanied by Abelard in his guise as the seedy old rental agent Xavier Bottereau who drives a 1900 Bugatti and who 'smells of mud' she pursues her quarry unnoticed by the indifferent Parisian crowds, for what does she look like in modern Paris but another thin dark-haired girl with bright red lips wearing fashionably outmoded clothes bought from a junk shop? The novel is a very witty parody of costume-gothic, for who would notice such a figure as extraordinary? Héloïse sitting beside the fountain in the place St-Michel drinking blood from a phial is indistinguishable from other pale young Parisians doing freakish things:

The world we live in receives, with the same air of weary unconcern, any peculiarity or perverse pleasure . . .
Quietly flaunting her crime and her need, amid general indifference, she decants the blood from her syringe into small glass flasks.
An ambulance streaks by, all sirens screaming. (84)[36]

In a modern world as indifferent to ambulances as to vampires, the past infiltrates the present without encountering much resistance. The same kind of confusion seems to infect the vampire population too, for we see them in their hangout at the café on the rue Gît-le-Coeur drinking Bloody Marys at room temperature, nothing stronger apparently being available.

However, ignorance and indifference offer no protection against the threat of the past, and this fantastic story inscribed within the boundaries of modern Paris is really about history and its victims. Just as traces of its past are written into the city above ground so, hidden below, the shadows of its past live their own impossible existences dependent for their very survival on draining the blood of the living. As a tale of terror and secret subversion *Héloïse* is truly gothic, but Hébert wears her rue with a difference, for this time it is the female figure who seduces and kills. Imprisoned within her own past history, Héloïse is both victim and *femme fatale* condemned to the endless re-enactment of her story of unfulfilled desire. Reminded from time to time by Abelard of the 'law' of her being (for he still occupies his tutorial role) Héloïse's is a shameful acquiescence in patterns laid down by the past so strong that they have become the very means of her unnatural existence. In Héloïse the traditional ambiguity of the gothic heroine as both victim and survivor assumes the status of paradox as the old romantic sexual games of pursuit and flight are turned around to reveal their other side as rape fantasies, only this time the victim is male. 'Here nothing is inconceivable' as one of Atwood's characters remarked in *Bodily Harm*,[37] nor is it in this gothic tale about a female vampire. Héloïse has to acquiesce in the 'law of the earth' in order to survive, just as the earlier Héloïse had to acquiesce in the religious law. She is truly an accomplice, one of the uncomfortable truths about the female victim complex which Atwood's fiction exposes. Though helpless she is not innocent but guilty, both victim and victimizer, a collaborator in the terrible process of vampiric colonization:

> 'Don't you long to have this marvel here with us?' [asks Bottereau].
> 'I have no choice have I? It is the price of my eternity' [answers Héloïse]. (87)[38]

Hébert's is another version of female gothic. She does not deal in women's subjective terrors nor does she set about revealing the female victim complex to be irresponsible fantasy like Atwood. Instead she focuses on the hidden gothic sub-text of female power and destructiveness which is usually veiled or displaced into fictions of helplessness rather than told as stories of betrayal. So she tells a more threatening story about a woman's desperate will to survive and about woman as double dealer. In her perversely double way Héloïse fulfils both her feminine roles as lover and mother towards her victim Bernard. Any psychological interest in the story has to focus on Bernard and his vulnerability to romantic dreams of the past, for Héloïse has no 'self' to be interested in; she is just a shadow of desire and it is as romantic image only that she seduces Bernard, surely a comment on the power of male sexual fantasy. Their few brief physical encounters are written in the double language of eroticism and death, for making love to Héloïse is like drowning:

> Bernard falls at Héloïse's feet. Buries his head in the young woman's skirts. Is captivated once more by the smell of the shore: rockweed, wrack, deep mud that steams and rages. Squeezes her legs so hard that she falls to the floor. They roll on the rug. A brief cry of pain.

Am I crying, Bernard wonders, as exquisite pleasure
crushes him and leads him to the gates of death. He is awash
in hot blood from his own slashed throat. He is swallowed up
in the night. (81–2)[39]

His obsession with Héloïse is also an obsession with dissolution and death so strong that even when he recognizes what she
is and even after the murder of his young wife by old Bottereau,
he cannot resist Héloïse. Once more he goes to seek her in the
underground, this time to shoot her, but she is of course an
unassailable target:

Here they are, both of them, on the platform, mingling with
the other travellers. The seduction of Héloïse. Her peverse
charm. She kisses Bernard.
Has he really whispered, against Héloïse's shoulder, 'I love
you?'
Has he really uttered these words, spoken the way one
speaks to a sick child?
'It's only the lure of death, my darling.' (101)[40]

Héloïse's final embrace is maternal – what else indeed did
Bernard ever really desire? 'A savage pieta, she wraps her arms
around him. While the crowd of the dead comes together,
tightly enclosing them' (244) ('Piéta sauvage, elle l'entoure de
ses bras. Tandis que la foule des morts se rapprochent, les
enferment étroitement', 123–4). As the blue mist rolls away
from the dark platform one can read the name of the station,
'Père-Lachaise'. Héloïse has returned once more to her burial
place for, her story having been told, she recedes into the dead
world of the past.
    The gothic world of *Héloïse* is not only a hidden world, it is a
fantasy world where the only order governing Héloïse's existence is the invented order of art. It is the fiction which grants
her an impossible life and her survival depends not only on her
power to seduce Bernard but on the power of the text to seduce

us as readers. What is our engagement with this story? Not anything so naïve as a 'willing suspension of disbelief' but rather the fascination of dream with its slippages and hidden connections, all the function of an elaborate displacement of female desire. It is fabrication, 'not real but true, as if I had discovered, not made up, such people and such a story, as if that town was lying close behind the one I walked through every day.' (Not Anne Hébert's words but Del Jordan's about her gothic story in Alice Munro's *Lives of Girls and Women*.[41] All that remains of Héloïse is words, the words of this text, no longer 'private' like her letters to Abelard eight hundred years ago when even then she had already written herself out of living into language, but 'fictional'. Hébert's tale is as much a memorial to a legendary figure as Pope's eighteenth-century poem 'Eloisa to Abelard':

> If such there be, who loves so long, so well;
> Let him our sad, our tender story tell;
> The well-sung woes will soothe my pensive ghost,
> He best can paint 'em, who shall feel 'em most.
>   (11.363–6)[42]

Though the gothic mode of *Héloïse* completely lacks Pope's complacency by conjuring up Héloïse's ghost rather than soothing it, Héloïse's story is placed as a tale to be told and retold. This is not a personal fiction like Laurence's, Kogawa's, Thomas's or Barfoot's, nor is it a life story; it is a death story, a no-exit fantasy more desperate than *Bodily Harm* or *The Handmaid's Tale* because no freedom is possible for Héloïse. Being neither imprisoned nor mad but dead, she no longer has a self or a future so that this story of a woman's entrapment can only be worked out as a celebration of death. Rather than story-telling being a way of coming to terms with the past, here the story is only fulfilling the terms already laid down by the past.

Yet *Héloïse* is writing as celebration: it celebrates the memory of a passionate woman through the kind of revisionist history which is such an important feature of modern feminism; it also celebrates the gothic, that most traditional form of women's writing. Most importantly it celebrates the power of fiction itself for Hébert has invented an identity for Héloïse through her writing, so liberating her into a whole new life more scandalous than her former one, for now she is truly subverting the order of things: the natural order of life and death within a fiction that transgresses the limits between realism and fantasy. In the end Héloïse does 'set down her title' to a kind of possession (though it is not the same as Margaret Laurence's heroine's) and her own name is the title of the book. It is also a triumph of an ambiguous sort in that unlike many of the protagonists discussed, Héloïse does not celebrate alone.

This freakish novella is neither 'private' nor Canadian but made of 'fictional words' entirely. Yet it is another woman's story, another way out of the silence of history, another way of making visible what has been hidden within the female psyche. *Héloïse* ends as confidently as *The Diviners* did on a moment of order created through writing, where it is the achievement and also the illusion of art to look like the order of life itself.

> The world is in order
> The dead below
> The living above.[43]

Conclusion

Any account of Canadian women's fiction in the 1970s and 1980s is likely to face the problems of duality signalled in Professor Lotta Gutsa's title, *Wilderness Womb: The Emergence of Canadian Women Writers*, for origins are important but so also are the varieties of narrative through which Canadian women's fiction has emerged. Contemporary women write within the traditions they have inherited but they also write in resistance to those traditions, recognizing the need for their revision in order to redefine national and gender identity. The fictions by the eleven writers I have considered in this book are variant versions of this attempt, resulting in a network of features through which Canadian women's writing is constituted. The possibilities for contradiction and multiple perspectives are obvious and indeed they are a necessary consequence of the limits and range of this study. What emerges is no fixed definition of either Canadianness or women's writing, but rather an open mesh of fictional responses to the influences that have shaped national and gender awareness in a number of individual writers.

The variety of cultural and regional backgrounds represented in these multivoiced fictions would seem to argue against any coherent concept of Canadian women's fiction. 'Canadian fiction' cannot be categorically defined by the place of origin of the writers nor of the texts themselves, nor by specifically Canadian references within the texts where even 'wilderness', that dominant cultural myth, is transformed into metaphor which merges geography with psychic landscape. 'Women's fiction' would seem to be less problematic but only in the sense that the writers are women, for these stories challenge traditional notions of gender encoded through social fictions and through narrative, unsettling the boundaries between masculine and feminine. Yet there is a sense in which these diverse narratives may be seen as sharing in a collaborative effort of revision and resistance. They are all responses to the pressures of colonial history and the contradictions within a colonized mentality where one's self-image is split between imposed traditional patterns and authentic experience which reveals the incompleteness or falsity of tradition. They all raise questions about inheritance, which is unmistakably plural in a culture like Canada's with its two mother cultures and two official languages in addition to its native cultures and the cultures of its waves of immigrants. Dispossession and disunity will be as important in these narratives about origins and inheritance as their attempts to forge a distinctive cultural identity which will in its turn be influenced by such awareness.

As I have suggested, there is a coincidence between stories of nationality and gender in Canada as strong as in any postcolonial Commonwealth literature. It is worth pursuing Canadian women writers' treatment of Canadian history in order to bring out these linkages. The novels of Laurence, Atwood, Kogawa and Hébert are obsessed with history and it was one of Engel's characters who said, 'It makes me boil with rage when people say Canadians have no history.'[1] Of course Canada has a history which like that of any New World country is full of stories of colonization and settlement, but that history was for a long time devalued and falsified because it did not fit with the official histories of the European colonizing powers. These writers are

all engaged in reassembling fragments from colonial history or
Canadian prehistory (which may be Indian or, in Hébert's case,
French from the twelfth century), fabricating a historical context within which to exist in the present – 'inheritance by
adoption' is what Laurence calls it, where 'the myths are my
reality'.[2] As Kroetsch writes in an important essay entitled
'Disunity as unity: a Canadian strategy', modern Canadian
writers' approach to history is 'archival' or 'archaeological',
recovering the stories that have been forgotten in
the interests of a coherent fiction of nationhood on the old
European or United States imperialist pattern.[3] Kroetsch
argues that postmodernist narratives celebrating disunity and
multiplicity are the most apt for Canada:

> In our happier moments, at least, we delight in the energy of
> the local, in the abundance that is diversity and difference, in
> the variety and life that exist on any coastline of human
> experience.
>   This willingness to refuse privilege to a restricted or
> restrictive cluster of metanarratives [i.e. stories which have
> traditionally been basic to nationhood] becomes a Canadian
> strategy for survival. (3)

As Kroetsch shows, this revisionist effort in the interests of
cultural nationalism is shared by male and female writers,
though it is worth pointing out women's difference here which
can be related to gender awareness or possibly gender conditioning. There are not many English-Canadian women's
fictions which could properly be called postmodernist, though
it is true that the feminist *nouvelle écriture* written out of
Quebec is much more radical in its language and fictional forms.
Most English-Canadian women's fiction is written within the
traditions of realism, though that framework is challenged with
the shifts into fantasy and the counterpoint of the voices of
tradition with the voices of female inheritors. They throw the
story-line of realism open to question by constructing narratives

that necessitate more open readings of male and female plots. Shifts of emphasis rather than revolution characterize these fictions in a traditional pattern of feminine resistance through evasive action beneath social and literary decorum.

Recognizing their role as inheritors, women writers are not arguing for the abolition of the categories of realism, nationality or gender, which would be hopelessly idealistic and counter-productive. Situated within a contemporary social and literary context, none of them is arguing for androgyny but again throwing the story-line of gender open to question and arguing for a redefinition of feminine gender identity to include many feelings and aspirations that have been rejected within tra-ditional definitions of the feminine. With their feminist aware-ness they are resisting their old 'colonized' gender status in the same way that Canada as a nation is resisting its definition as British cultural colony or American cultural colony, where 'Canadian' is obliterated by the imperialist assertions of the United States.

It is obvious that language is the site of the power struggle and that writing fiction may be seen as an ideological act in the Canadian process of national and gender redefinition. This does not mean a reduction of difference among Canadian women's fictions but a recognition that difference implies instability and multiplicity and works against separateness or conclusions. Writing fiction is in part at least a social project bearing witness to the fact of one's existence ('Tell someone I'm here'), just as it is always an aesthetic project in its attempts to create an alternative order which both mirrors and transforms the chaos of lived experience. All these fictions formulate order through narrative yet they are all aware of the limits of narrative order. They are pervaded by images of unfathomable depths like the Manawaka River in *The Diviners* or the Wachakwa in *Lives of Girls and Women*, or of dismemberment and unbridgeable gaps, and there are secrets and secret lives in them all. They must contain these resistant and subversive elements within their fictional structures in the recognition that any narrative is only partially successful and that any story is always in the process of emerging.

The distinctive combination of optimism and scepticism which characterizes contemporary Canadian women's fiction finds one of its many possible forms of expression in the voice of the narrator of *Dancing in the Dark*:

> What good is it to know these things now?
> I cannot say. But I keep busy, I write on.[4]

Notes

Date in square brackets immediately after title indicates original publication (for Canadian authors first Canadian publication). Where possible, quotations are taken from British editions.

Introduction

1 Alice Munro, 'Simon's Luck', *The Beggar Maid: Stories of Flo and Rose* (London: Penguin, 1980), 177.
2 Margaret Atwood, *The Journals of Susanna Moodie* (Toronto: Oxford University Press, 1970), 63.
3 See Toril Moi, *Sexual/Textual Politics* (London: Methuen, 1985) for a subtle analysis of current French and Anglo-American feminist theory.
4 See Ellen Moers, *Literary Women* (London: Women's Press, 1978), ch. 7, 'Traveling heroinism' for an early feminist discussion of inner adventuring.
5 Alice Munro, 'Baptising', *Lives of Girls and Women* (London: Penguin, 1982), 207.
6 Patrick Parrinder, 'Making Poison', *London Review of Books*, 20 March, 1986, 20–2.
7 Margaret Laurence, *The Diviners* (Toronto: McClelland & Stewart, New Canadian Library, 1978), 350.

1 Canadianness and women's fiction

1 Lecture given by Prof. Clara Thomas at conference on 'Women's studies in Canada: researching, publishing and teaching', York University (Downsview, Ontario), 19–20 April, 1985.

2 Robert Kroetsch, 'Death is a happy ending' [1978]: reprinted in *Canadian Novelists and the Novel*, eds D. Daymond and L. Monkman (Ottawa: Borealis, 1981), 248.

3 Margaret Laurence, 'Ivory tower or grassroots? The novelist as socio-political being' [1978], reprinted in Daymond and Monkman (eds) *Canadian Novelists and the Novel*, 258.

4 Margaret Atwood, *True Stories* [1981] (London: Cape, 1982), 11.

5 Gaile McGregor, *The Wacousta Syndrome: Explorations in the Canadian Landscape* (Toronto: University of Toronto Press, 1985).

6 Susanna Moodie, *Roughing It In The Bush: or, Life in Canada* [1852], (reprinted London: Virago, 1986), 83, 467. I should point out that my view of *Roughing It In The Bush* is problematized by recent Canadian scholarship which shows that this text was a collaborative effort between Susanna Moodie, her husband and her London publishers Bentley and Bruce. As a multivoiced narrative it assumes a new importance in the Canadian literary tradition, exemplifying a pattern not confined to women's fiction. For this information I am indebted to John Thurston's paper, 'Rewriting *Roughing It*,' given at the symposium 'Future indicative: literary theory and Canadian literature' at the University of Ottawa in April, 1986. Neither the 1962 New Canadian Library edition nor the 1986 Virago re-edition of the original 1852 text indicates its multiple authorship.

7 Marian Fowler, *The Embroidered Tent: Five Gentlewomen in Early Canada* (Toronto: Anansi, 1982), 11.

8 Elaine Showalter, 'Feminist criticism in the wilderness', in *Writing and Sexual Difference*, ed. Elizabeth Abel (Brighton: Harvester, 1982), 9–35.

9 Marian Engel, *No Clouds of Glory* (New York: Harcourt Brace & World, 1968), 8. Republished 1974 as *Sarah Bastard's Notebook*.

10 Margaret Atwood, *The Journals of Susanna Moodie*, 'Afterword', 62.

11 See John Moss, 'Invisible in the house of mirrors' (London: Canada House Lecture Series 21, November 1983).

12 D. H. Lawrence, *Studies in Classic American Literature* (London: Heinemann, 1923), 7.

13 Robert Kroetsch, 'Contemporary standards in the Canadian novel', *Taking Stock: The Calgary Conference on the Canadian Novel*, ed. C. Steele (Downsview: ECW Press, 1982), 13.

14 W. J. Keith, *Canadian Literature in English* (London and New York: Longman, 1985), 2. I am much indebted to Prof. Keith's first chapter for my summary of Canadian colonization.

15 Both wrote novels. Moodie's include *Mark Hurdlestone* [1853], *Flora Lyndsay* [1854], *Matrimonial Speculations* [1854]; Traill's output includes *Canadian Crusoes* [1852] as well as her earlier letters *The Backwoods of Canada* [1846] and several botany books.

16 Clara Thomas, 'Commonwealth albums: family resemblance in Derek Walcott's *Another Life* and Margaret Laurence's *The Diviners*, *World Literature Written in English*, 21(2), Summer 1982, 262–8.

17 Maggie Butcher, 'From *Maurice Guest* to *Martha Quest*: the emergence of the female *Bildungsroman* in Commonwealth Literature', *World Literature Written in English*, 21(2), Summer 1982, 254–62.

18 Carol Shields, *Susanna Moodie: Voices and Vision* (Ottawa: Borealis, 1977), quoted in Butcher, 'From *Maurice Guest*', 260.

19 Anna Jameson, quoted in Fowler, *The Embroidered Tent*, 171.

20 Emily Carr, 'D' Sonaqua', *Klee Wyck* (Toronto: Oxford University Press, 1941).

21 V. Strong-Boag, 'Discovering the home: the last 150 years of domestic work in Canada', *Women's Paid and Unpaid Work*, ed. P. Bourne (Toronto: New Hogtown Press, 1985, published for the Centre for Women's Studies in Education, Ontario Institute for Studies in Education), 36.

22 A similar pattern could be traced through prairie women's fiction, moving from the 1920s fiction of Laura Salverson and Martha Ostenso. A recent anthology of modern prairie women's stories is significantly titled *Double Bond*, ed. Caroline Heath (Saskatoon: Fifth House, 1984).

23 See Keith, *Canadian Literature in English*, 209; Robert Kroetsch, 'Beyond nationalism: a prologue,' *Open Letter*, Fifth Series, no. 4: Spring 1983, 83–9; Northrop Frye, 'Haunted by

lack of ghosts,' *The Canadian Imagination*, ed. David Staines (Cambridge and London: Harvard University Press, 1977), 22–45; W. H. New, 'Beyond nationalism: on regionalism', *World Literature Written in English*, 23(1), Winter 1984, 12–18.

24 Staines, introductory essay to *The Canadian Imagination*, 1–21.

25 Mavis Gallant, 'In Youth Is Pleasure', quoted by Keith, *Canadian Literature in English*, 159.

26 Robert Kroetsch, 'Disunity as unity: a Canadian strategy,' *Canadian Story and History 1885–1985*, ed P. Easingwood and C. Nicholson (Edinburgh: Centre for Canadian Studies, 1986), 1–11.

27 The question of gender difference is one that has obsessed feminist criticism and I am writing within a critical context that includes Elaine Showalter, *A Literature of Their Own* (Princeton: Princeton University Press, 1977) and her critical essays like 'Feminist criticism in the wilderness' and 'Towards a feminist poetics,' in *Women Writing and Writing about Women*, ed. M. Jacobus (London: Croom Helm, 1979); Annette Kolodny, 'Some notes on defining a feminist criticism,' *Critical Inquiry*, 2 (1975), 75–92, and 'Dancing through the minefield: some observations on the theory, practice and politics by feminist literary criticism', *Feminist Studies*, VI, i (1980), 1–25; *Women Writing and Writing about Women* (1979); J. Culler's chapter on feminist criticism in *On Deconstruction: Theory and Criticism after Structuralism* (London: Routledge & Kegan Paul, 1983); K. K. Ruthven, *Feminist Literary Studies* (Cambridge: Cambridge University Press, 1984); Toril Moi, *Sexual/Textual Politics* (London: Methuen, 1985).

28 Margaret Laurence, *The Diviners* [1974] (Toronto: New Canadian Library, 1978), 25.

29 Audrey Thomas, *Latakia* (Vancouver: Talonbooks, 1979), 118.

30 Alice Munro, *Lives of Girls and Women* [1971] (Harmondsworth: Penguin, 1982), 247.

31 Joan Barfoot, *Dancing in the Dark* (London: Women's Press, 1982), 67.

32 Alice Munro, 'The Colonel's Hash Resettled', in *The Narrative Voice* ed. J. Metcalf (Toronto: McGraw-Hill Ryerson, 1972), 181–2.

33 I am indebted for this historical insight to Ann Van Sant's paper

on Samuel Richardson, 'Probing the heart: experiments in sensibility', given at the Sixteenth Annual Meeting of the American Society for Eighteenth-Century Studies, Toronto, April 1985.
34 Margaret Atwood, 'Bluebeard's Egg', *Bluebeard's Egg* (Toronto: McClelland & Stewart, 1983), 147.
35 Alice Munro, 'The Moons of Jupiter', *The Moons of Jupiter* (Toronto: Macmillan, 1982), 216.
36 Margaret Laurence, *The Diviners*, 453.

2 Margaret Laurence

1 Margaret Laurence, *The Diviners* [1974] (Toronto: McClelland & Stewart, New Canadian Library, 1978; reprinted 1984), 453. All references to the novel are taken from this edition and included in the text.
2 Margaret Laurence, *Heart of a Stranger* [1976] (Toronto: McClelland & Stewart, Seal edition, 1981), 5.
3 Clara Thomas, *The Manawaka World of Margaret Laurence* (Toronto: McClelland & Stewart, New Canadian Library, 1976), ch. 9.
4 Quoted by P. Easingwood in 'Margaret Laurence, Manawaka and the edge of the unknown', *World Literature Written in English*, XXII, Autumn 1983, 254–63.
5 M. Fabre, 'From *The Stone Angel* to *The Diviners*: an interview with Margaret Laurence', reprinted in *A Place to Stand On: Essays by and about Margaret Laurence*, ed. G. Woodcock (Edmonton: NeWest, 1983), 193–209.
6 Margaret Laurence, *A Bird in the House* [1970] (New Canadian Library, 1978; reprinted 1984), 115. All references to the stories are taken from this edition.
7 Kent Thompson first used the term 'whole-book story sequence' to describe *A Bird in the House* in his 'Review of *A Bird in the House* [1970]', reprinted in Woodcock (ed.) *A Place to Stand On*, 232–5.
8 Margaret Laurence, *Heart of a Stranger*, 5.
9 Margaret Laurence, 'Gadgetry or growing: form and voice in the novel', reprinted in Woodcock (ed.) *A Place to Stand On*, 80–9.
10 Margaret Laurence, *Heart of a Stranger*, 7.

11 Interview with Margaret Laurence in G. Gibson, *Eleven Canadian Novelists* (Toronto: Anansi, 1973), 203.

12 Virginia Woolf, entry for 4 January 1929 in *A Writer's Diary*, ed. L. Woolf (London: Hogarth, 1953), 141.

13 *The Diviners* shares many points of similarity with Virginia Woolf's *To the Lighthouse* in its presentation of doubleness and ambiguity, and I am indebted to a lecture on *To the Lighthouse* given by Professor Isobel Armstrong at the University of London Summer School in August 1984 for stimulating my awareness of the possible parallels between them.

14 Gibson, *Eleven Canadian Novelists*, 190–1.

3 Margaret Atwood

1 Margaret Atwood, 'An end to audience?' [8 October 1980], reprinted in *Second Words: Selected Critical Prose* (Toronto: Anansi, 1982), 334–57.

2 Margaret Atwood's statement as a creative artist is closely related to modern reader response theories. See L. Hutcheon, *Narcissistic Narrative: The Metafictional Paradox* (London: Methuen, 1984), J. Culler, *The Pursuit of Signs* (London: Routledge & Kegan Paul, 1981) and *On Deconstruction* (London: Routledge & Kegan Paul, 1983).

3 Margaret Atwood, *Bodily Harm* [1981] (London: Virago, 1983) and *The Handmaid's Tale* [1985] (London: Cape, 1986). All page references will be to these editions and included in the text.

4 Margaret Atwood, *Survival: A Thematic Guide to Canadian Literature* (Toronto: Anansi, 1972), 13. I am indebted to V. Redman's unpublished essay, 'Margaret Atwood, language and the popular form' submitted at the Polytechnic of North London (1986) for drawing this image to my attention.

5 Toril Moi, *Sexual/Textual Politics* (London: Methuen, 1985), 158.

6 Margaret Atwood, 'Witches' [1980], reprinted in *Second Words*, 329–33.

7 See Coral Ann Howells, *Love, Mystery and Misery* (London: Athlone, 1978) for a fuller discussion of the Radcliffean heroine.

8 Patrick Parrinder, *London Review of Books*, 20 March 1986, 20–2.

9 Quoted from Atwood's address delivered at a conference,

'Imagined realities in contemporary women's writing', held at Dyffryn House near Cardiff (October 1982).

10 This gesture of female bonding is also a revision of Rennie's relationship with her mother and grandmother where hands are very important. For a fascinating essay on mothers and daughters, see B. Godard, 'My (m)other, my self: strategies for subversion in Atwood and Hébert', *Essays in Canadian Writing*, 26, Summer 1983, 13– 44

11 J. McCoombs, 'Atwood's haunted sequences: *The Circle Game, The Journals of Susanna Moodie*, and *Power Politics*', in *The Art of Margaret Atwood: Essays in Criticism*, ed A. E. Davidson and C. N. Davidson (Toronto: Anansi, 1981), pp. 35–54.

12 C. Stimpson, 'Atwood woman', *The Nation*, 31 May 1986, 764–7.

13 Atwood's warning against matriarchal power is developed in her futurist short story 'Freeforall', *Toronto Star*, 20 September 1986, J1–J4.

14 E. M. Forster, 'What I believe', *Two Cheers for Democracy* (London: Edward Arnold, 1951), pp. 77–85.

15 Marilyn French, *Beyond Power: On Women, Men and Morals* [1985] (London: Cape, 1986). French's theoretical discussion and Atwood's novel share many common features in their feminist analyses of patriarchy.

16 Margaret Atwood, 'Writing the male character' [1982], reprinted in *Second Words*, pp. 412–30.

4 Alice Munro

1 'Bardon Bus' is from Alice Munro's collection of short stories, *The Moons of Jupiter* [1982] available in England in King Penguin, 1984, 111. My references to *The Moons of Jupiter, Lives of Girls and Women* [1971] (Harmondsworth: Penguin, 1984) and *The Beggar Maid: Stories of Flo and Rose* [published in Canada as *Who Do You Think You Are?* [1978] (Harmondsworth: Penguin, 1980) are all taken from the English paperback texts.

2 J. Metcalf (ed), *Making It New: Contemporary Canadian Stories* (Toronto and London: Methuen, 1982), 224.

3 Alice Munro's 'Appreciation of Marian Engel', *Room of One's Own* (Special Issue on Marian Engel), 9(2), June 1984, 12–13.

4 Alice Munro, 'Everything here is touchable and mysterious', *Weekend Magazine*, 11 May 1947, 33.

5 Alice Munro described her writing as a kind of 'super realism' like the paintings of Edward Hopper or Andrew Wyeth in her interview with Graeme Gibson in *Eleven Canadian Novelists* 256.

6 Jennifer Waelti-Walters in *Fairy Tales and the Female Imagination* (Montreal: Eden Press, 1982) also uses the term 'split-level discourse' to describe the contradictory structures within Québécois women's narratives.

7 For full-length discussions of fantasy and realism, see C. Brooke-Rose, *A Rhetoric of the Unreal: Studies in Narrative and Structure, especially of the Fantastic* (Cambridge: Cambridge University Press, 1981) and R. Jackson, *Fantasy: The Literature of Subversion* (London and New York: Methuen New Accents series, 1981).

8 Virginia Woolf, *A Room of One's Own* [1929] (London: Panther, 1977), 63.

9 Munro has called *Lives of Girls and Women* a novel, though it is structurally a short-story sequence like the semi-autobiographical fictions of Laurence's *A Bird in the House* and Thomas's *Songs My Mother Taught Me*. It is an interesting example of mixed genre coding in the collection as a whole.

10 Barbara Godard, 'Heirs of the living body: Alice Munro and the question of a female aesthetic', *The Art of Alice Munro: Saying the Unsayable*, ed. J. Miller (Waterloo: University of Waterloo Press, 1984), 43–71.

11 Nancy K. Miller, 'Emphasis added: plots and plausibilities in women's fiction', *PMLA*, 96 (1981), 36–48.

12 'The progress of love', *The New Yorker*, October, 1985, 35–58. I am indebted to Dr Rosalie Osmond's paper, 'Arrangements, disarrangements and earnest deceptions: changing narrative patterns in the work of Alice Munro' given at the BACS Literature Group Conference, University of Birmingham in May 1986, for bringing this story to my attention and for her insightful presentation of Munro's narrative methods.

13 *Lives of Girls and Women*, 250.

14 *The Beggar Maid*, 210.

5 Mavis Gallant

1 Mavis Gallant, *Home Truths: Selected Canadian Stories* (Toronto: Macmillan, 1981), xiii. All my textual references are to this edition.

2 Mavis Gallant lived in Montreal as a young adult, but is generally regarded as an expatriate. See Biographical Note.

3 I am indebted for this phrase, as for several of my ideas on expatriate writers, to A. J. Gurr, *Writers in Exile: The Identity of Home in Modern Literature* (Sussex: Harvester, 1981).

4 For original publication dates of Mavis Gallant's stories and other bibliographical details, see the excellent Annotated Bibliography of Mavis Gallant by Judith Skelton Grant and Douglas Malcolm in *The Annotated Bibliography of Canada's Major Authors*, vol. 5, eds. R. Lecker and J. David (Downsview, Ontario: ECW Press, 1984), 179–230.

5 See G. Hancock, 'An interview with Mavis Gallant', *Canadian Fiction Magazine*: Special Issue on Mavis Gallant, 28 (1978), 46.

6 Gurr, *Writers in Exile*, 145.

7 Patrick Parrinder, *James Joyce* (Cambridge: Cambridge University Press, 1984), 42.

8 Mavis Gallant, 'The Moslem Wife', *From The Fifteenth District* (Toronto: Macmillan, 1979), 76.

9 This story was first published in *The New Yorker*, 14 December 1963; reprinted in *My Heart Is Broken* (1964).

10 First published in *The New Yorker*, 30 January 1965. This story of refusal has striking similarities with Mavis Gallant's earlier story 'The Other Paris' (1953). See Ronald B. Hatch, 'Mavis Gallant: returning home', *Atlantis*, 4(1), Fall 1978, 95–102 for a discussion of 'The Other Paris'.

11 See Michel Fabre, '"Orphans' Progress": reader's progress – Le "on-dit" et le "non-dit" chez Mavis Gallant', *Recherches Anglaises et Américaines* (Strasbourg), XVI (1983), 57–67.

12 Lottie's unwritten letter has a similar function to Erika's in 'An Autobiography', *The Pegnitz Junction* (1973) which ends with a parallel sense of unfulfilment: 'There has been such a waste of everything, such a waste.'

13 First published in *The New Yorker*, 3 April 1965. My analysis will be brief as Fabre has discussed this story at some length in his

article, though he has not considered the manipulations of language here.

14 George Woodcock, 'Memory, imagination, artifice: the late short fiction of Mavis Gallant', *Canadian Fiction Magazine*, 28 (1978), 74–91.

15 First published in *The New Yorker*, 20 June 1977.

16 Del Jordan stares at the same picture by Sir Luke Fildes on the wall of her room in Jubilee, Ontario, in Alice Munro's *Lives of Girls and Women*, 173, which incidentally substantiates Mavis Gallant's claim that 'reproductions of this work flowed into every crevice and corner of North America and the British Empire, swamping continents.' Dr J. Skelton Grant has pointed out to me a reference by Robertson Davies to the same picture in his editorial, 'The Doctor', *Peterborough Examiner*, 6 July 1962, 4.

17 Mavis Gallant, 'What is style?', *Canadian Forum*, XLII, (721), September 1982, 6–7, 37.

18 George Woodcock, 'Memory, imagination, artifice', 77.

19 Mavis Gallant uses this phrase in her novella, 'Its Image in the Mirror', *My Heart Is Broken* [1964]: reprinted in New Press Canadian Classics (Toronto: General Pub. Co. Ltd., 1982), 153.

6   Marian Engel; Joy Kogawa; Janette Turner Hospital

1 Janette Turner Hospital, 'The Interview', *The Weekend Australian*, 29–30 March 1986, 4.

2 ibid.

3 Graeme Gibson, *Eleven Canadian Novelists*, 113. See also Alice Munro's 'Appreciation' of Marian Engel in *Room of One's Own*, 9(2) June 1984, 12–13: 'She knew what we were getting at.'

4 Marian Engel, *Bear* [1976]. All references in the text will be taken from the McClelland & Stewart New Canadian Library paperback, 1982.

5 I am indebted in my thinking about demarcation lines and transgression in this novel to Jeanne Delbaere-Garant's essay 'Decolonizing the self in *Surfacing*, *Bear* and *A Fringe of Leaves*', *Colonisations: Rencontres Australie–Canada* (Travaux de l'Université de Toulouse-Le Mirail, série B, tome 07, 1985), 67–78.

6 See Jay Macpherson's Canadian chapter, 'Epilogue: this swan neck of the woods', in *The Spirit of Solitude* (Yale, 1982) for a scholarly and imaginative account of this tradition; also the chapters on 'Animals and landscape' in Margaret Atwood's *Survival* (Toronto: Anansi, 1972). The old Indian woman Lucy in *Bear* is an elusive reminder of the affinity between wilderness creatures in this novel.

7 Macpherson, 'Epilogue', 255.

8 Anne Barr Snitow, 'Mass market romance: pornography for women is different', in *Desire: The Politics of Sexuality*, eds. A. Snitow, C. Stansell, S. Thompson [1983] published in England by Virago, London, 1984), 269.

9 Rosalind Coward, *Female Desire* (London: Paladin, 1984), 196.

10 The central situation of *Bear* has interesting similarities with D. H. Lawrence's *St Mawr* [1925] and in both stories the heroine is called Lou. J. Delbaere-Garant comments on this similarity in 'Decolonizing the self', 67. In a conversation with Carroll Klein Marian Engel spoke of herself as a reader of Lawrence, 'I gobbled him up when I was young', *Room of One's Own*, 9(1) June 1984, 5–30. Here Engel has told the love story from a woman's perspective.

11 Snitow, 'Mass market romance' 270–1; Coward, *Female Desire*, 196.

12 In her Jungian reading of *Bear* Patricia Monk highlights these gender transformations, seeing the source of the book's energy in the symbolic ambivalence of the bear itself: 'Engel's *Bear*: a furry tale', *Atlantis*, 5(1), Fall 1979, 29–39.

13 Anne Cameron, *Daughters of Copper Woman* (Vancouver: Press Gang Publishers, 1981), 119.

14 Margaret Atwood refers to this poem in her chapter on animal victims in *Survival*, 84–5, though she uses it to emphasize the possibility of resistance to the victim image. I am more interested in the constellation as transformation effected through art.

15 Macpherson, 'Epilogue', 264.

16 Interview with Carole Corbeil, *Toronto Globe and Mail*, 14 May 1983.

17 *Obasan* [1981] (Harmondsworth: Penguin 1983, distributed in UK 1984). All references will be to the Penguin text.

18 Maxine Hong Kingston, *The Woman Warrior: Memoirs of a*

Girlhood among Ghosts (1975). My references are taken from the Picador paperback edition published by Pan Books Ltd, London, 1981.

19 Virginia Woolf, *To the Lighthouse* [1927]. My page reference is to Penguin Modern Classics paperback edition (1964), 194.

20 Janette Turner Hospital, *The Ivory Swing* [1982]. All my references are to the McClelland & Stewart Bantam-Seal paperback, 1983; 207.

21 Audrey Thomas, *Latakia* (Vancouver and Los Angeles: Talonbooks, 1979), 167. I shall be discussing this novel in the following chapter.

22 Elizabeth Waterston, 'Women in Canadian fiction', a paper presented at the Canadian Literature Conference, University of Aarhus, Denmark, May 1984. Now published in *Canadiana*, ed. Jørn Carlsen and Knud Larson, Aarhus, 1984, 100–8.

23 Anita Desai, *Clear Light of Day* [1980]. All my references are to the Penguin paperback, 1980.

24 For a fuller discussion on the value of history and tradition see D. Riemenschneider, 'History and the individual in Anita Desai's *Clear Light of Day* and Salman Rushdie's *Midnight's Children*', *World Literature Written in English* XXXIII (i), Winter 1984, 196–207.

7 Audrey Thomas; Joan Barfoot

1 Audrey Thomas, *Intertidal Life* (Toronto: Stoddart (General Publishing Co. Ltd), 1984), 170.

2 Urjo Kareda, 'Sense and Sensibility', *Saturday Night*, January 1985, 50–1, uses this phrase to describe *Intertidal Life*.

3 Rachel's effort is similar to Isobel's, the adolescent narrator in *Songs My Mother Taught Me* and to Alice's, another middle-aged narrator in *Intertidal Life*.

4 See my essay, 'Margaret Laurence: *The Diviners* and Audrey Thomas: *Latakia*', *Canadian Woman Studies*, VI (i), 1985, 98–100.

5 A. Thomas, *Latakia* (Vancouver: Talonbooks, 1979), 152. All references will be to this edition and included in the text.

6 See P. Butling, 'The Cretan paradox, or where the truth lies in *Latakia*', *Room of One's Own*, 10(3 & 4), 1986, 105–10.

7 Virginia Woolf, *The Waves* [1931] (Harmondsworth: Penguin, 1971), 139. Thomas succeeds better than Woolf in her sustained use of a female narrator.

8 Joan Barfoot, *Dancing in the Dark* (Toronto: Macmillan, 1982; London: Women's Press, 1982), 67. All references will be taken from the London edition and included in the text.

9 Doubtless one could find clinical diagnoses of Edna's mental state in the accounts of psychiatric disorders in R. D. Laing, *The Divided Self* [1959]. However her state is so vividly realized in her account that naming and classifying do not seem particularly necessary.

8 Marie-Claire Blais; Anne Hébert

1 For a neat discussion of this point about conquest or betrayal, see the feature review by I. M. Owen of Susan Mann Trofimenkoff's *The Dream of Nation: A Social and Intellectual History of Quebec*, in *Books in Canada*, XII, 5, May 1983, 10–12.

2 I take this quotation from Ralph Sarkonak's excellent essay, 'Accentuating the differences', in *The Language of Difference: Writing in Québéc(ois)*, *Yale French Studies*, 65, 1983, 3–20. I am greatly indebted for the facts of my potted history to this essay. See also G. L. Symons, 'Quebec nationalism and Canadian unity: a phenomenological excursion in the Québécois and Canadian realities', paper presented at Tenth Anniversary Conference of British Association for Canadian Studies, Edinburgh, April 1985.

3 Sherry Simon, 'Feminist writing in Quebec', in *Canadian Forum*, LX (701), August 1980, 5–8.

4 Two attempts at interrelatedness between French and English Canadian feminist writing are *Les Stratégies du réel/The story so far*, ed. Nicole Brossard (Toronto: Coach House Press, 1980) and *Tessera: Room of One's Own*, special issue on Quebec women's writing, VIII(4), 1984. Four of Nicole Brossard's novels have been translated into English (Coach House Press).

5 Patricia Smart, 'Culture, revolution and politics in Quebec', *Canadian Forum*, LXII(718), May 1982, 7–10; Michelle Jean, 'Two decades of feminism in Quebec: 1960–1979', *Fireweed*, 5 and 6, Winter 1979/80 and Spring 1980, 189–93.

6 Sarkonak, 'Accentuating the differences', 12.

7 This question appears at the end of M. J. Green's essay, 'Structures of liberation', in *Yale French Studies* (1983), 124–36. In her answer to this question Green points to parallels between Quebec's history and women's writing, though given her autobiographical material her answer is different from mine.

8 Mais la faim de la nuit, c'était aussi la faim des femmes, le goût de leurs désirs, la joie de les revoir, de les connaître . . . pendant que les vents d'hiver poussaient vers une commune cérémonie célébrée dans une cave, ces cheveux, ces corps, ces âmes épars qu'un seul mot unissait et faisait vibrer : aimer.
Marie-Claire Blais, *Les Nuits de l'underground* (Montreal: Stanké, 1978), 159. The English edition is entitled *Nights in the Underground*, trans. R. Ellenwood (Toronto: Musson, 1979), 117. Further page references to these editions will appear in the text.

9 Blais had shown the lives of male homosexuals in *Le Loup/The Wolf* (1972) but I am not concerned with that novel here.

10 Jane Rule's *Lesbian Images* (New York: Doubleday, 1975) is an excellent critical study of writing within a lesbian tradition. See also Catherine Stimpson, 'Zero degree deviancy: the lesbian novel in English', *Writing and Sexual Difference*, ed. E. Abel (Brighton: Harvester, 1982), 243–59.

11 See Mary Daly, *Gyn/Ecology: The Metaethics of Radical Feminism* (Boston: Beacon Press, 1979); also Marilyn R. Shuster, 'Strategies for survival: the subtle subversion of Jane Rule', *Feminist Studies* (Fall 1981), 431–50.

12 Bonnie Zimmerman, 'What has never been: an overview of lesbian feminist literary criticism', *Feminist Studies*, Fall 1981, 451–75.

13 Shuster, 'Strategies for survival', 447.

14 Madeleine Gagnon, 'My body in writing', trans. Wendy Johnson, in *Feminism in Canada: From Pressure to Politics*, eds. Angela Miles and Geraldine Finn (Montreal: Black Rose, 1982), 269–82.

15 For a thought-provoking discussion of this structuralist principle in relation to gender definitions, see Alice Echols, 'The new feminism of Yin and Yang', in *Desire: The Politics of Sexuality*, ed. A. Snitow, C. Stansell, S. Thompson (London: Virago, 1983), 62–81.

16   Adrienne Rich, 'Compulsory heterosexuality and lesbian exist-
      ence', in Snitow, Stansell, Thompson (eds) *Desire*, 212–41.
      Further page references to this essay will be included in the text.
17   Elle n'aimait pas Lali, elle aimait en elle la beauté, la perfection
      de l'art. Mais ce qui la désemparait, c'était de comprendre que
      l'art est partout vivant et charnel, que ce qu'elle avait vu au loin
      et sans danger, dans la confiance des musées, vivait et frémissait
      tout près d'elle, dans sa vie même, cette oeuvre vivante c'était
      Lali, vulnérable, soumise à toutes les puissances contraires à
      l'amour de la vie et de l'art, la violence, la guerre, la bêtise. (21)
18   Il y avait une grande cheminée dans la maison, et il y avait,
      comment t'appelles donc ça? un tour, une fissure dans la
      cheminée, et je regardais pendant des heures, ah! je pensais with
      terror' . . . Geneviève songeait que c'était peut-être, encore
      aujourd'hui, cette brèche infime dans la cheminée que con-
      templait par instants le regard désolé de Lali, lorsqu'elle buvait
      seule au bar; de cette brèche, n'était-ce pas tout un monde
      sépulcral qui s'échappait? Celui des victimes dont on ne se
      souvient plus des visages, de refugiés, d'errants dont les dos
      courbés, les pieds vêtus de loques longtemps vous persecutent?
      Toute l'enfance de Lali allait et venait par cette fente
      apocalyptique. (31)
19   Ce doute qui lui rappelait dans sa sêcheresse, son aigreur même
      que tout amour est peut-être un don, une merveille, mais un don
      marqué par nous du signe de sa propre folie, de sa propre perte?
      (68)
20   Ainsi ces rayons de soleil qui tombaient sur le visage de Lali
      traversaeint comme une voile cette soie qui recouvrait ses joues
      et qui ressemblait si peu à de la chair pour faire saillir au dehors
      une ossature diaphane, fantôme d'un autre visage privé de toute
      vie, dont Lali elle-même paraissait ignorer la présence. (96)
21   On eût dit que toutes les femmes qui l'avaient aimée, ces
      étrangères multiples . . . avaient déposé en Lali toute leur
      ardeur, et que le bruissement de leurs voix, la chaleur de leur
      haleine passaient par la voix, le souffle de Lali pour mieux fêter
      avec elle cette idée pourtant très cérébrale que Lali se faisait des
      corps, laquelle ne pouvait se délivrer que par sa chair à la fois
      ardue et frémissante. (130)
22   Et Lali, plus qu'une autre, même si elle avait initié Geneviève, à

travers elle-même, à tout un cortège de femmes appartenant à la communauté homosexuelle . . . abandonnait Geneviève à cette ignorance bénie où, devenue son propre maître, Geneviève ne subissait plus les lois de Lali, mais les siennes. (180)

23 It seems clear that the model for Françoise is Vita Sackville-West, herself a lesbian and a diplomatic wife and mother – a hunch confirmed I think by the epigraph of the novel, Vita Sackville-West's words quoted by Nigel Nicholson in *Portrait of a Marriage* (1973).

24 C'était, dans son achèvement, la plénitude de sa jeunesse, da sa sensuelle audace, le portrait de Lali, passant du côté de la lumière de Van Eyck, lumière presque rose et qui a l'effet d'une insupportable douceur, à la brune violence d'un visage de Goya. (197)

25 Car l'été semblait triompher de tout, même de Lali qui avait quitté l'armure sévère de son manteau pour un short de garçon . . . rayonnant de ce bonheur simple animal, qui était le sien, ce bonheur qui vous apportait tant d'illusions, en ces jours de transparence, qu'on croyait ne jamais pouvoir le perdre . . . Pourtant, au-delà de cette certitude qu'était Lali aujourd'hui, dans son insouciante jeunesse, un autre être, Françoise, marchait vers Geneviève, encore obscurcie par l'ombre de la forêt, un autre être, fait lui aussi de beautés et de doutes, ce que deviendrait Lali demain, peut-être, lorsque le défi de son sourire l'aurait à jamais quittée . . . (266–7)

26 Imagery of the seasonal cycle is also an important thematic image in Jane Rule, *Against the Season* (1975) and *The Young in One Another's Arms* (1978).

27 Jane Rule, 'Sexuality in literature', *Fireweed*, (5 and 6), Winter 1979/80 and Spring 1980, 22–7.

28 'Anne Hébert et les racines de l'imaginaire', in Donald Smith, *L'Ecrivain devant son oeuvre* (Montreal: Collections Literature d'Amerique, 1983), 36–58. The translations of the Hébert interview are my own.

29 Smith, 'Anne Hébert', 56.

30 Anne Hébert, *Héloïse* (Paris: Editions du Seuil, 1980), 9. The English edition is entitled *Héloïse*, trans. S. Fischman (Toronto: Stoddart, 1982), 13. Further page references to these editions will appear in the text.

31 Smith, *L'Ecrivain*, 55.

32 Le trou d'air. Oui, c'est cela la même impression de tomber dans le vide. Ma vieille horreur du métro me reprend. Je m'enforce au plus creux de lrdeura terre. Son coeur de feu et de glace. Au niveau des morts.
    Les murailles grises défilent dans l'obscurité. Un instant les stations éclairent la nuit. Puis à nouveau le noir, les murs gris, les espèces de tuyaux rouges et bleus. Parfois la réclame Dubonnet à moitié effacée comme une fresque perdue. (19)

33 See Janet M. Paterson, 'Anne Hébert and the discourse of the unreal', *The Language of Difference: Writing in Québéc(ois)*, 172–86.

34 Peggy Kamuf, *Fictions of Feminine Desire: Disclosures of Héloïse* (Lincoln and London: University of Nebraska Press, 1982), 19.

35 I am indebted to Kamuf, *Fictions of Feminine Desire*, ch. 1, for these details.

36 Ce monde dans lequel nous vivons accueille d'un même air indifférent et las toute singularité et jouissance perverse . . .
    Tranquillement, étalant son crime et sa nécessité, parmi l'indifférence générale, elle transvase le sang de sa séringue dans des flacons de verre. Sur la place une ambulance passe en trombe, toutes sirènes hurlantes. (102–3)

37 Margaret Atwood, *Bodily Harm*, 133.

38 —Ne vous tarde-t-il pas de ramener cette merveille parmi nous?
    —Je n'ai pas le choix, n'est-ce pas? Mon éternité est à ce prix. (107)

39 Bernard tombe aux pieds d'Héloïse. Il enfouit sa tête dans les jupes de la jeune femme. Retrouve l'odeur prenante des grèves; varech, goémon, vase profonde qui fume et se déchaîne. Il enserre les jambes d'Héloïse jusqu'à la faire tomber par terre. Ils roulent tous les deux sur le tapis. Un bref cri de douleur.
    Est-ce moi qui crie, pense Bernard, pendant que la volupté le broie et l'emmène jusqu'aux portes de la mort. Le sang chaud l'inonde venant de sa gorge tranchée. Il sombre dans la nuit. (100)

40 Les voici, tous les deux, sur le quai, mêlés aux autres voyageurs. La séduction d'Héloïse. Son charme pervers. Elle embrasse Bernard.

Les a-t-il vraiment chuchotés ces mots, contre l'epaule
d'Héloïse?
—Je t'aime Héloïse, je t'aime.
Les a-t-elle vraiment prononcées ces paroles, comme on
s'adresse à un enfant malade.
—Ce n'est que la fascination de la mort, mon chéri.' (123)
41 Alice Munro, *Lives of Girls and Women*, 244.
42 Alexander Pope, 'Eloisa to Abelard', *The Poems of Alexander Pope*, ed. J. Butt (London: Methuen, 1963), 261.
43 Le monde est en ordre
   Les morts dessous
   Les vivants dessus.
Anne Hébert, 'A Kind of Feast', *Poems by Anne Hébert*, trans. A. Brown (Don Mills, Ontario: Musson, 1975). These lines are also the epigraph to *Héloïse*.

Conclusion

1 'Could I have Found a Better Love than You?' in *The Tattooed Woman* (Harmondsworth: Penguin, 1985), 144.
2 Margaret Laurence, *The Diviner*, 390.
3 Robert Kroetsch, 'Disunity as unity: a Canadian strategy', in *Canadian Story and History 1885–1985*, ed. P. Easingwood and C. Nicholson (Edinburgh: Centre for Canadian Studies), 1–11.
4 Joan Barfoot, *Dancing in the Dark*, 19.

Biographical Sketches

Margaret Atwood (b. 1939). Born in Ottawa, she grew up in Ottawa and Toronto and in the northern Ontario and Quebec bush country. She took her BA at the University of Toronto and was a graduate student at Harvard. During the 1960s she lived in Boston, Vancouver, Montreal, Edmonton, and since 1970 she has lived mainly in Ontario (in or near Toronto) with numerous excursions to Britain, Europe and Australia. She has taught English Literature and been Writer in Residence at York University, the University of Toronto, the University of Alabama and New York University. In 1981–2 she was Chairperson of the Writers' Union of Canada. She has published six novels, two collections of short stories, a critical study of Canadian literature, several children's books and a collection of essays. Also a poet of world-wide reputation, her early collection *The Circle Game* won the Governor-General's Award in 1966; she is the editor of the *New Oxford Book of Canadian Verse in English.* Her work has been translated into fourteen languages and her numerous awards include several honorary degrees, the Welsh Arts Council's International Writers' Prize in 1982 and the Governor-General's Award for *The Handmaid's Tale.* She and novelist Graeme Gibson have one young daughter and live in Toronto.

Joan Barfoot (b. 1946). Born in Owen Sound, Ontario, she graduated in English Literature from the University of Western Ontario. She has always worked as a journalist, first on the campus newspaper then in Windsor and London, Ontario. Her first novel was published in 1978. She is unmarried and lives in London, Ontario.

Marie-Claire Blais (b. 1939). Born and brought up in Quebec City, she left school at sixteen to be a writer and worked at nine jobs over the next three years; she also attended courses in literature and the social sciences at Laval University. Her first novel *La Belle Bête* was published in 1959, and in 1963 she obtained a Guggenheim Fellowship to Cambridge, Mass. She lived in New England till 1971, then in Brittany till 1975. Since then she has settled in Quebec and continues to make numerous trips throughout Canada, the United States and Europe. Marie-Claire Blais has published fifteen novels plus plays, poems and stories, and unlike Anne Hébert all her novels have been published first in Montreal. Her work (all written in French) has been translated into twelve languages. She has won many literary prizes, including the *Prix Médici* and two Governor-General's Awards: in 1969 for *Les Manuscrits de Pauline Archange* and in 1979 for *Le Sourd dans la ville*.

Marian Engel (b. 1933; d. February 1985). Born in Toronto, she spent her childhood in Ontario and took her BA in French and German at McMaster University, Ontario and her MA at McGill University, Montreal. (Her thesis topic was 'The English-Canadian novel since 1939.') After teaching briefly in Montreal and Montana she visited Belgium, Holland, Sweden, France and England in the early 1960s, and in 1962 she married a Canadian in London and worked in London and in Cyprus before returning to Canada. Her twins were born in 1964 and her first novel appeared in 1968. She was the first Chairperson of the Writers' Union of Canada 1973–4, and she won the

Governor-General's Award for *Bear* in 1976. Divorced, she lived in Toronto with her children until her death from cancer. She has been posthumously awarded the Order of Canada.

Mavis Gallant (b. 1922). Born in Quebec and brought up bilingually, she lived there until she was ten, then in Ontario and the United States till the age of eighteen. She was back in Canada in 1941 and worked briefly for the National Film Board and then as a feature writer for the *Montreal Standard*. She married but had separated from her husband before 1950 when she left Canada for Europe where she has lived and worked as a writer, mainly in Paris. She has long been a contributor of short stories and essays to *The New Yorker* and the *New York Times Book Review*, and her books have been regularly published since 1956 in the United States and in London. Her first book to be published in Canada was *The End of the World and Other Stories* (1974). Only with *From the Fifteenth District* (1979) and *Home Truths* (1981) has she been widely read in Canada. She received the Governor-General's Award for *Home Truths* and was awarded the Order of Canada in 1981. She was Writer in Residence at the University of Toronto 1983–4 and has since returned to Paris.

Anne Hébert (b. 1916). Born and brought up in Quebec, she started publishing poems in 1939 and her first collection was published in 1942. In 1950 her first collection of short stories appeared, published at her own expense. She worked for Radio Canada and the National Film Board till 1954 when she won a scholarship to Paris, where she lived for three years and wrote her first novel *Les Chambres de Bois* (published in Paris in 1958). She divided her time between Paris and Quebec till 1965, since when she has lived in Paris, returning to Quebec frequently for visits. Her five novels have all been published in France. In 1960 her third volume of poems won the Governor-General's Award, and she won it again in 1975 for her novel *Les Enfants du Sabbat*. She has won numerous literary prizes in Canada, Belgium and France, including the Prix Femina in

1982 for her novel *Les Fous de Bassan*. Translated into English in 1983 as *In the Shadow of the Wind* it is the first of her novels to be published in Britain.

Janette Turner Hospital (b. 1942). Born and brought up in Australia, she taught school there until her husband's research took the family abroad. She has two teenage children and an MA in Medieval English literature from Queen's University, Ontario. She began her writing career in her late 30s with short stories, and *The Ivory Swing* won the Seal First Novel Award in 1982. She frequently revisits Australia and was Writer-in-Residence at MIT in Boston 1985–6. She lives in Kingston, Ontario.

Joy Kogawa (b. 1935). A third-generation Japanese-Canadian born in Vancouver, she and her family were interned during World War II and then transported first to the ghost town of Slocan in the Rockies of British Columbia and then to Alberta. She attended the Universities of Saskatchewan and Alberta, and the Royal Conservatory of Music and the Anglican Women's Training College in Toronto. Married with two children and now divorced, she lives in Toronto. A member of the League of Canadian Poets and the Writers' Union of Canada, she has also been a school teacher and Writer in Residence at the University of Ottawa.

Margaret Laurence (b. 1926, d. January 1987). Born and brought up in Neepawa, Manitoba, she took her BA with Honours in English in Winnipeg. She married in 1947 and had two children. During her early married life she lived in Somaliland and Ghana where she translated a collection of Somali folktales and wrote her first novel and a book of short stories, both about Africa; she returned to Canada in 1957 and then lived in England in the mid-1960s after separating from her husband. Until her death she lived in Lakefield, Ontario. During the 1960s and early 1970s she wrote the Manawaka novels. She was Writer in Residence at several Canadian universities, she had twelve honorary degrees, and was Chancellor of Trent University, Ontario. Margaret Laurence was actively involved in the Peace Movement for years and she also worked earnestly for Canadian writing. She won two Governor-General's Awards: in 1967 for *A Jest of God* and in 1975 for *The Diviners*.

Alice Munro (b. 1931). Born and brought up in Wingham, Ontario, she was an undergraduate at the University of Western Ontario. Her first story was published in the university's literary magazine in 1950. In 1951 she married and moved to the West Coast; she lived for twenty years in Vancouver and Victoria where her three daughters were born. In the early 1970s she returned to Ontario and now lives in Clinton, not far from Wingham, with her second husband. Her first collection of short stories *Dance of the Happy Shades* was published in 1968 and won a Governor-General's Award; she won it a second time in 1978 for *Who Do You Think You Are?* (published in England under the title *The Beggar Maid*). She has been Writer in Residence at the University of Queensland, Australia.

Audrey Thomas (b. 1935). Born in Binghampton, New York, she took her BA at Smith College and came to Canada in 1959, where she took her MA at the University of British Columbia. At this stage she was married with one child. She lived in Ghana 1964–6 and it was while she was in Africa that she sold her first short story. In 1976 she lived in Greece. She has been Visiting Professor of Creative Writing at several Canadian universities and Writer in Residence at the University of Edinburgh 1985–6. Divorced, she lives near Vancouver and has three daughters.

Bibliography

This bibliography includes a complete list of books published by the women writers whose works I have discussed. I include details of publication in Canada, England and the United States for English-Canadians. I have listed new editions (most of them in paperback) but not reprintings. For French-Canadians I list date and place of first publication in Canada and in France; date, place and title of first translation into English, and some subsequent editions in English though these last publication details are not necessarily complete.

These lists are based on information provided by a search of the Canadian National Library Database in Ottawa up to October 1983. This material has been supplemented from many sources: information given by the writers themselves; catalogues of the Canadian collection held by the Thomas Fisher Rare Book Library at the University of Toronto and the Women's Educational Resource Centre, Ontario Institute for Studies in Education. Additional searches for British and French imprints have been made at the Bibliothèque Nationale in Paris, and in the British Library, the libraries of the Canadian High Commission and the Québec Délégation générale in London.

The principal critical and scholarly books and articles that have been consulted in writing this book are indicated in the Notes to individual chapters.

Margaret Laurence

The Manawaka cycle

The Stone Angel. Toronto: McClelland & Stewart, 1964; London: Macmillan, 1964; New York: Knopf, 1964; Toronto: New Canadian Library (McClelland & Stewart), 1968; London: Panther, 1970; Toronto: Seal Books (McClelland & Stewart-Bantam), 1978.

A Jest of God. Toronto: McClelland & Stewart, 1966; London: Macmillan, 1966; New York: Knopf, 1966; New York: Popular Library, 1966; Toronto: NCL, 1974; Toronto: Seal, 1977. Also published as *Rachel, Rachel*, Toronto and New York: Popular Library, 1966; London: Panther, 1968.

The Fire-Dwellers. Toronto: McClelland & Stewart, 1969; London: Macmillan, 1969; New York: Knopf, 1969; New York: Popular Library, 1969; Toronto: NCL, 1973; London: Panther, 1973; Toronto: Seal, 1978.

A Bird in the House. Toronto: McClelland & Stewart, 1970; London: Macmillan, 1970; New York: Knopf, 1970; Toronto: NCL, 1974; Toronto: Seal, 1978.

The Diviners. Toronto: McClelland & Stewart, 1974; London: Macmillan, 1974; New York: Knopf, 1974; Toronto: Seal, 1975; London: Bantam, 1976; Toronto: NCL, 1978.

African Writings

A Tree for Poverty: Somali Poetry and Prose. Nairobi: Eagle Press, 1954; Dublin: Irish University Press, 1970; Hamilton: McMaster University, 1970.

This Side Jordan. Toronto: McClelland & Stewart, 1960; London: Macmillan, 1961; New York: St Martins Press, 1960; Toronto: NCL, 1976.

The Tomorrow-Tamer. Toronto: McClelland & Stewart, 1963;

London: Macmillan, 1963; New York: Knopf, 1964; Toronto: NCL, 1970.

The Prophet's Camel Bell. Toronto: McClelland & Stewart, 1963; London: Macmillan, 1963; Toronto: McClelland & Stewart, 1975. Also published as *New Wind in a Dry Land*, New York: Knopf, 1964.

Long Drums and Cannons: Nigerian Dramatists and Novelists 1952–1966. London: Macmillan, 1968; New York: Praeger, 1969.

Essays

Heart of a Stranger. Toronto: McClelland & Stewart, 1976; Toronto: Seal, 1980.

Children's books

Jason's Quest. Toronto: McClelland & Stewart, 1970; London: Macmillan, 1970; New York: Knopf, 1970; Toronto: Seal, 1981.

The Olden-Days Coat. Toronto: McClelland & Stewart, 1979.

Six Darn Cows. Toronto: James Lorimer, 1979.

The Christmas Birthday Story. Toronto: McClelland & Stewart, 1980; New York: Knopf, 1980.

Margaret Atwood

Poetry

Double Persephone. Toronto: Hawkshead Press, 1961.

The Circle Game. Toronto: Contact Press, 1966; Toronto: Anansi, 1967.

The Animals in that Country. Toronto: Oxford University Press, 1968; Boston: Little, Brown, 1968.

The Journals of Susanna Moodie. Toronto: Oxford University Press, 1970.

Procedures for Underground. Toronto: Oxford University Press, 1970; Boston: Little, Brown, 1970.

Power Politics. Toronto: Anansi, 1971; New York: Harper & Row, 1971.

You Are Happy. Toronto: Oxford University Press, 1974; New York: Harper and Row, 1974.

Selected Poems. Toronto: Oxford University Press, 1976; New York: Simon & Shuster, 1976.

Two-Headed Poems. Toronto: Oxford University Press, 1978; New York: Simon & Shuster, 1978.

True Stories. Toronto: Oxford University Press, 1981; New York: Simon & Shuster, 1981; London: Jonathan Cape, 1982.

The New Oxford Book of Canadian Verse in English. Toronto, London, New York: Oxford University Press, 1982.

Murder in the Dark: Short Fictions and Prose Poems. Toronto: Coach House Press, 1983; London: Jonathan Cape, 1984.

Interlunar. Toronto: Oxford University Press, 1984.

Novels

The Edible Woman. Toronto: McClelland & Stewart, 1969; Boston: Little, Brown, 1969; London: André Deutsch, 1969; Toronto: NCL, 1973; New York: Popular Library, 1976; Toronto: Seal, 1978; London: Virago, 1979.

Surfacing. Toronto: McClelland & Stewart, 1972; New York: Simon & Shuster, 1972; New York: Popular Library, 1972; Don Mills, Ontario: PaperJacks, 1973; London: André Deutsch, 1973; London: Virago, 1979; Toronto: New Press Canadian Classics (General Publishing Co. Ltd), 1983.

Lady Oracle. Toronto: McClelland & Stewart, 1976; New York: Simon & Shuster, 1976; Toronto: Seal, 1977; London: André Deutsch, 1977; New York: Avon, 1978; London: Virago, 1980.

Life Before Man. Toronto: McClelland & Stewart, 1979; New York: Simon & Shuster, 1979; Toronto: Seal, 1980; London: Jonathan Cape, 1980; New York: Fawcett Popular Library, 1981; London: Virago, 1982.

Bodily Harm. Toronto: McClelland & Stewart, 1981; New York: Simon & Shuster, 1982; London: Jonathan Cape, 1982; Toronto: Seal, 1982; London: Virago, 1983.

The Handmaid's Tale. Toronto: McClelland & Stewart, 1985;

London: Jonathan Cape, 1986; New York: Houghton Mifflin, 1986.

Short stories

Dancing Girls. Toronto: McClelland & Stewart, 1977; Toronto: Seal, 1978; New York: Simon & Shuster, 1982; London: Jonathan Cape, 1982; London: Virago, 1984.
Bluebeard's Egg. Toronto: McClelland & Stewart, 1983; Toronto: Seal, 1984.

Criticism

Survival: A Thematic Guide to Canadian Literature. Toronto: Anansi, 1972.
Second Words: Selected Critical Prose. Toronto: Anansi, 1982; Boston: Beacon Press, 1984.

Children's books

Up in the Tree. Toronto: McClelland & Stewart, 1978.
Anna's Pet. Toronto: James Lorimer, 1980.

Alice Munro

Short stories

Dance of the Happy Shades. Toronto: Ryerson, 1968; New York: McGraw-Hill, 1973; London: Allen Lane, 1974; Harmondsworth, Middlesex: Penguin, 1983.
Something I've Been Meaning to Tell You. Toronto: McGraw-Hill Ryerson, 1974; New York: McGraw-Hill, 1974; New York and Scarborough, Ontario: Signet, 1975.
Who Do You Think You Are? Toronto: Macmillan, 1978; Scarborough, Ontario: Signet, 1979. Published in England and the United States under the title *The Beggar Maid: Stories of Flo and Rose.* London: Allen Lane, 1980; New York: Knopf, 1982; Harmondsworth, Middlesex: Penguin, 1980.
The Moons of Jupiter. Toronto: Macmillan, 1982; Markham, Ontario: Penguin, 1983; New York: Knopf, 1983; Harmondsworth, Middlesex: Penguin, 1984.

The Progress of Love. Toronto: McClelland & Stewart, 1986;
New York, Knopf, 1986; London: Chatto & Windus, 1987.

Novel

Lives of Girls and Women. Toronto: McGraw-Hill Ryerson,
1971; New York: McGraw-Hill, 1972; Boston: G. K. Hall,
1973; London: Allen Lane, 1973; New York and Scarborough,
Ontario: Signet, 1974; London: Women's Press, 1978;
Harmondsworth: Penguin, 1982.

Non-fiction

Alice Munro and Charles E. Israel, *The Newcomers*. Toronto:
McClelland & Stewart, 1979. (*The Newcomers* is a TV series on
immigrants in Canada. Alice Munro did the Irish. The scripts
were turned into narrative and published as a book.)

Mavis Gallant

Short stories

The Other Paris. Cambridge, Mass.: Houghton Mifflin, 1956;
London: André Deutsch, 1957; Freeport, New York: Books
for Libraries, 1970.

My Heart is Broken, eight stories and a short novel. New York:
Random House, 1964; Don Mills, Ontario: PaperJacks, 1974;
Toronto: New Press Canadian Classics, 1982. Published
in England under the title *An Unmarried Man's Summer*,
London: Heinemann, 1965.

The Pegnitz Junction, a novella and five short stories. New
York: Random House, 1973; London: Cape, 1974; Toronto:
Laurentian Library (Macmillan), 1982.

The End of the World and Other Stories. Toronto: NCL, 1974.

From the Fifteenth District, a novella and eight short stories.
Toronto: Macmillan, 1979; New York: Random House, 1979;
London: Cape, 1980; Toronto: Laurentian Library, 1981.

Home Truths, Selected Canadian Stories. Toronto: Macmillan, 1981; Toronto: Laurentian Library, 1982; London:
Cape, 1985.

Overhead in a Balloon: Stories of Paris. Toronto: Macmillan, 1985.

Novels

Green Water, Green Sky. Cambridge, Mass.: Houghton Mifflin, 1959; London: André Deutsch, 1960; Toronto: Laurentian Library, 1983.
A Fairly Good Time. New York: Random House, 1970; London: Heinemann, 1970; Toronto: Laurentian Library, 1983.

Play

What Is To Be Done? Dunvegan, Ontario: Quadrant Editions, 1983.

Essays

'Things overlooked before', Introduction to *The Affair of Gabrielle Russier*, by Gabriella Russier. Trans. Ghislaine Boulanger. Preface Raymond Jean. New York: Knopf, 1971; Toronto: Popular Library, 1971; London: Gollancz, 1973.
Paris Notebooks: Essays and Reviews. Toronto: Macmillan, 1986.

Marian Engel

Novels

No Clouds of Glory. Don Mills, Ontario: Longmans, 1968; New York: Harcourt Brace & World, 1968. Re-issued as *Sarah Bastard's Notebook*, Don Mills, Ontario: PaperJacks, 1974.
The Honeyman Festival. Toronto: Anansi, 1970; New York: St Martins Press, 1972.
Monodromos. Toronto: Anansi, 1973. Re-issued as *One-Way Street*, Don Mills, Ontario: PaperJacks, 1974; London: Hamish Hamilton, 1975.
Joanne. (First commissioned as a radio-novel for CBC's 'This Country in the Morning', 1973). Don Mills, Ontario: Paper-Jacks, 1975.

Bear. Toronto: McClelland & Stewart, 1976; New York: Atheneum, 1976; London: Routledge & Kegan Paul, 1977; Toronto: Seal, 1977; Toronto: NCL, 1982.
The Glassy Sea. Toronto: McClelland & Stewart, 1978; New York: St Martins Press, 1979; Toronto: Seal, 1979.
Lunatic Villas. Toronto: McClelland & Stewart, 1981; Toronto: Seal, 1982.

Short stories

Inside the Easter Egg. Toronto: Anansi, 1975.
The Tattooed Woman. Toronto: Penguin, 1985.

Children's books

Adventure at Moon Bay Towers. Toronto: Clarke Irwin, 1974.
My Name Is Not Odessa Yarker. Toronto: Kids Can Press, 1977.

Non-fiction

Islands of Canada. Edmonton: Hurtig, 1981.

Joy Kogawa

Poetry

The Splintered Moon. Fredericton: Fiddlehead Poetry Books, 1967.
A Choice of Dreams. Toronto: McClelland & Stewart, 1974.
Jericho Road. Toronto: McClelland & Stewart, 1977.

Novel

Obasan. Toronto: Lester & Orpen Dennys, 1981; Boston: Godine, 1982; Toronto: Penguin, 1983; Harmondsworth: Penguin, 1984; Japan: Futumi Shobo, 1983.

Janette Turner Hospital

Novels

The Ivory Swing. Toronto: McClelland & Stewart, 1982; New York: Dutton, 1983; London: Hodder & Stoughton, 1983;

Toronto: Seal, 1983; New York: Bantam, 1984; London: Sphere, 1984.
The Tiger in the Tiger Pit. Toronto: McClelland & Stewart, 1983; New York: Dutton, 1984; London: Hodder & Stoughton, 1984; Toronto: Seal, 1984; New York: Bantam, 1985; London: Sphere, 1985.
Borderlines. Toronto: McClelland & Stewart, 1985.

Audrey Thomas

Novels

Mrs Blood. New York: Bobbs-Merrill, 1970; Vancouver: Talonbooks, 1975.
Munchmeyer and Prospero on the Island. New York: Bobbs-Merrill, 1972.
Songs My Mother Taught Me. New York: Bobbs-Merrill, 1973; Vancouver: Talonbooks, 1973; New York: Ballantine, 1975.
Blown Figures. New York: Knopf, 1975; Vancouver: Talonbooks, 1976.
Latakia. Vancouver and Los Angeles: Talonbooks, 1979.
Intertidal Life. Toronto: Stoddart (General Publishing Co. Ltd), 1985; New York: Beaufort, 1985; Toronto: General, New Press Canadian Classics, 1986.

Short stories

Ten Green Bottles. New York: Bobbs-Merrill, 1967; Ottawa: Oberon, 1977.
Ladies and Escorts. Ottawa: Oberon, 1977.
Real Mothers. Vancouver: Talonbooks, 1981.
Two in the Bush and Other Stories. Toronto: NCL, 1982.
Goodbye Harold, Good Luck. Toronto: Viking Penguin, 1986.

Radio plays

(all commissioned for CBC Radio)
Once Your Submarine Cable is Gone. CBC Stage, 1973.
Mrs Blood (an adaptation of the novel). CBC Stage, 1975.
The Milky Way. CBC Stage Theatre, 1984.

The Man with Clam Eyes. CBC Anthology, 1983.
Stopover Point, 1983. (Produced but never broadcast.)
The Woman in Black Velvet (based on Thomas's short story, 'Joseph and His Brother'). Vanishing Point, 1984.
The Axe of God. Disasters, 1985.
In the Groove. Vanishing Point, 1985.
On the Immediate Level of Events Occurring in Meadows. CBC Stereo Theatre, 1986.

Joan Barfoot

Novels

Abra. Toronto: McGraw-Hill Ryerson, 1978; Toronto: Signet, 1979; Published in England under the title *Gaining Ground.* London: Women's Press, 1980.
Dancing in the Dark. Toronto: Macmillan, 1982; London: Women's Press, 1982; Toronto and New York: Avon, 1984.
Duet for Three. Toronto: Macmillan, 1985; London: Women's Press, 1986.

Marie-Claire Blais

Novels

La Belle Bête. Quebec: Institut littéraire du Québec, 1959; Paris: Flammarion, 1961. Translation: *Mad Shadows* (trans. Merloyd Lawrence) Toronto: McClelland & Stewart, 1960; Toronto: New Canadian Library, 1981.
Tête Blanche. Quebec: Institut littéraire du Québec, 1960. Translation: *Tête Blanche* (trans. Charles Fullman). Toronto: McClelland & Stewart, 1961; Toronto: NCL, 1974.
Le Jour est noir. Montreal: Editions du Jour, 1962; Paris: Grasset, 1970; Montreal: Livre de Poche (Stanké), 1981. Translation: *The Day is Dark* (trans. Derek Coltman) New York: Farrar, Strauss & Giroux, 1967.
Une Saison dans la vie d'Emmanuel. Montreal: Editions du Jour, 1965; Paris: Grasset, 1966. Translation: *A Season in the Life of Emmanuel* (trans. Derek Coltman) New York. Farrar,

Strauss & Giroux, 1966; London: Jonathan Cape, 1967; Toronto: Bantam, 1976.

L'Insoumise. Montreal: Editions du Jour, 1966; Paris: Grasset, 1970. Translation: *The Fugitive* (trans. David Lobdell) Ottawa: Oberon Press, 1978.

L'Insoumise, suivi de Le Jour est noir. Paris: Grasset, 1971.

Le Jour est noir, suivi de L'Insoumise. Montreal: Stanké, 1979.

David Sterne. Montreal: Editions du Jour, 1967; Montreal: Livre de Poche, 1983. Translation: *David Sterne* (trans. David Lobdell) Toronto: McClelland & Stewart, 1973.

Les Manuscrits de Pauline Archange. Montreal: Editions du Jour, 1968; Paris: Grasset, 1968; Montreal: Livre de Poche, 1983. Translation: *The Manuscripts of Pauline Archange* (trans. Derek Coltman) New York: Farrar, Strauss & Giroux, 1969; Toronto: NCL, 1982.

Vivre! Vivre! Montreal: Editions du Jour, 1969; Montreal: Livre de Poche, 1983. Translation: Included as Part II of *The Manuscripts of Pauline Archange.* New York: Farrar, Strauss & Giroux, 1969; Toronto: NCL, 1982.

Les Apparences. (Tome III des *Manuscrits de Pauline Archange*) Montreal: Editions du Jour, 1970; Montreal: Livre de Poche, 1983. Translation: *Durer's Angel* (trans. David Lobdell) Toronto: McClelland & Stewart, 1974; Vancouver: Talonbooks, 1976.

Le Loup. Montreal: Editions du Jour, 1972; Paris: Laffont, 1973; Montreal: Livre de Poche, 1980. Translation: *The Wolf* (trans. Sheila Fischman) Toronto: McClelland & Stewart, 1974.

Un Joualonais, sa joualonie. Montreal: Editions du Jour, 1973; Paris: Laffont, 1974, under the title, *A coeur joual*; Montreal: Livre de Poche, 1981. Translation: *St Lawrence Blues* (trans. Ralph Manheim) New York: Farrar, Strauss & Giroux, 1974; Toronto and New York: Bantam, 1976; London: Harrap, 1976.

Une Liaison Parisienne. Montreal: Stanké, 1975; Paris:

Laffont, 1976. Translation: *A Literary Affair* (trans. Sheila Fischman) Toronto: McClelland & Stewart, 1979.
Les Nuits de l'Underground. Montreal: Stanké, 1978; Paris: Diffusion Hachette. Translation: *Nights in the Underground* (trans. Ray Ellenwood) Toronto: Musson, 1979. Toronto: New Press Canadian Classics, 1982.
Le Sourd dans la ville. Montreal: Stanké, 1979; Paris: Gallimard, 1980. Translation: *Deaf to the City* (trans. Carol Dunlop) Toronto: Lester & Orpen Dennys, 1981.
Visions d'Anna. Montreal: Stanké, 1982; Paris: Gallimard, 1982. Translation: *Anna's World* (trans. Sheila Fischman) Toronto: Lester & Orpen Dennys, 1983.
Pierre ou la Guerre du Printemps. Montreal: Editions Primeur, 1984.

Plays

L'Exécution. Pièce en deux actes. Montreal: Editions du Jour, 1968. Translation: *The Execution* (trans. David Lobdell) Vancouver: Talonbooks, 1976.
Fièvre et autres textes dramatiques. Montreal: Editions du Jour, 1974.
L'Océan, suivi de Murmures. Montreal: Editions Quinze, 1977.
Sommeil d'hiver. Montreal: Editions Pleine Lune, 1984.

Short stories

Les Voyageurs sacrés. Ecrits du Canada Français, XIV (1962), 193–257. Translation: *Three Travellers* (trans. Derek Coltman) and published with *The Day Is Dark*. New York: Farrar, Strauss and Giroux, 1967; Toronto: Penguin, 1985. Re-edition *Les Voyageurs Sacrés.* Montreal: Editions NMH, 1969.
La Fin d'une Enfance (en appendix dans T. Fabi, *Le Monde perturbé des jeunes dans l'oeuvre de Marie-Claire Blais: sa vie, son oeuvre, la critique, essai*) Montreal: Editions agence d'Arc, 1973.

Poetry

Pays voilés. Quebec: Garneau, 1963.
Existences. Quebec: Garneau, 1964. Re-edition: *Pays voilés, existences.* Montreal: Editions de l'Homme, 1967; Montreal: Stanké, 1983. Translation: *Veiled Countries/Lives* (trans. Michael Harris) Montreal: Vehicule Press, 1985.

Anne Hébert

Poetry

Les Songes en equilibre. Montreal: l'Arbre, 1942.
Le Tombeau des rois. Quebec: Le Soleil, 1953. Translation: *The Tomb of the Kings* (trans. Peter Miller) Toronto: Contact Press, 1967.
Poèmes. (*Le Tombeau des rois; Mystère de la parole*) Paris: Seuil, 1960. Translation: *Poems by Anne Hébert* (trans. Alan Brown) Toronto: Musson Book Company, 1975.

Novels

Les Chambres de bois. Paris: Seuil, 1958. Translation: *The Silent Rooms* (trans. Kathy Mezei) Toronto: Musson, 1974; Don Mills, Ontario: PaperJacks, 1975.
Kamouraska. Paris: Seuil, 1970. Translation: *Kamouraska* (trans. Norman Shapiro) Toronto: Musson, 1973; New York: Crown Publishers, 1974; Markham, Ontario: PaperJacks, 1974; Toronto: New Press Canadian Classics, 1982.
Les Enfants du Sabbat. Paris: Seuil, 1975. Translation: *Children of the Black Sabbath* (trans. Carol Dunlop-Hébert) Toronto: Musson, 1977; Ontario: PaperJacks, 1978.
Héloïse. Paris: Seuil, 1980. Translation: *Héloïse* (trans. Sheila Fischman) Toronto: Stoddart, 1982; Toronto: New Press Canadian Classics, 1983.
Le Fous de Bassan. Paris: Seuil, 1982; Translation: *In the Shadow of the Wind* (trans. Sheila Fischman) Toronto: Stoddart, 1983; London: Dent, 1984; London: Paladin, 1986.

Short stories

Le Torrent. Montreal: Editions Beauchemin, 1950. Slightly altered edition Paris: Seuil, 1965. Translation: *The Torrent: Novellas and Short Stories* (trans. Gwendolyn Moore) Montreal: Harvest House, 1973.

Plays

Le Temps sauvage. La Mercière assassinée. Les Invités au procès. Montreal: Editions Hurtubise, 1967.

Index